POSTCARD HISTORY SERIES

Muncie Indiana in Vintage Postcards

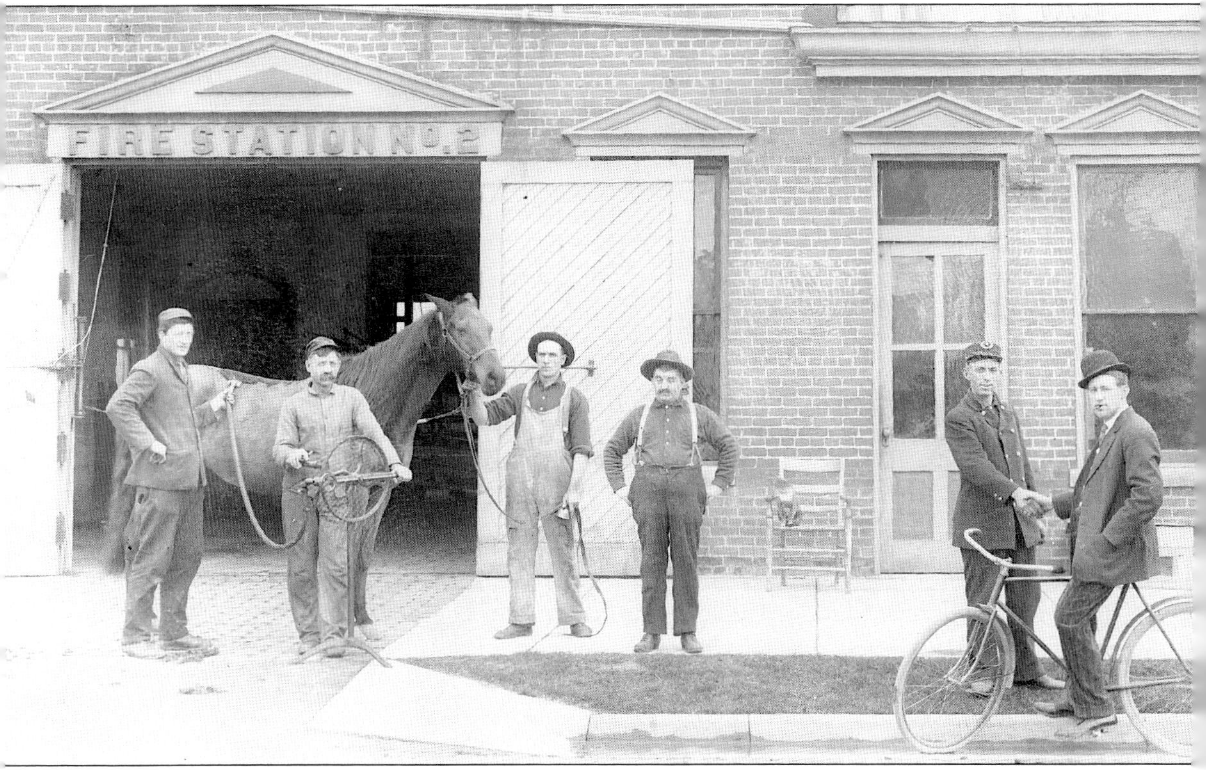

Firehouse Number Two. This photo of the station on the northeast corner of Willard and Ebright Streets was taken around 1910. The station had two horses to pull the hose wagon. The firemen, identified in a Muncie newspaper column called "Album of Yesteryear," are from left to right as follows: Charles Treon, Been Koontz, Frank Doerr, Thomas McFadden, and William Jones. The man on the bicycle is Ralph Huff, who was the superintendent of the Hemingway Glass Company. The building was razed in the mid-1960s. (Real Photo, unidentified photographer.)

Front Cover Photo: **Peach-Canning Time—on the Farm.** Exaggeration postcards were used in the early part of the century as humorous applications of everyday situations, objects, and events. In the cover photo of this volume the feature is an emphasis upon a Ball Brothers' canning jar and the seasonal, but common practice of canning fruits and vegetables for use later in the year. Photographic tricks were used to create the pictures. (Real Photo, published in 1910 by the Martin Post Card Company.)

Back Cover Photo: See page 11.

POSTCARD HISTORY SERIES

Muncie Indiana in Vintage Postcards

Milton A. Masing and Jeffrey Koenker

ARCADIA PUBLISHING

ISBN 978-0-7385-0111-6

Published by Arcadia Publishing
Charleston, South Carolina

Printed in the United States of America

Library of Congress Catalog Card Number: 99-61276

For all general information contact Arcadia Publishing at:
Telephone 843-853-2070
Fax 843-853-0044
E-Mail sales@arcadiapublishing.com
For customer service and orders:
Toll-Free 1-888-313-2665

Visit us on the Internet at www.arcadiapublishing.com

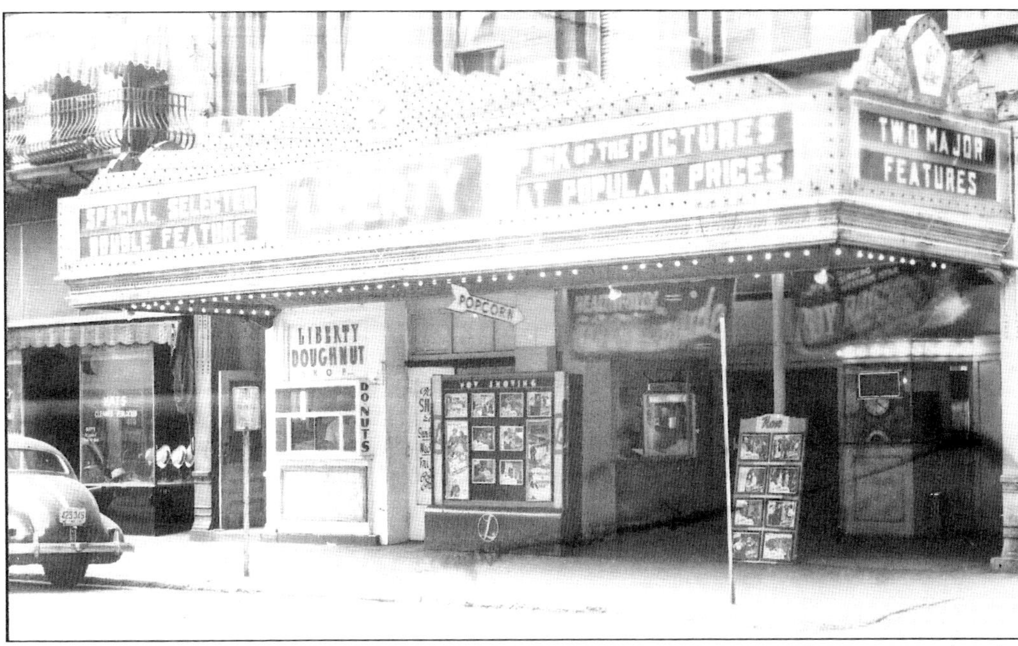

Liberty Theater. Located at 415 South Walnut Street, the Liberty was known in its heyday as one of the theaters that specialized in western films. At the time of this photo, the 1944 film *Song of Nevada*, starring Roy Rogers and Dale Evans, was one of the two features showing. (Real Photo, unidentified photographer.)

CONTENTS

ACKNOWLEDGMENTS

Numerous individuals have assisted the editors of this volume by providing suggestions and information important to the formulation of the final result. Some of these individuals, knowledgeable about Muncie and Delaware County, provided assistance in areas where the authors lacked background. Others provided ideas regarding the actual structure and production of the volume.

The following are people that contributed information about various subjects relating to Muncie: Pat Steinfield; Bill Reiter and Don Salughter, for data regarding the Muncie Schools; William Spurgeon, David R. Hermansen, posthumously, for help with architectural data and identifications on several pages; the Reference Department staff at the Muncie Public Library; Henry J. Ratican, Jenny Lockard, Philip Clark, and James L. Masing.

The following are people that contributed background assistance relating to the structure and production of this volume:
Stan and Sharon Waggoner Zukowski, Emmaus, PA
Nancy Turner & staff, Stoelkel Archives, Ball State University
John Straw & staff, Stoelkel Archives, Ball State University

The authors would like to express our sincere appreciation to all those mentioned above for their invaluable help in producing this volume of Muncie history.

INTRODUCTION

This book is about Muncie, Indiana, during the "Golden Age" of picture postcards, lasting roughly from 1904 through the 1940s. Chrome cards that started being manufactured in the late 1940s are not included in the book. The book has been illustrated with postcards from the personal collections of the authors, who have collected cards for a combined total of around 50 years. Both authors can boast a collection of over a thousand different views, with more than 200 appearing in this book.

In a sense, this book is also about history, although neither author claims to be a dedicated historian. Collecting, not history, is the major interest. Consequently, information about the cards tends to be somewhat brief in most cases. Where there is considerable text, the focus is usually upon facts and data rather than personal recollections. Since many of the cards selected for this book are pictures of buildings and other structures, emphasis is placed upon architecture and architects. Moreover, to justify this focus, Muncie has the largest architecture school in the state.

The authors of this book first began discussing the possibility of co-authoring a book some 15 or 20 years ago. At that time, we began to realize that many of the images that we were acquiring were actually quite rare and had never before been reproduced in other books. Also, each author has several images that the other does not, making a combined collection all the more necessary.

Postcards of the smaller communities and townships that surround the city have not been included in this volume. It is hoped that another volume about Delaware County will follow.

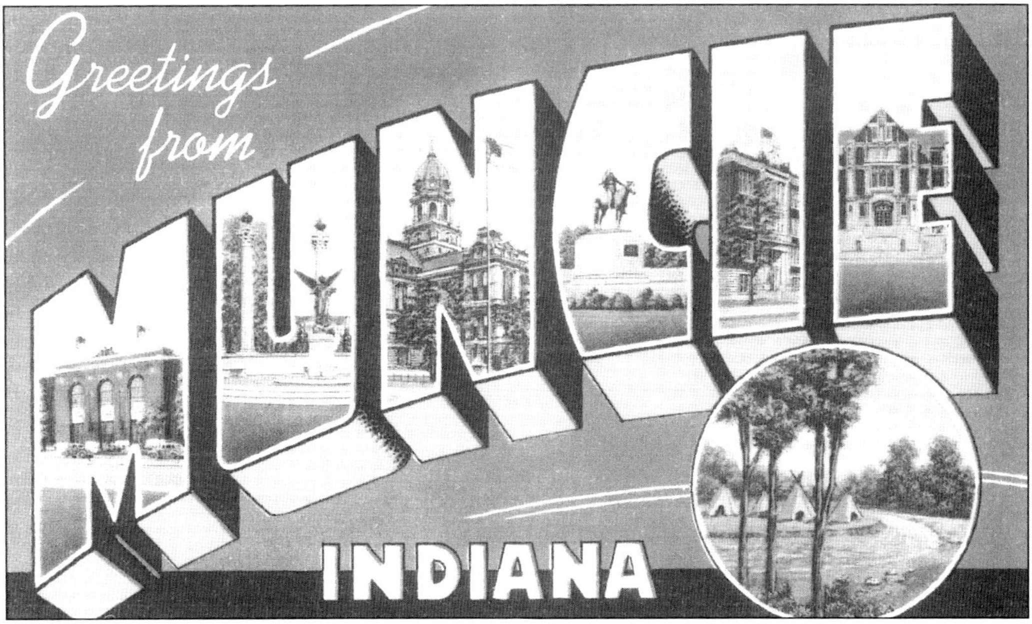

GREETINGS FROM MUNCIE, INDIANA, C. 1940. This card includes the following views: (M) Vocational and Physical Education Building; (U) The Ball Memorial Statue at Ball State Teacher's College; (N) Court House; (C) "Appeal to the Great Spirit" Ball Memorial; (I) Central High School; and (E) Arts Building at Ball State. (Curt Teich Co., for Muncie News Co.)

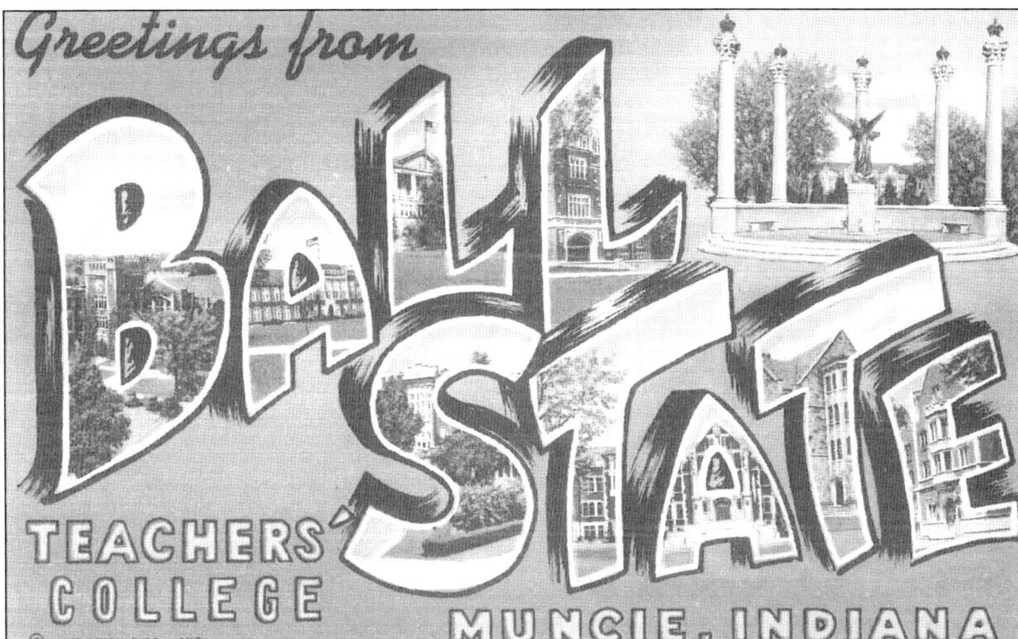

GREETINGS FROM BALL STATE TEACHERS' COLLEGE, C. 1940. Scenes included in this card are as follows: (B) Library and Assembly Hall; (A) Burris Laboratory School; (L) Administration Building; (L) Ball Gymnasium; (S) Science Hall; (T, A) Arts Building; (T) Frank Elliott Ball Memorial Hall; and (E) Lucina Hall. (Curt Teich Co., for Muncie News Co.)

One

Public Buildings and Structures

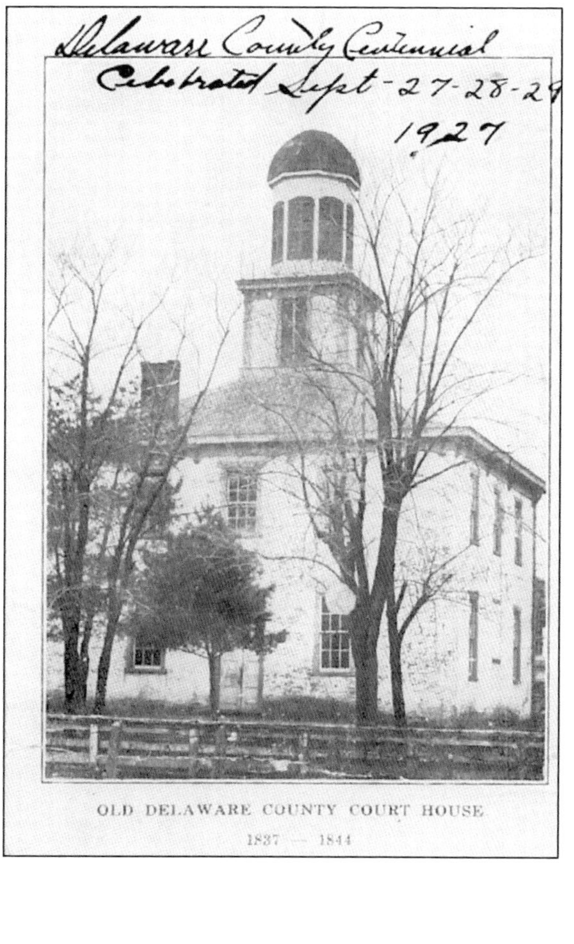

Old Delaware County Court House. Constructed from 1836 until 1837, this was the second structure in Delaware County to be used as a courthouse. It was built by Muncie's own Morgan John to be similar in plan with the Wayne County Court House in Centerville. The building was demolished by D.C. Mitchell in 1884 to make room for a new structure. (Unidentified printer for the Delaware County Centennial Celebration, September 27–29, 1927.)

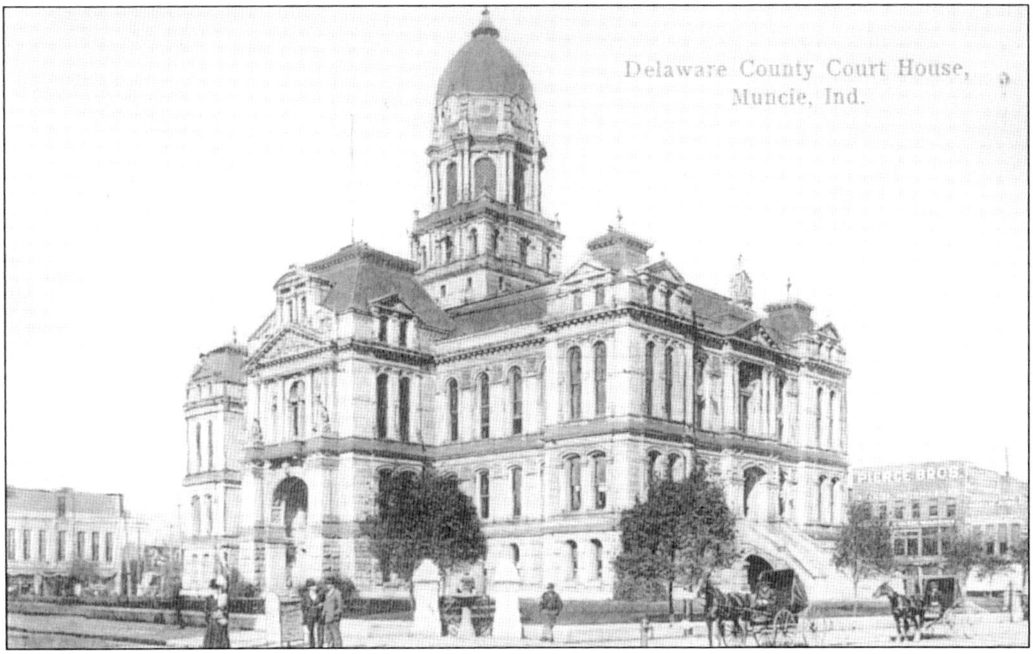

Delaware County Court House. The third structure used as a Delaware County Court House was designed by the Fort Wayne architect Brentwood S. Tolan, who was employed by the county board of commissioners on April 25, 1884. On November 7, 1884, the contract for construction of the building was awarded to Charles Pearce & Co. of Indianapolis for $195,618.46. This second Empire structure was demolished in 1967 to make room for the present building. (Kraemer Art Co., for C.A. Penzel.)

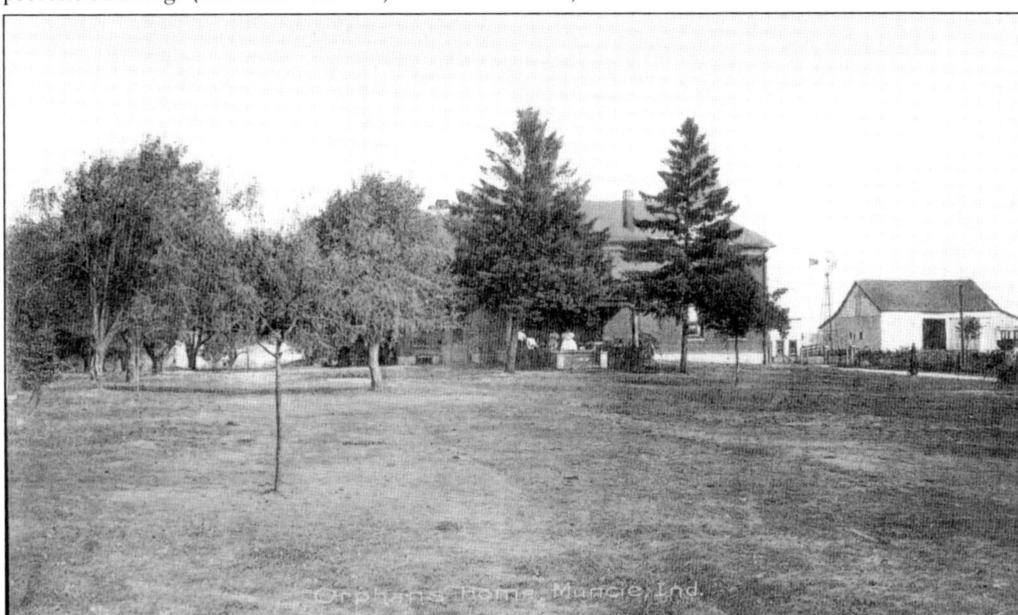

Orphans Home. The Orphans Home, constructed between 1906 and 1907, was located on West 3316 Kilgore Avenue. In 1991, construction began on cottage-style buildings that were to replace the old building. (Kraemer Art Co., for C.A. Penzel.)

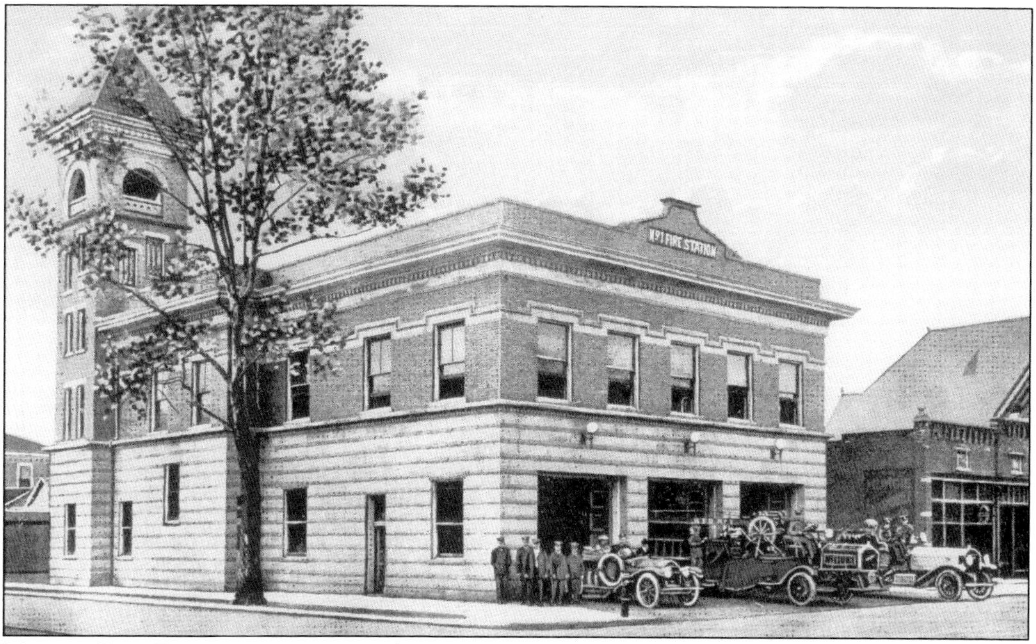

MUNCIE FIRE DEPARTMENT. Located at 421 East Jackson Street, the Muncie Fire Department, later known as Firehouse Number One, was completed in 1913. The contractor was Leslie Colvin of Brookville, Indiana. Cost for the building was $22,450. (Harry H. Hamm.)

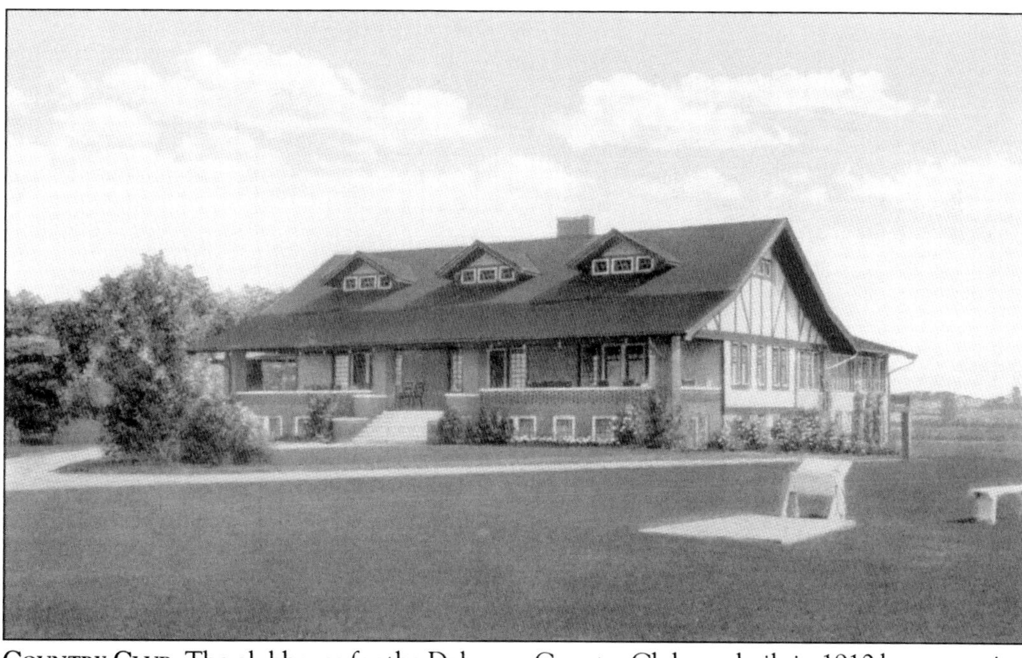

COUNTRY CLUB. The clubhouse for the Delaware Country Club was built in 1910 by converting an old farm house. Additions were made as major remodeling took place in the 1940s, 1960s, and 1980s. (Harry H. Hamm.)

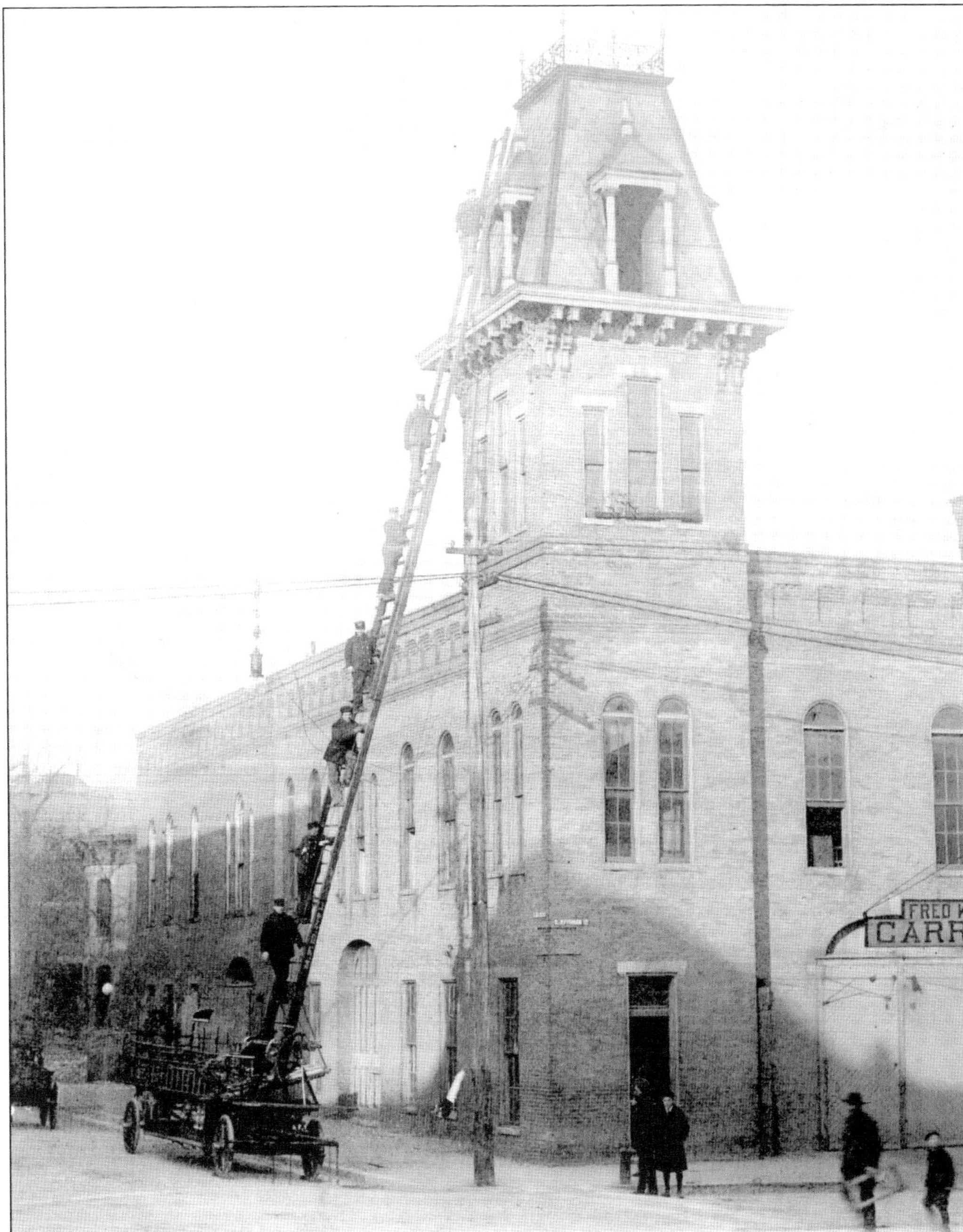

MUNCIE CITY HALL. The first Muncie City Hall was erected in the fall of 1873. Excavation work for the building was contracted to Davis & Branson. Brick and stone work was contracted to Hamilton & Sons. Upon completion, the building was immediately determined to be too small. In 1875, an addition made to the building nearly doubled its capacity. Demolition of the building made room for the erection of the next city hall. (Real Photo, unidentified photographer.)

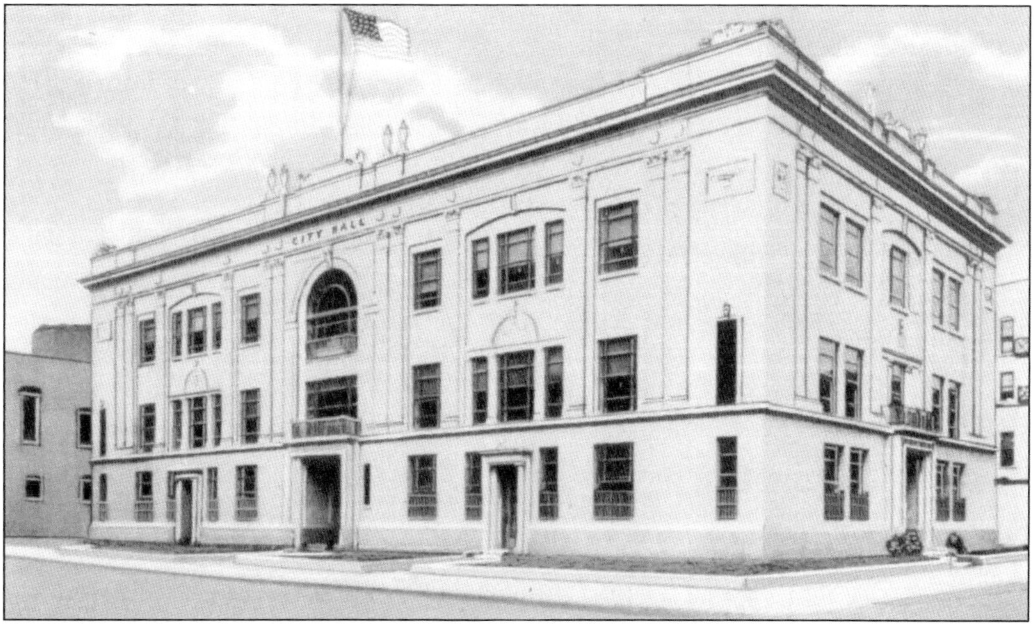

City Hall. The second Muncie City Hall was completed in 1925 following the design and plans of Muncie architects Kibele and Garrard. It was located at 210 East Jackson Street. The building was torn down in 1994 after the current city hall was completed. (Curt Teich Co., for Muncie News Co.)

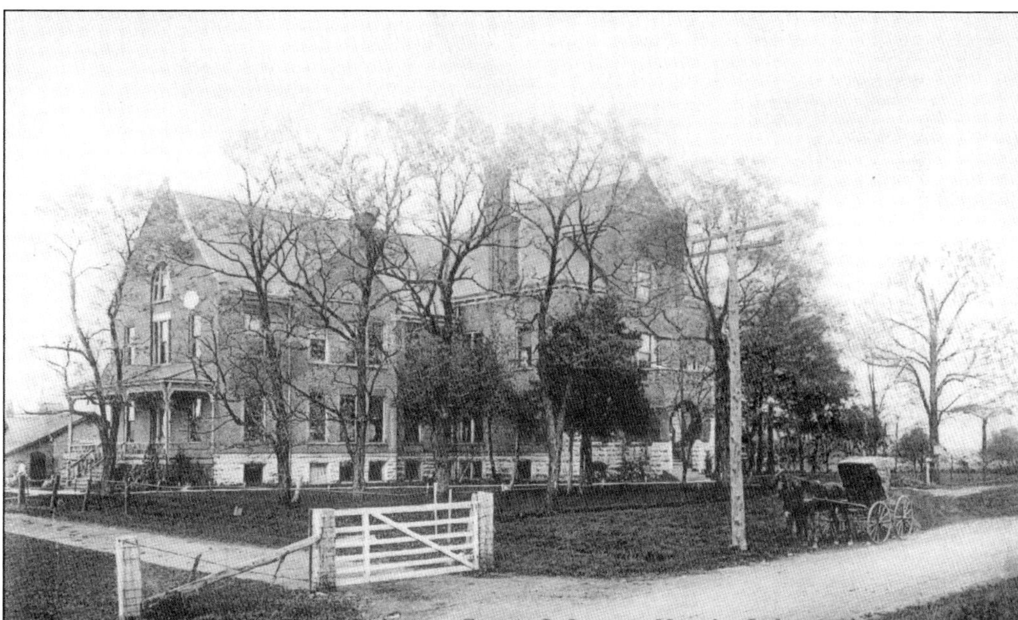

Delaware County Infirmary. The county infirmary, or poor farm, was located on the Winchester Pike about 4 miles from the city. The building is no longer used as a home for the poor. (Kraemer Art Co., for C.A. Penzel.)

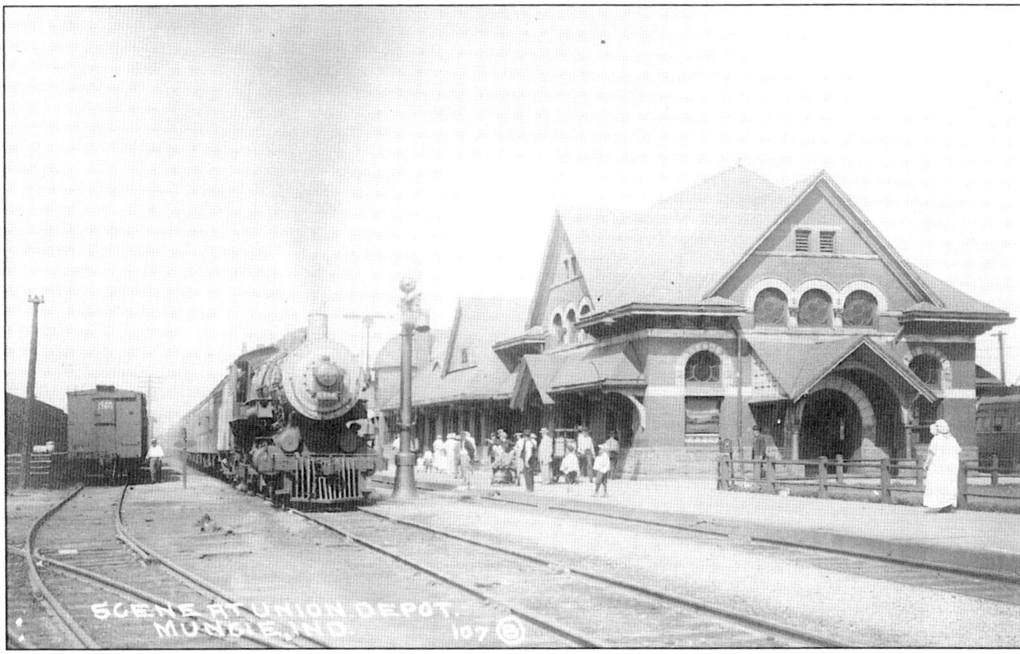

SCENE AT UNION DEPOT. Original construction on this Romanesque Revival-style building, located at 630 South High Street, was completed in 1883. Additions were made in 1892 and again in 1902, resulting in the east wing that is prominent in this view. The building was torn down in 1990. (Real Photo, published by M.L. Photo, Chicago.)

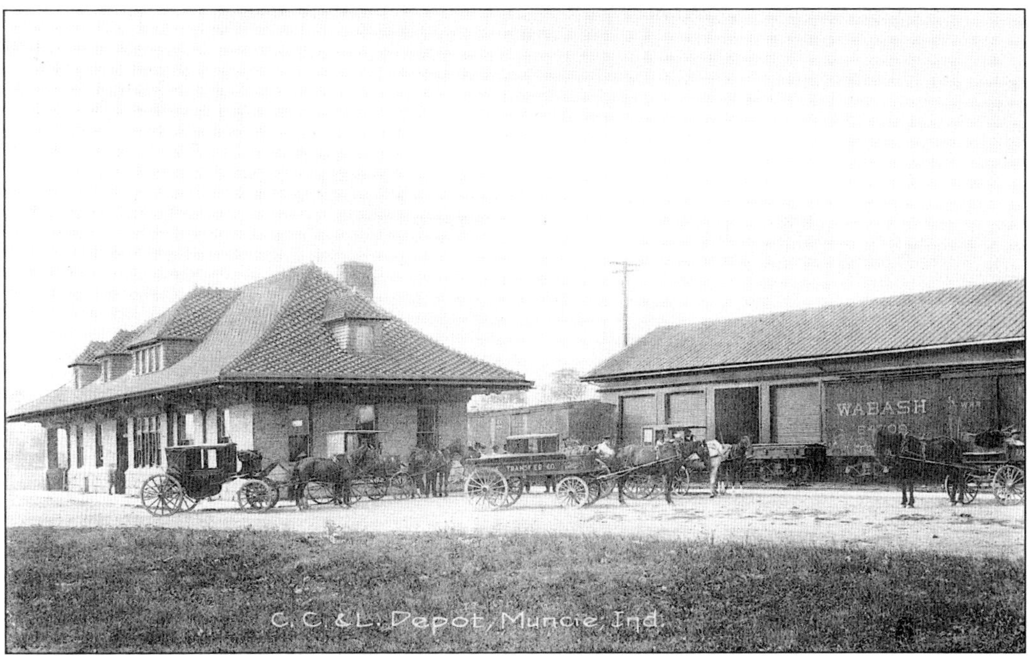

C.C. & L DEPOT. Located at 700 East Wysor Street, this depot has had many different names throughout its history. For the majority of the twentieth century, it was known as the Chesapeake & Ohio Railway Passenger Depot. Construction of the building was completed in 1902. (Kraemer Art Co., for C.A. Penzel.)

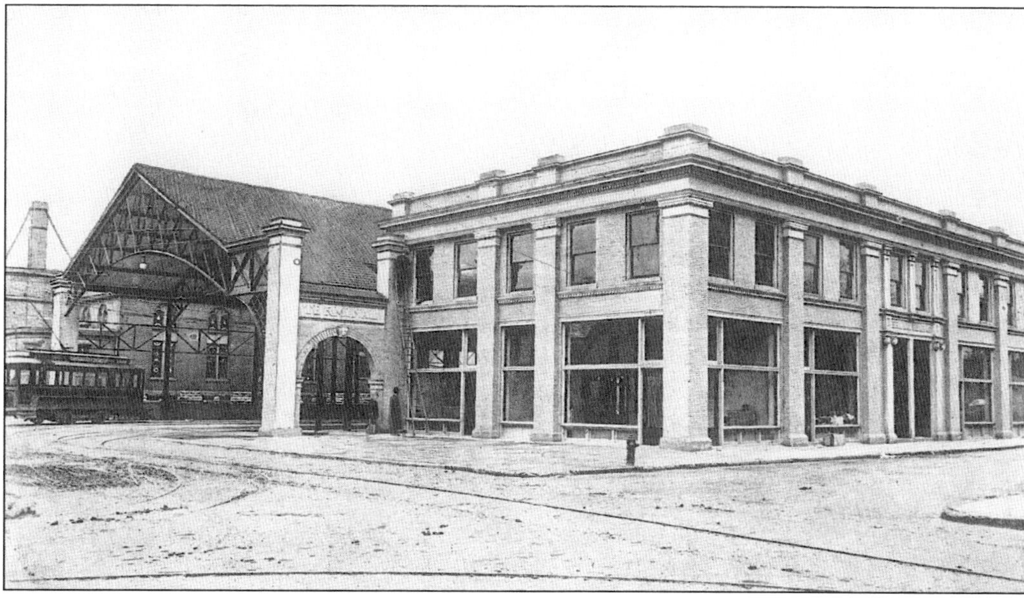

TERMINAL STATION. The architects for the Muncie Terminal Station came from the architectural firm of Grindle and Stiles. It was completed in 1906 at a cost of $20,000. The building was demolished in 1959 and replaced by a J.C. Penney department store. (Excelsior News Company, also marked A.N.C., New York.)

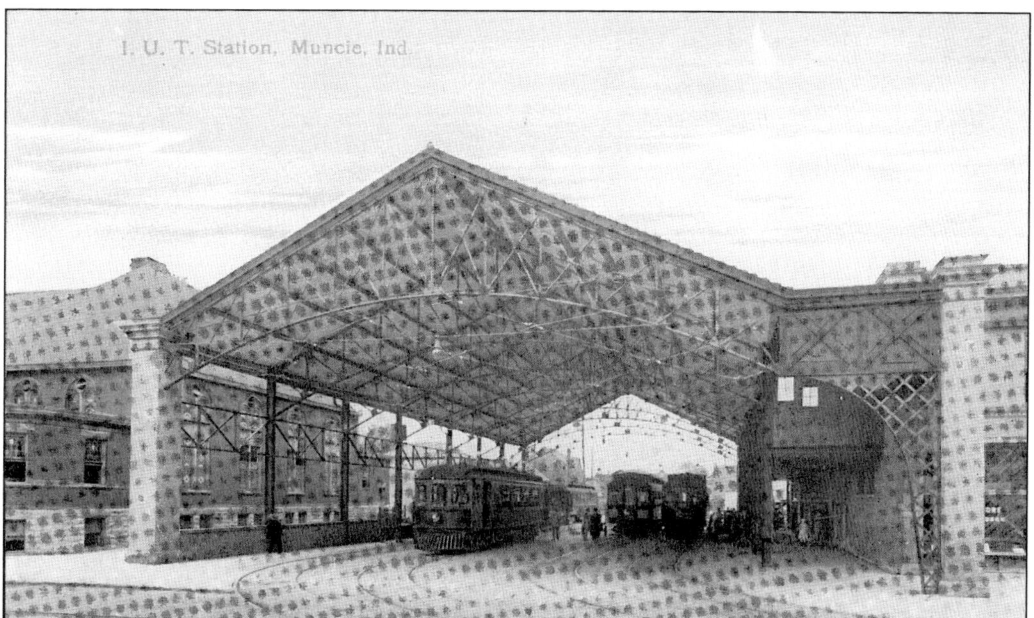

I. U. T. STATION. In the late years of its existence, this train shed and the adjoining terminal station were used as a bus station for the Muncie city buses. (Superior Post Card Company.)

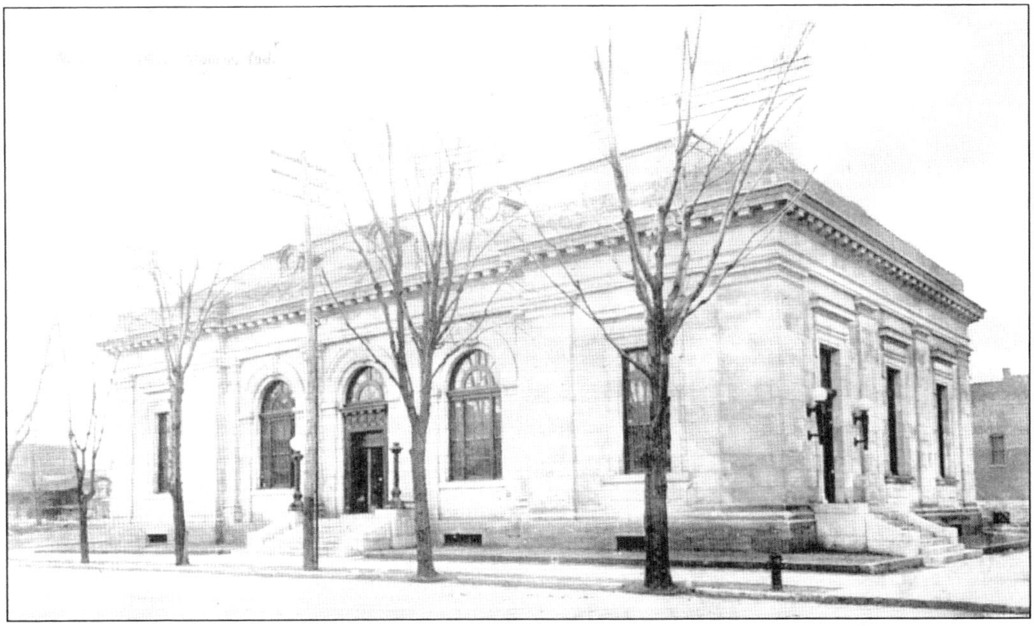

New Post Office. Located at 401 South High Street, this structure was under construction from 1906 until 1907. The architect for the building was James Knox Taylor of Washington, D.C. The contract for this Beaux arts-style building was awarded to Morrow and Morrow Construction for $55,003.50. It officially opened on April 28, 1907. (Tom Jones.)

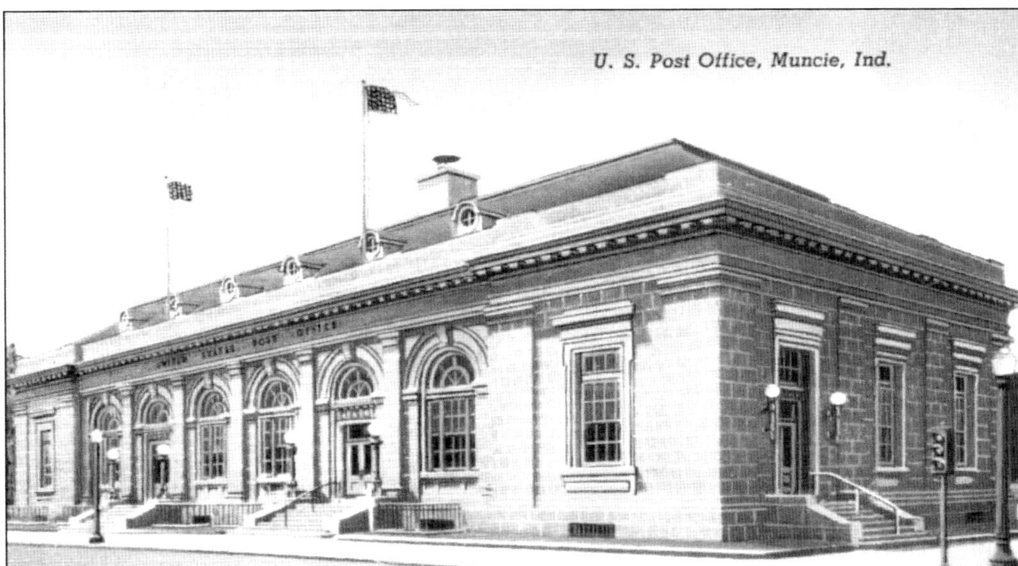

U.S. Post Office. In 1931, the post office shown at the top of this page was enlarged to the size shown here. Ideal Construction Co. built the enlargement at a cost of $158,671.98. In 1988, it became a part of the plans for the Horizon Convention Center designed by Gooden Associates. (Curt Teich Co., for Muncie News Co.)

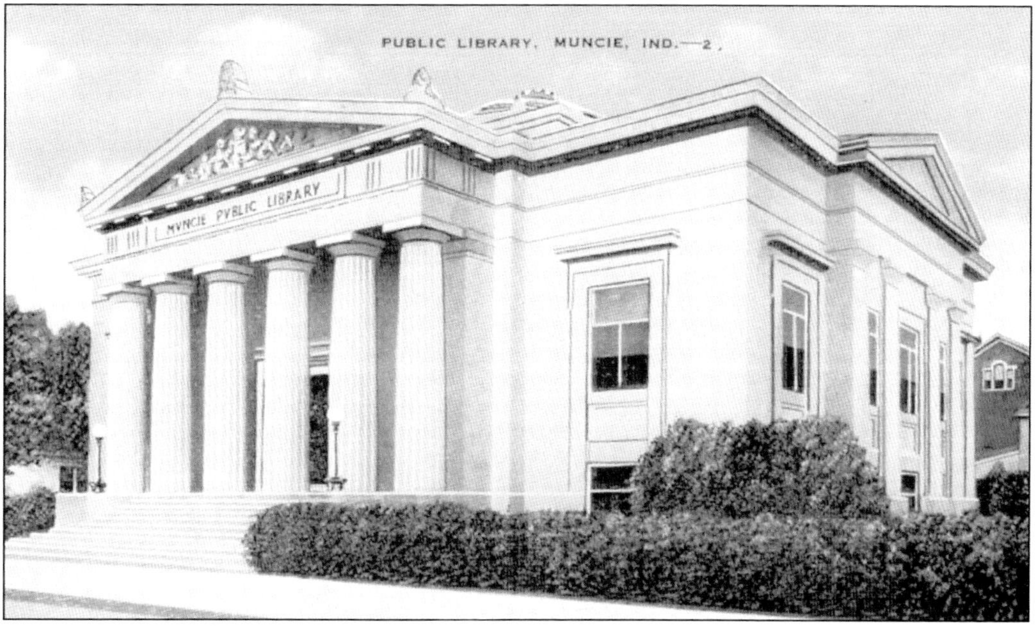

PUBLIC LIBRARY. The years 1902 and 1903 witnessed the construction of a new Muncie Public Library. Dedicated on January 1, 1904, the cost of the building was $55,900.85. The plans were prepared by the Fort Wayne, Indiana architectural firm Wing and Mahurin. The outside of the building was designed in the Doric order of Classic Revival architecture. (Curt Teich Co., for Muncie News Co.)

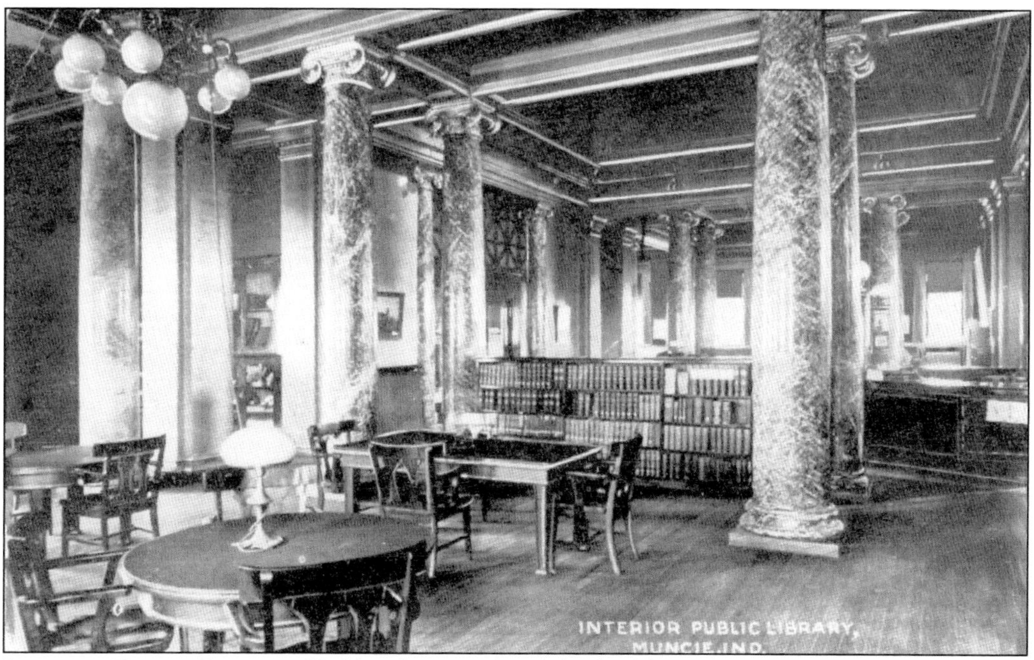

INTERIOR PUBLIC LIBRARY. Unlike the outside of the building, the inside of the building was designed in the Ionic order of Classic Revival architecture. Morrow & Morrow of Muncie was the general contractor for the building at 301 East Jackson Street. (Weltpostverein-Union postale universelle, for Watson Stationer.)

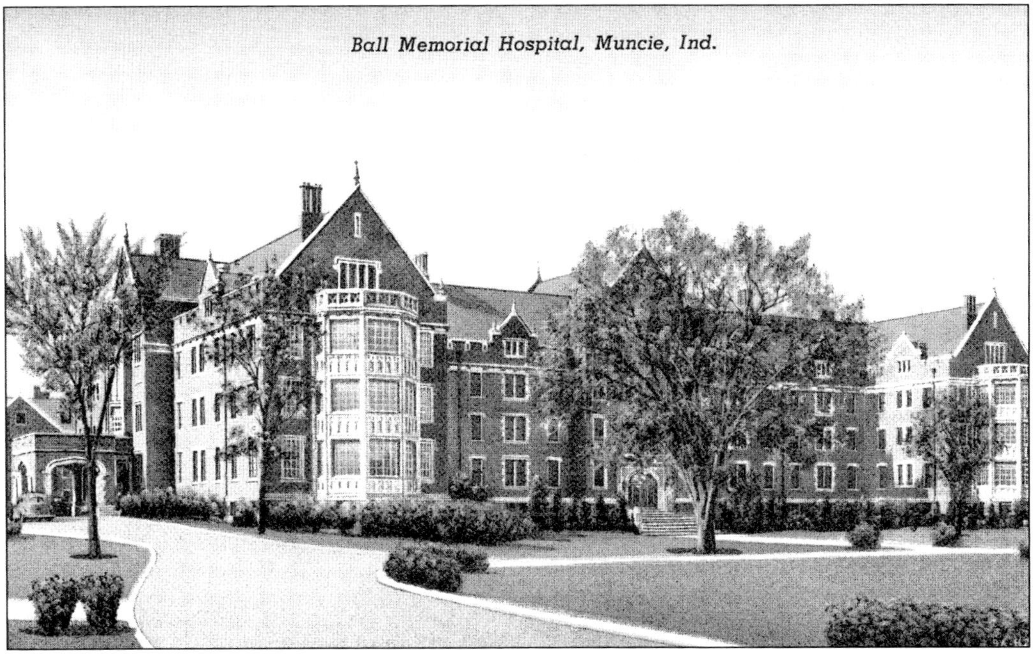

BALL MEMORIAL HOSPITAL. This view shows the original wing of the Ball Memorial Hospital that was designed by Kibele and Garrard of Muncie and built between 1927 and 1929 at a cost of $ 1,170,000.00. The hospital was named after the five Ball brothers that settled in Muncie to establish a glass factory in the late 1880s. (Curt Teich Co., for Muncie News Co.)

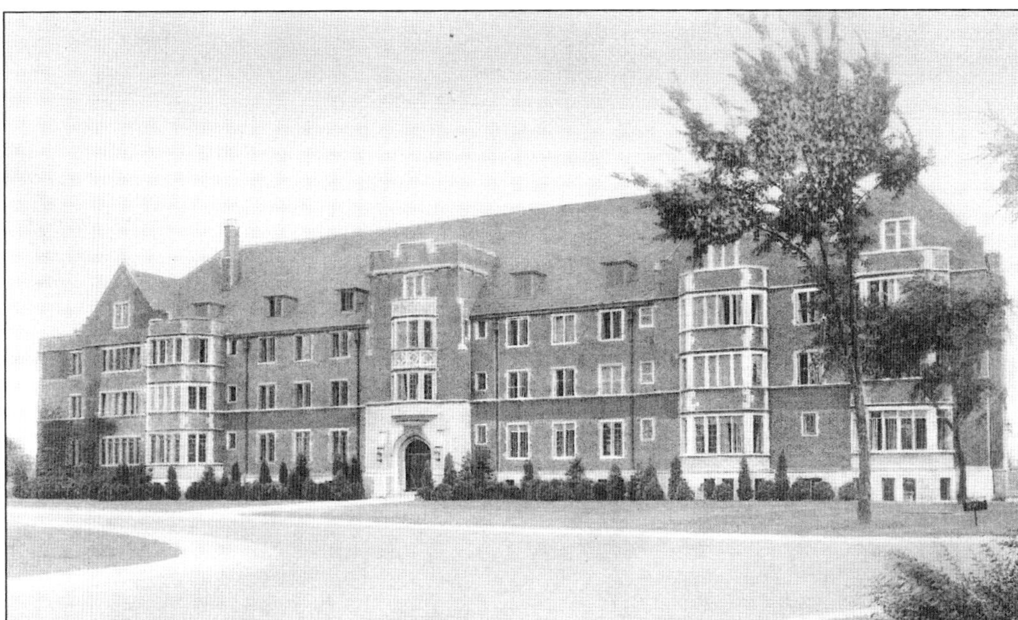

MARIA BINGHAM HALL, NURSES' RESIDENCE, BALL MEMORIAL HOSPITAL. Also designed by Kibele and Garrard, the nurses' residence for the hospital was completed in 1930. It was named for Maria Bingham Ball, mother of the five brothers. (The Albertype Co., probably for the Ball State Bookstore.)

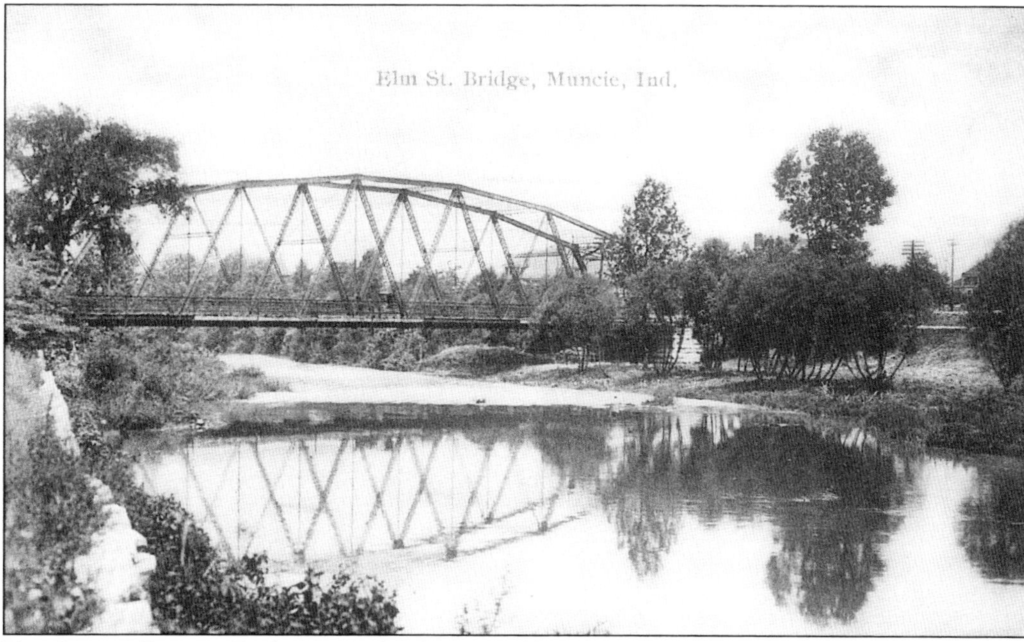

Elm Street Bridge. Built in 1889 by the McCullough Co. to span the White River, this bridge connected northern Muncie with downtown by way of Elm Street. The bridge is also referred to as Bridge #506. It was demolished and replaced with a modern WPA bridge in 1936. (Kraemer Art Co.)

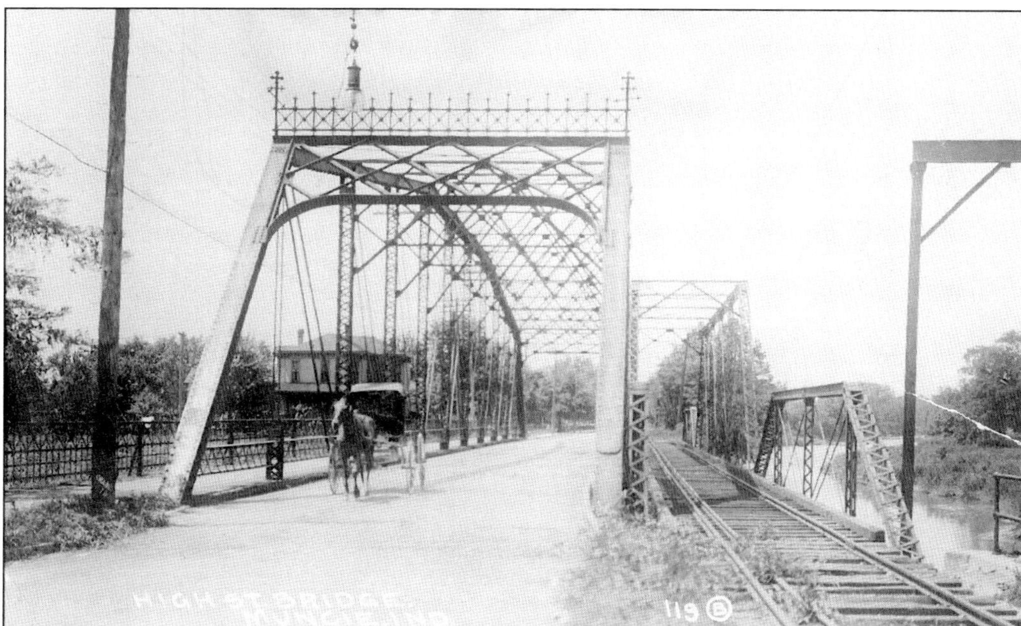

High Street Bridge. Also built to span the White River, this bridge represents the meeting place of High Street and Wheeling Avenue. Both this bridge and the traction one beside it were replaced by a modern bridge in 1937 through the Federal Emergency Assistance Program (F.E.A.). It is also referred to as Bridge #511. (Real Photo, produced by M.L. Photo Co., Chicago.)

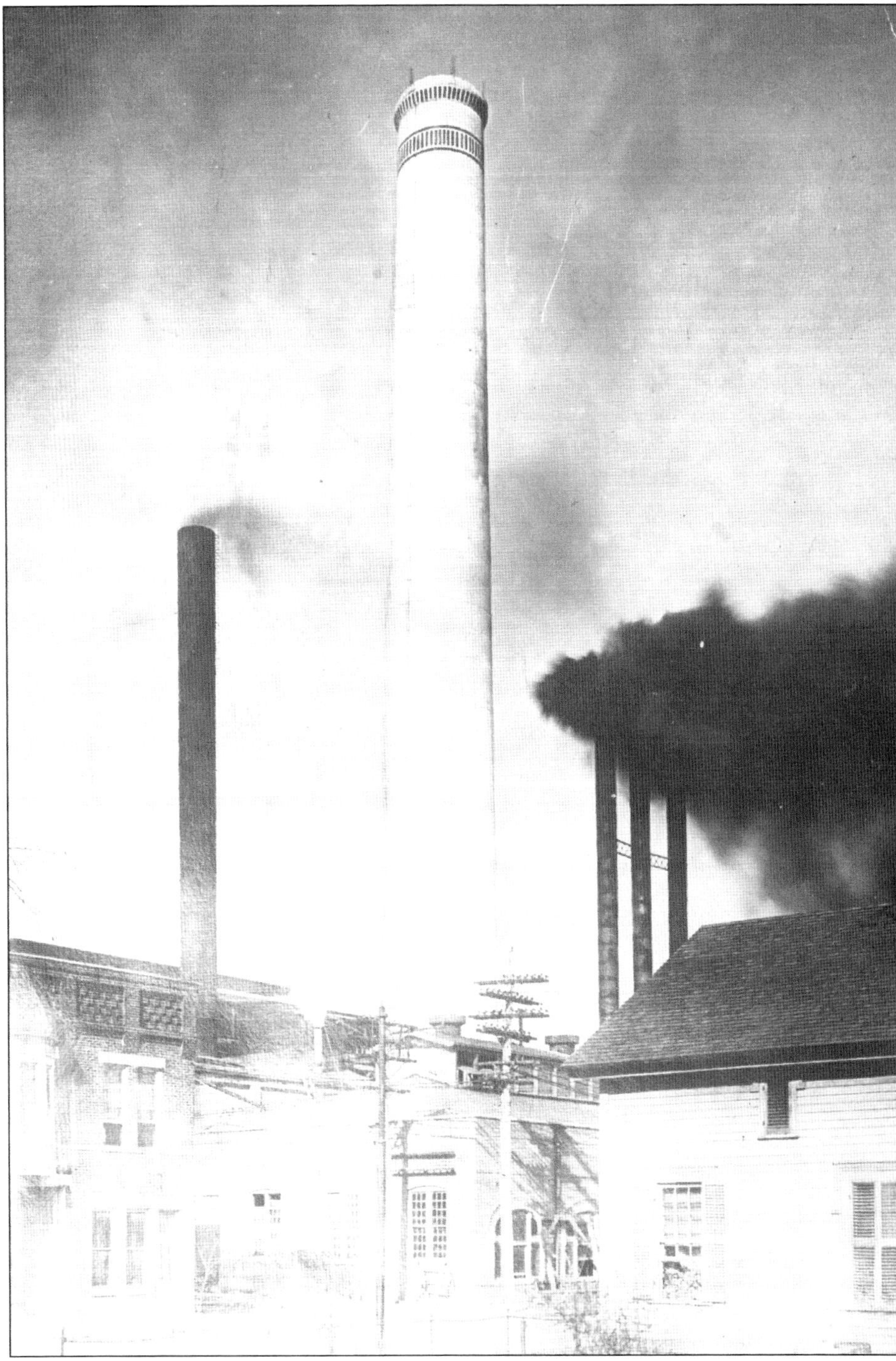

MUNCIE HEAT, LIGHT, AND POWER COMPANY PLANT. The Muncie Electric Power Plant was built on a large city block bounded by Wysor, North, High, and Walnut Streets. The company was promoted by Mr. James Boyce in February of 1888. The stack shown in this photo was 250 feet high. In the 1960s, the plant was demolished. The present Muncie City Hall stands on the site of the plant. (Real Photo, unidentified photographer.)

Two

People and Organizations

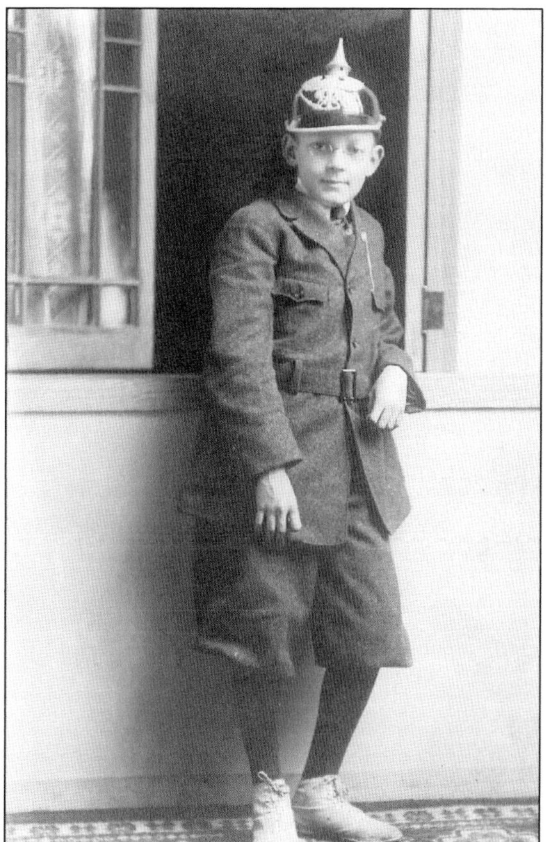

Stanley C. Nossett. Stanley C. Nossett posed for this photo postcard after winning a German helmet for selling war bonds during World War I. The Nossett family owned a printing business for a number of years at 116 North Mulberry. Later, the business moved to 117 North Franklin Street. (Real Photo, unidentified photographer.)

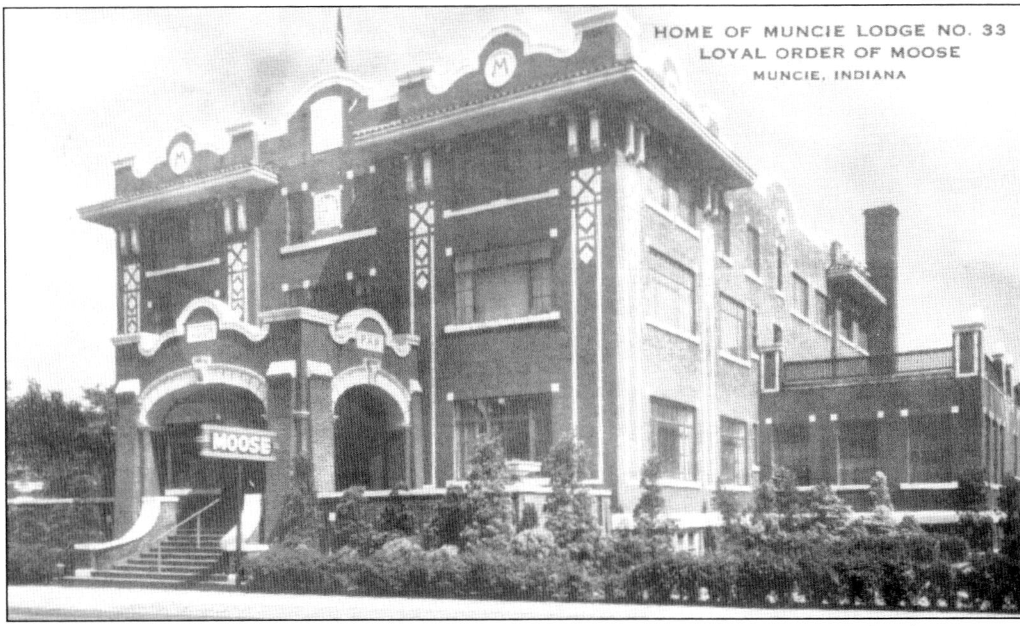

HOME OF MUNCIE LODGE NO. 33, LOYAL ORDER OF MOOSE. Originally built by the Muncie Elks in 1921, this lodge building, located at the northeast corner of Main and Franklin Streets, was designed by Houck & Smenner of Muncie. The building was razed in 1970. (Unidentified printer and publisher.)

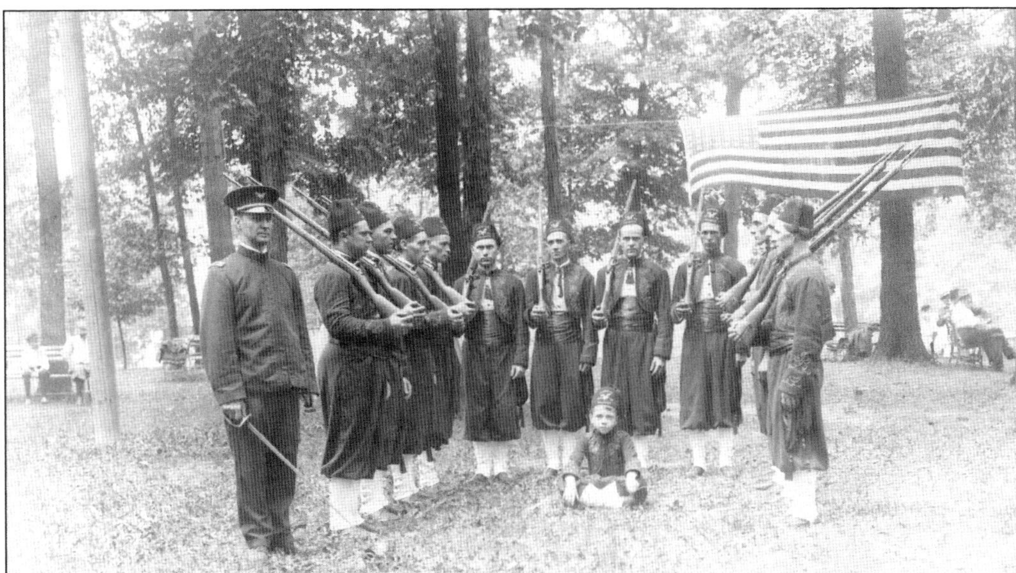

MOOSE LODGE NO. 33. The above real photo postcard was of a gathering of Muncie's Loyal Order of Moose, perhaps in McCullough Park. Each member is wearing a hat with Muncie Lodge No. 33 and the word "Zouaves" on it. What the word specifies is uncertain. (Real photo, unidentified photographer.)

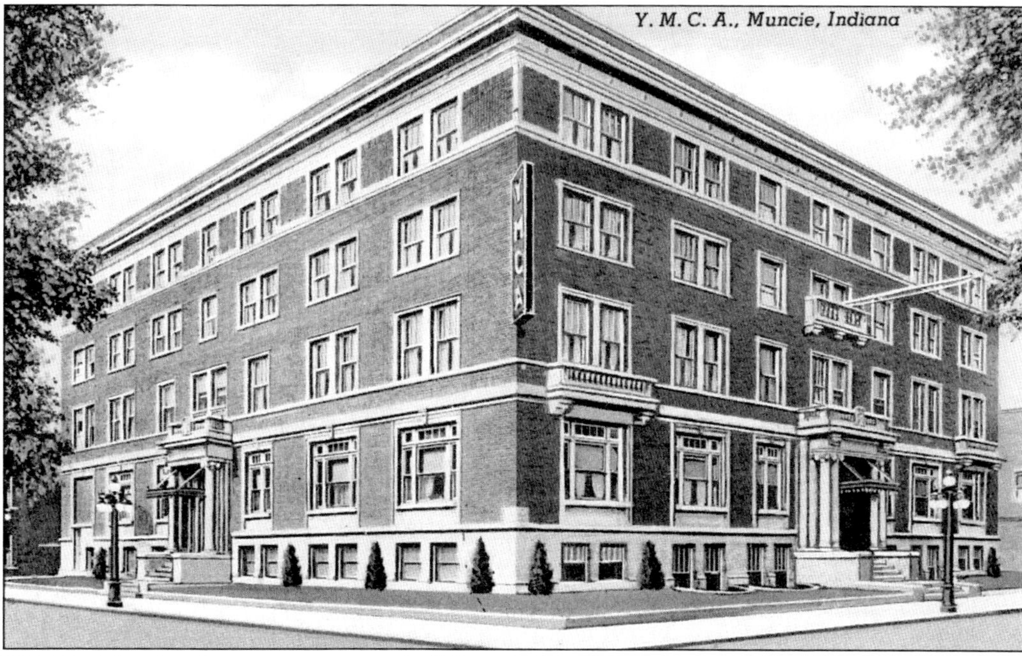

YMCA. This handsome structure at 225 East Adams Street was completed in 1926 from plans drawn by Kibele & Garrard of Muncie. The building was razed sometime around 1976 to make room for a new structure with more "modern" and complete facilities. (Curt Teich Co., for Muncie News Co.)

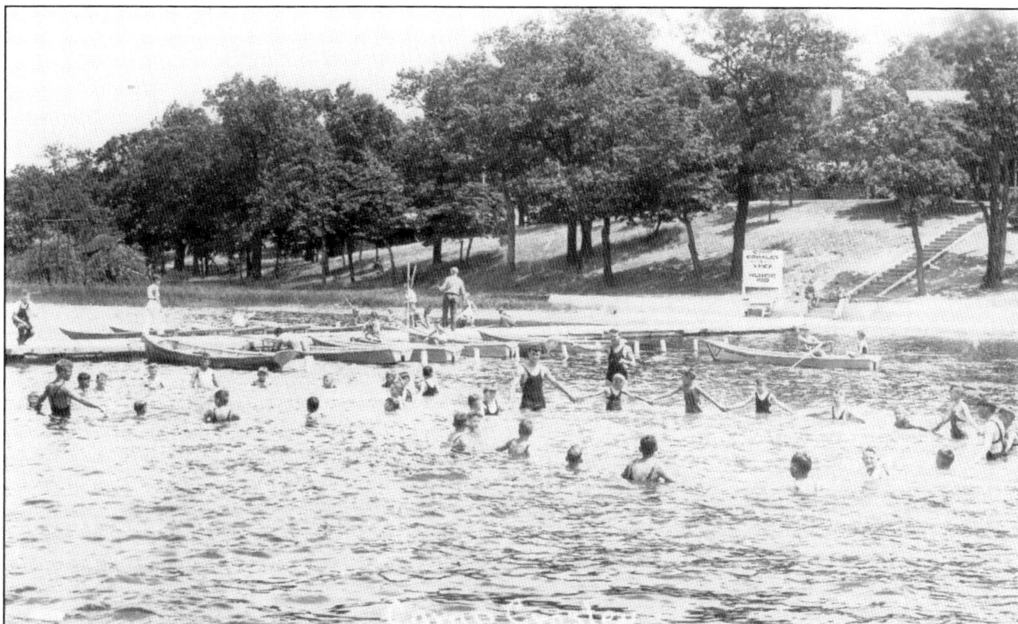

CAMP CROSLEY. Camp Crosley is owned and operated by the Muncie YMCA as a summer camp. It is located on little Tippecanoe Lake in Kosciusko County near the town of North Webster. Construction was subsidized by the Ball family by individual gifts and collective gifts from the Ball Brothers Foundation. (Real photo, unidentified photographer.)

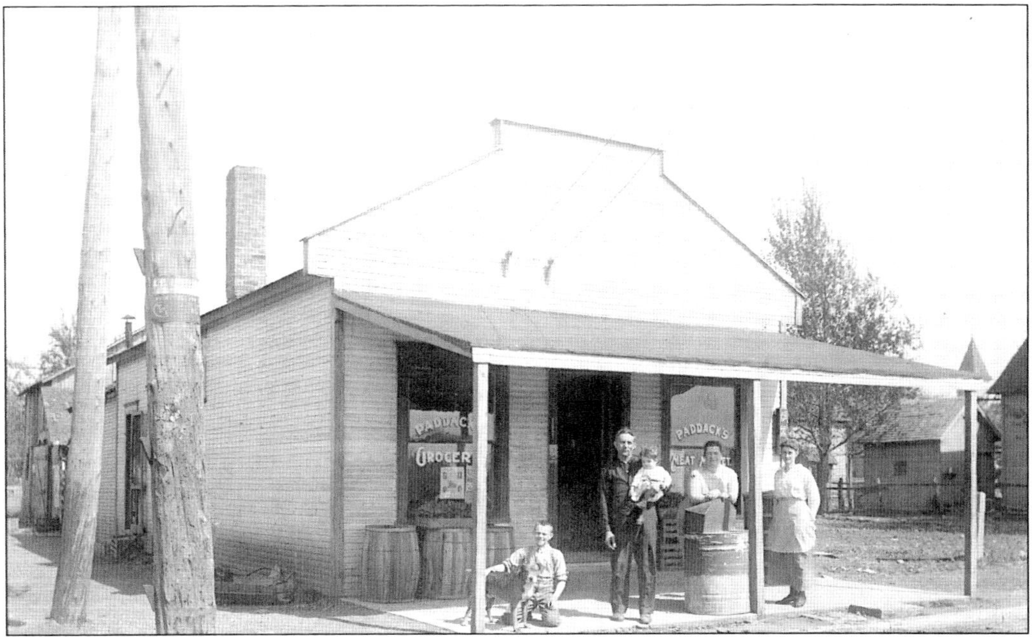

Paddock's Grocery and Meat Market. The family of Otterbein Paddock is shown in this postcard dated May 18, 1916. Mr. Paddock and his wife Elizabeth owned this small grocery store at 2800 South Walnut Street. The card was mailed to Otterbein's father, Reverend C.R. Paddock. (Real Photo, unidentified photographer.)

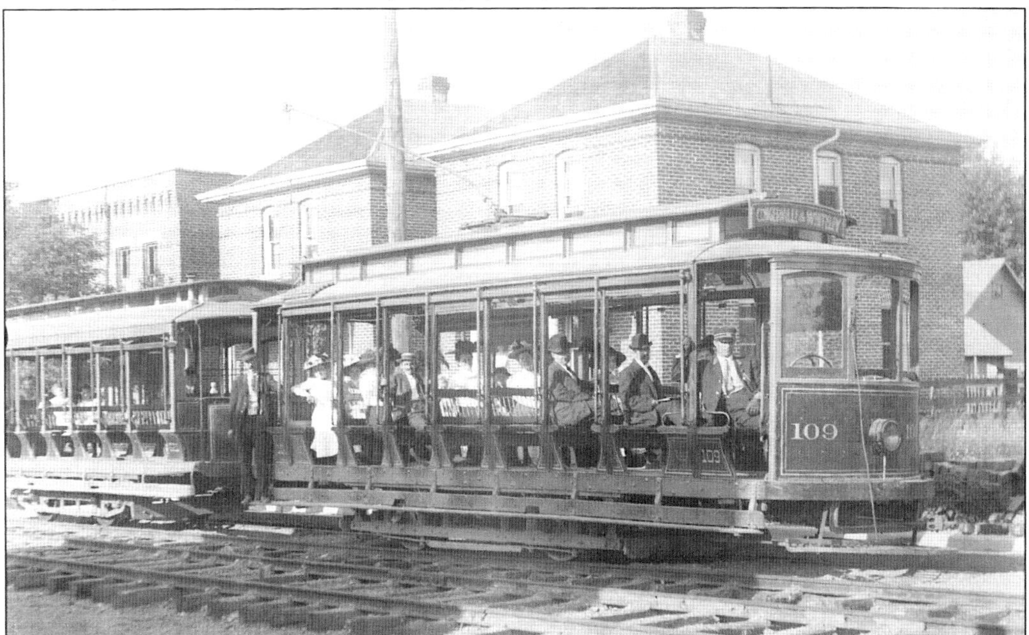

Congerville and Whiteley Summer Trolley Car. During the hot summer months, the trolleys often became "summer cars" because the sides were left open to cool off passengers. In the event of rain, curtains could be pulled down. Fares were 5¢. (Real Photo, published by Burkey's Post Card Shop, Muncie, Indiana.)

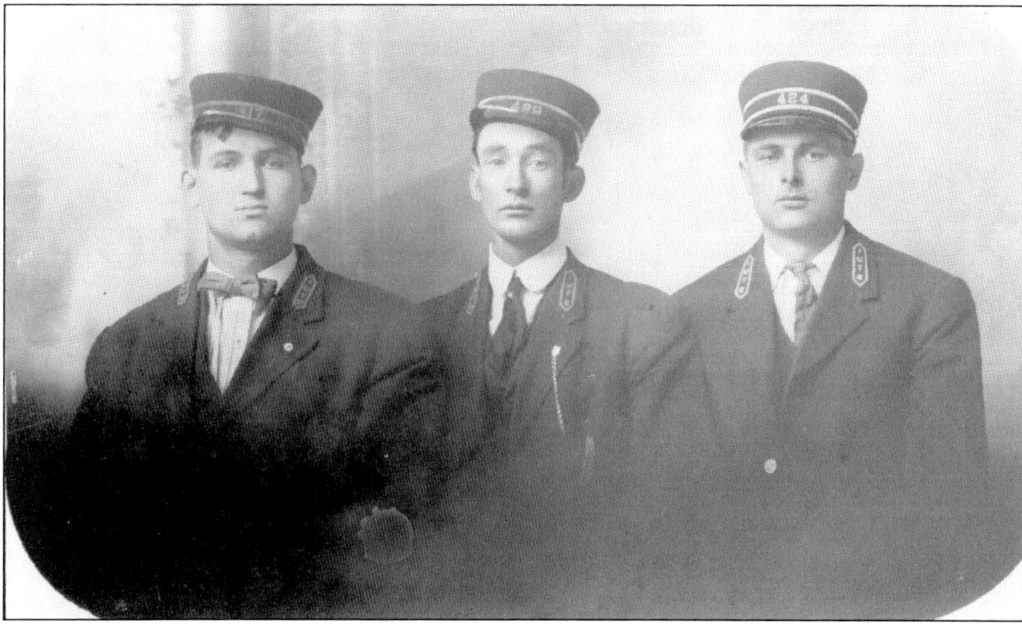

Indiana Union Traction Company Employees. These three fellows, all Indiana Union Traction Company employees, posed for this photo, which was later made into a postcard. The conductor, or motorman, on the left can also be seen in the photo shown below. (Real Photo, unidentified photographer.)

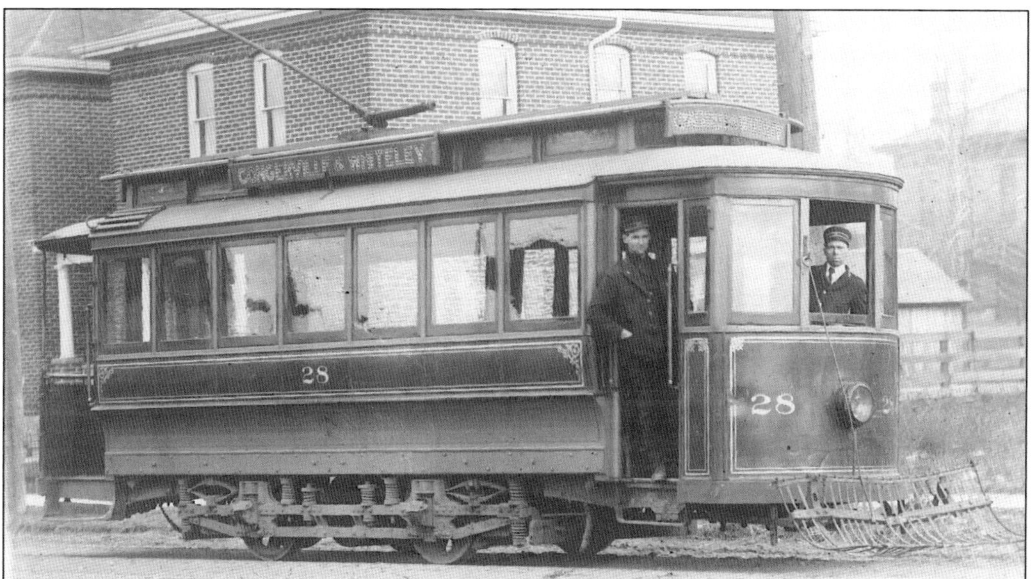

Congerville & Whiteley Trolley Car. Trolleys ran six different lines: Avondale, Congerville, Heeken Park, Industry, Whiteley, and the West Side known as Normal City. Electric streetcars appeared in Muncie in the spring of 1893 and were discontinued on October 11, 1931. (Real Photo, unidentified photographer.)

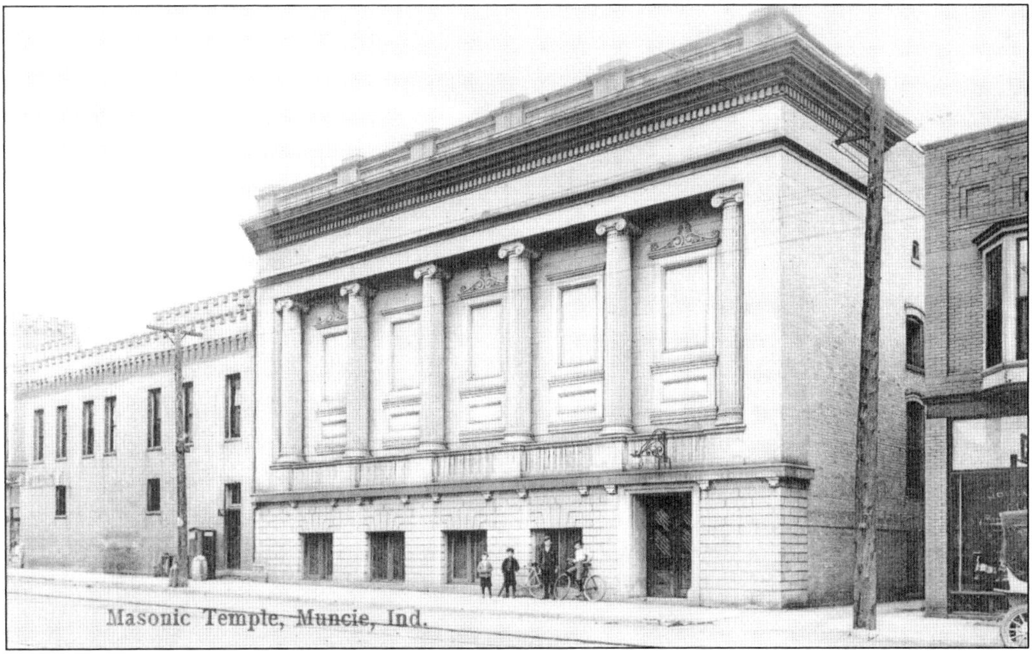

MASONIC TEMPLE. This building, designed in the Classic Revival style, was constructed on West Main Street in 1905–07 as the second Muncie Masonic Temple. The cost of the building was $25,000. In later years, it was used as a Buick automobile dealership. (Kraemer Art Co., for C.A. Penzel.)

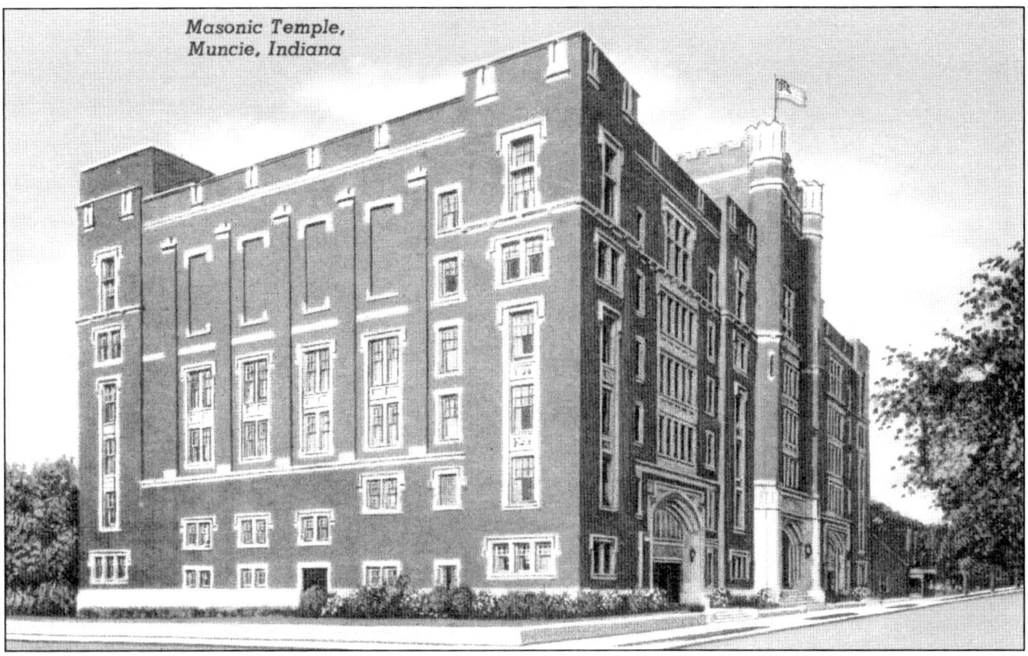

MASONIC TEMPLE. The 1929 Muncie Masonic Temple was and still remains one of Muncie's finest architectural designs. Kibele & Garrard were the architects of the masterpiece. On October 30, 1923, the cornerstone was laid for the building, and on November 26, 1929, it was dedicated. (Curt Teich Co., for Muncie News Co.)

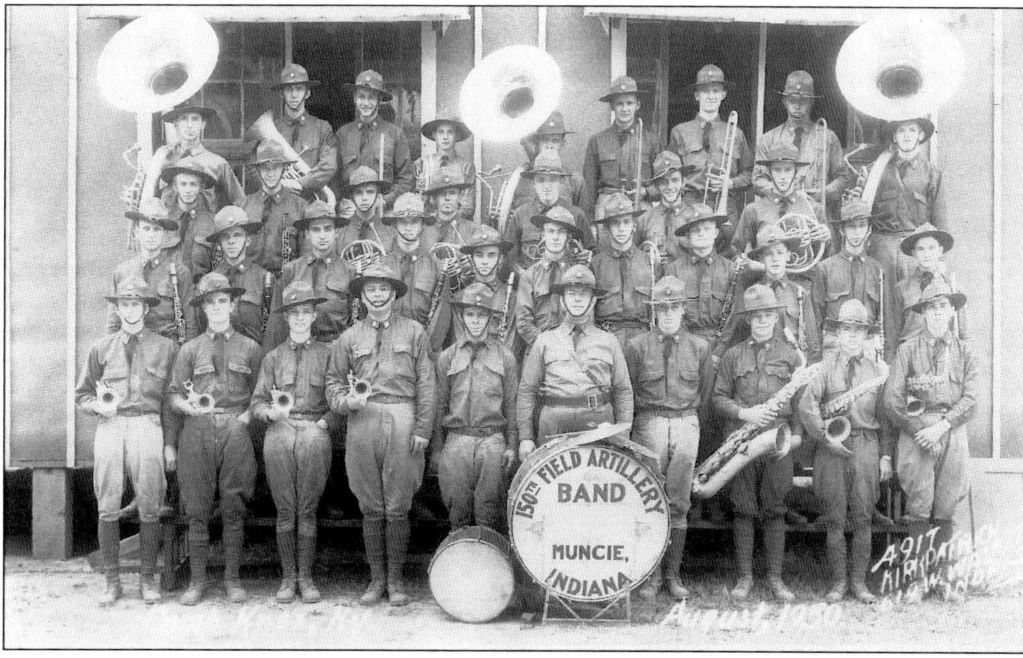

150TH FIELD ARTILLERY BAND. Muncie's 150th Field Artillery Band posed for this photo postcard in August of 1930 at Camp Knox near Louisville, Kentucky. (Real Photo, by Kirkpatrick, Indianapolis, Indiana.)

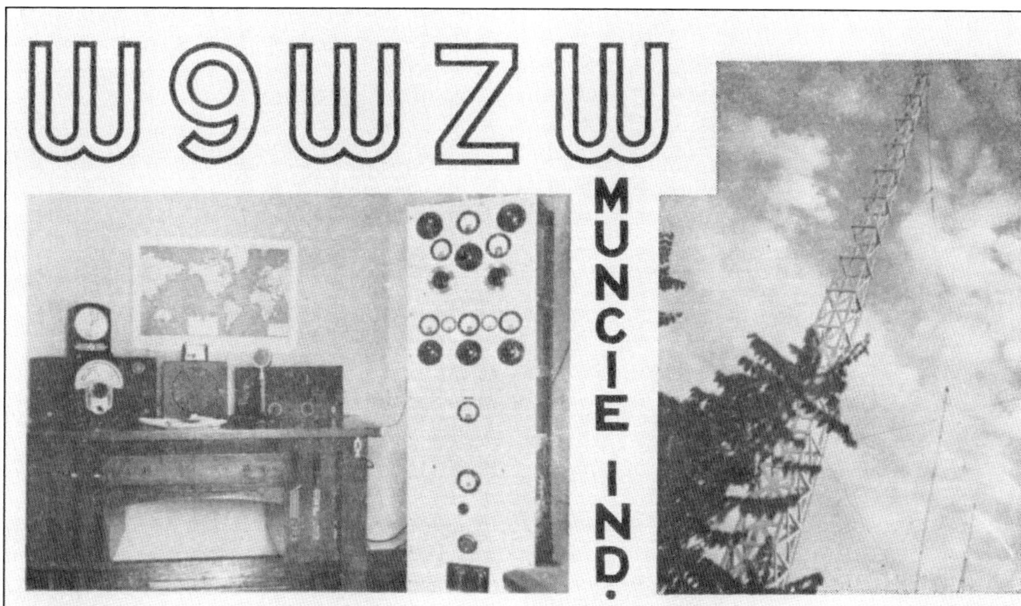

W9WZW. The ham radio station and tower pictured on the front of this card were located at 2506 Ethel Avenue. The station was owned and operated by the father of this author and had a 500-kilowatt transmitter and S X 16 receiver. When a new home was purchased on Woodridge Drive in the Maplewood addition, the station was closed. (Unidentified printer, for George W. Masing.)

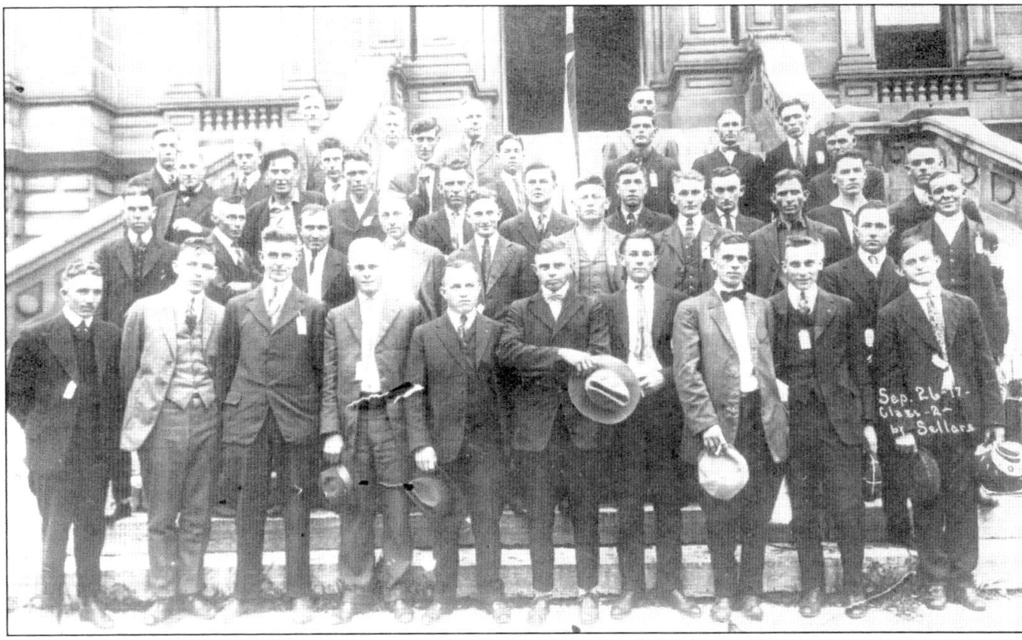

WORLD WAR I GROUP. During WW I, men often gathered on the steps of the Muncie Courthouse to have their pictures taken before going off to war. This image was taken on September 26, 1917, by local photographer Otto Sellers. (Real Photo, produced by Sellers of Muncie, Indiana.)

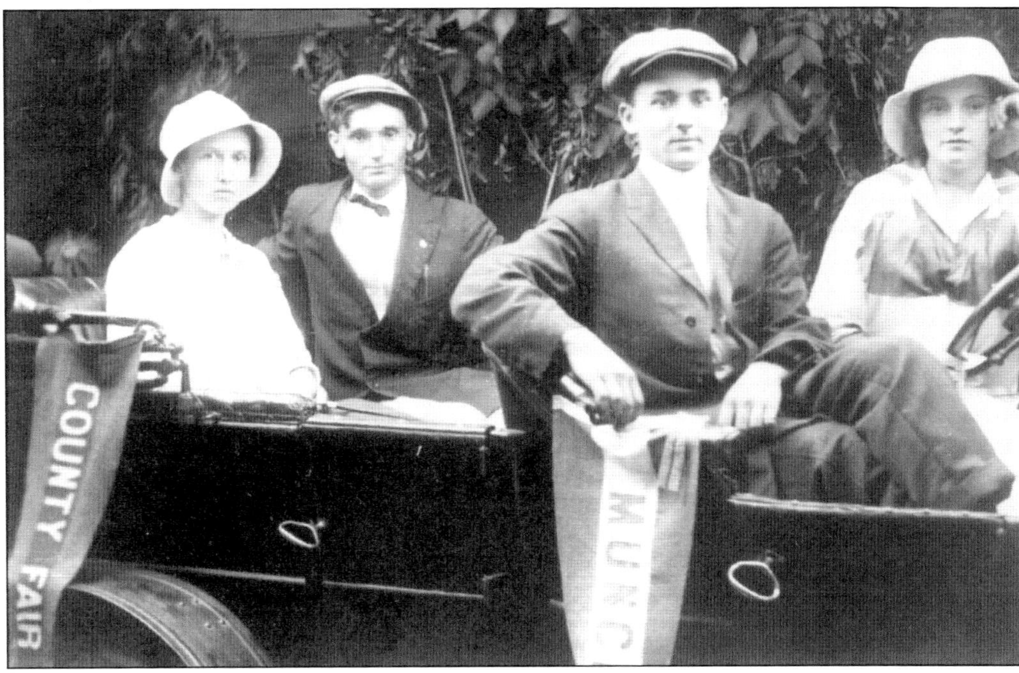

GROUP PHOTO, DELAWARE COUNTY FAIR. During the early nineteenth century—before everyone had a car—it was common to have pictures taken at the Delaware County Fair while sitting in one of the newfangled motorcars. This picture dates from between 1915 and 1920. (Real Photo, unidentified photographer.)

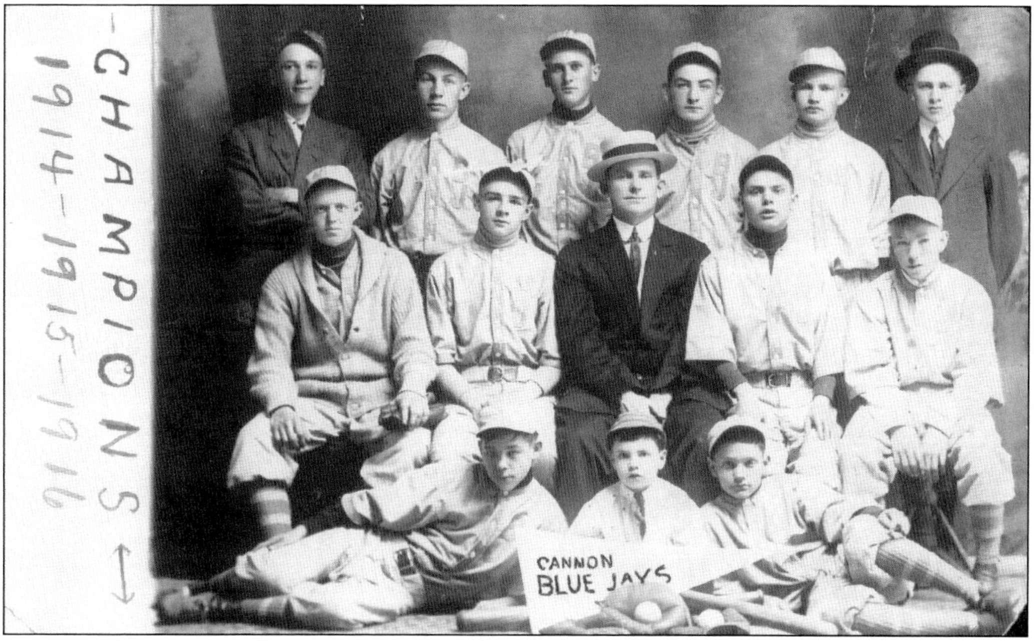

CANNON BLUE JAYS BASEBALL TEAM. The Cannon Blue Jays baseball team played in Muncie prior to WW I. According to writing on the back and front of this card, they were league champions in 1914, 1915, and 1916. (Real Photo, published by Peoples Studio, Muncie, Indiana).

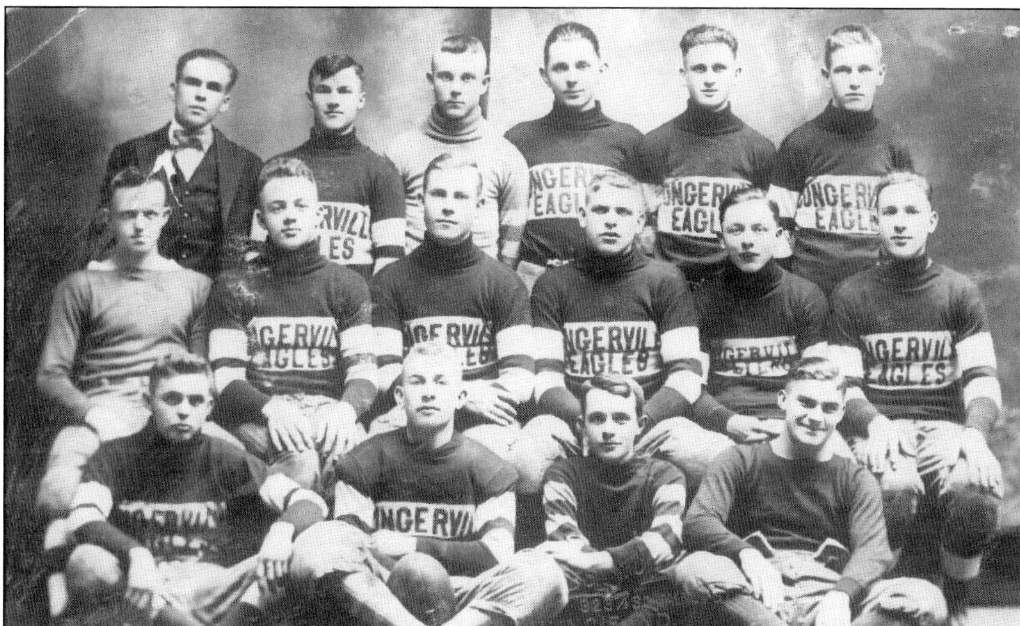

CONGERVILLE EAGLES FOOTBALL TEAM. Some of the individuals identified in this photo include Charles Gildea, Red Rogers, Henry Ratican, Hope Mullen, Murvin Collins, John Golden, and Earl Getz. The team played football in Muncie around the time of WW I. (Real photo, published by Peoples Studio, Muncie, Indiana.)

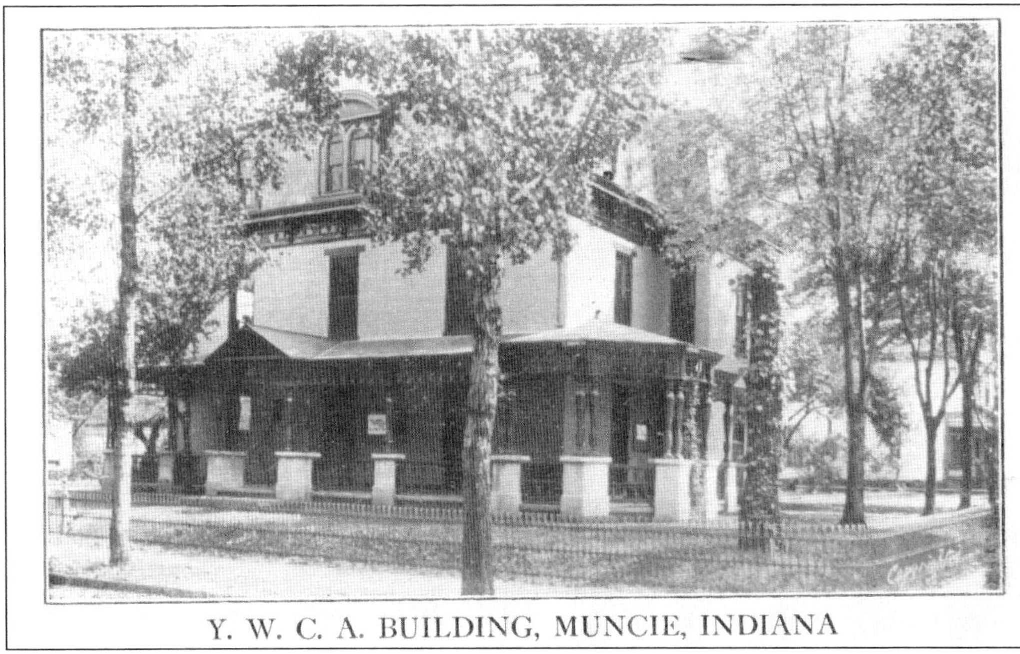

YWCA Building. This was the first building used as a YWCA in Muncie. It was used from 1912 until 1925, when the current building was completed at the northeast corner of Jefferson and Charles Streets. This card was used to promote "YWCA at Home" on Friday, January 24, 1913. (Unidentified publisher and printer.)

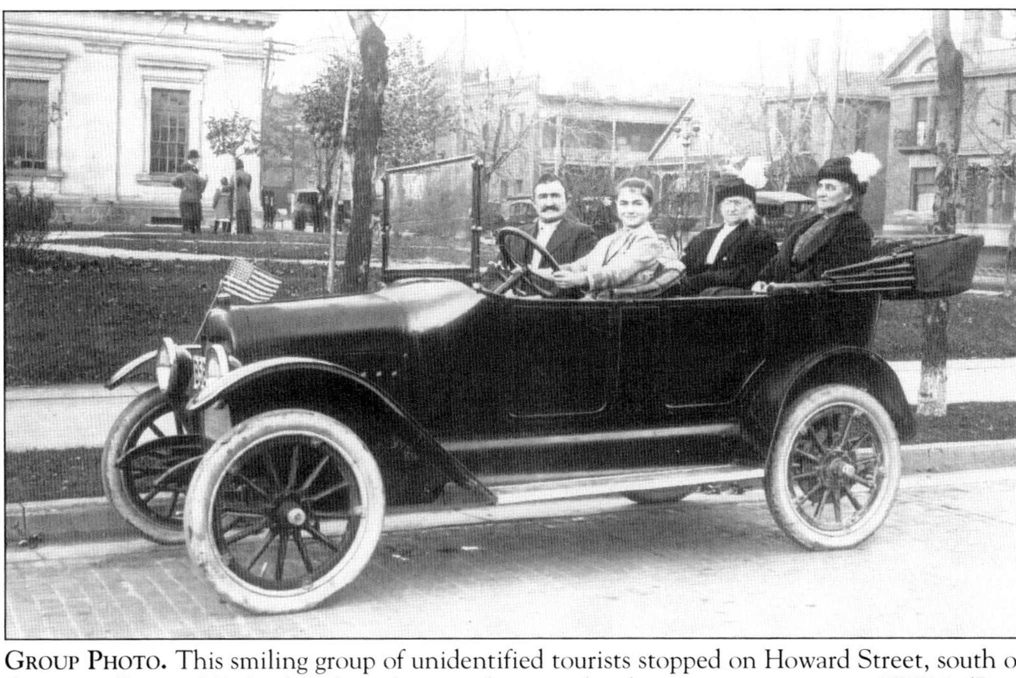

Group Photo. This smiling group of unidentified tourists stopped on Howard Street, south of the post office and Federal Park, to have a photograph taken sometime prior to WW I. (Real photo, unidentified photographer.)

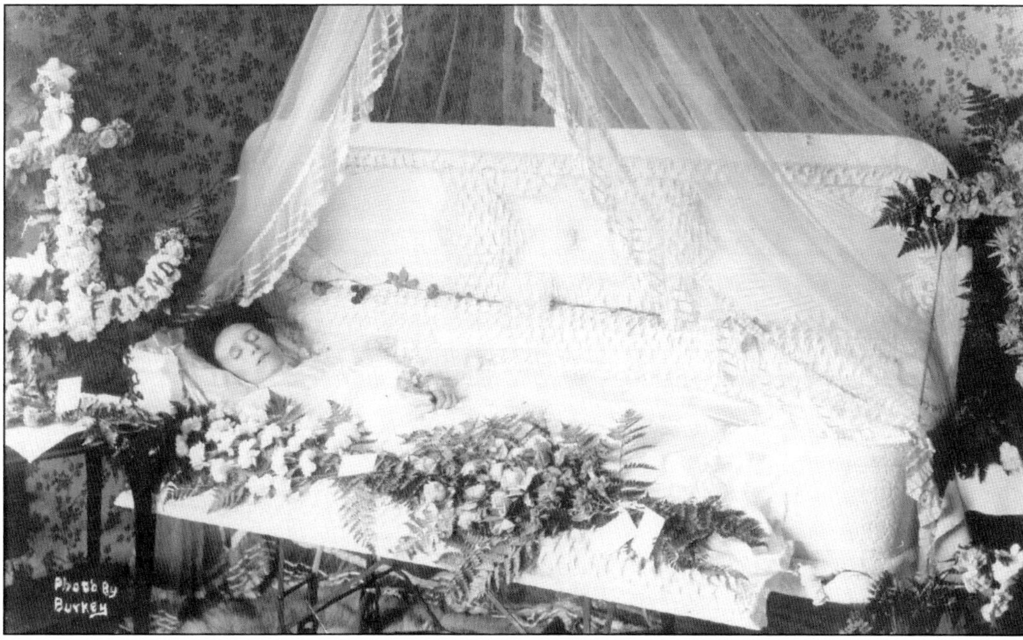

UNKNOWN WOMAN IN CASKET. As unusual as it might seem today, just after the turn of the century, the dearly departed were often photographed in their caskets. This photo was probably taken around 1910 or 1915 in a private home, where funerals were usually held at the time. The deceased woman in the photo is unidentified. (Real photo, published by Burkey Brothers Studio, Muncie, Indiana.)

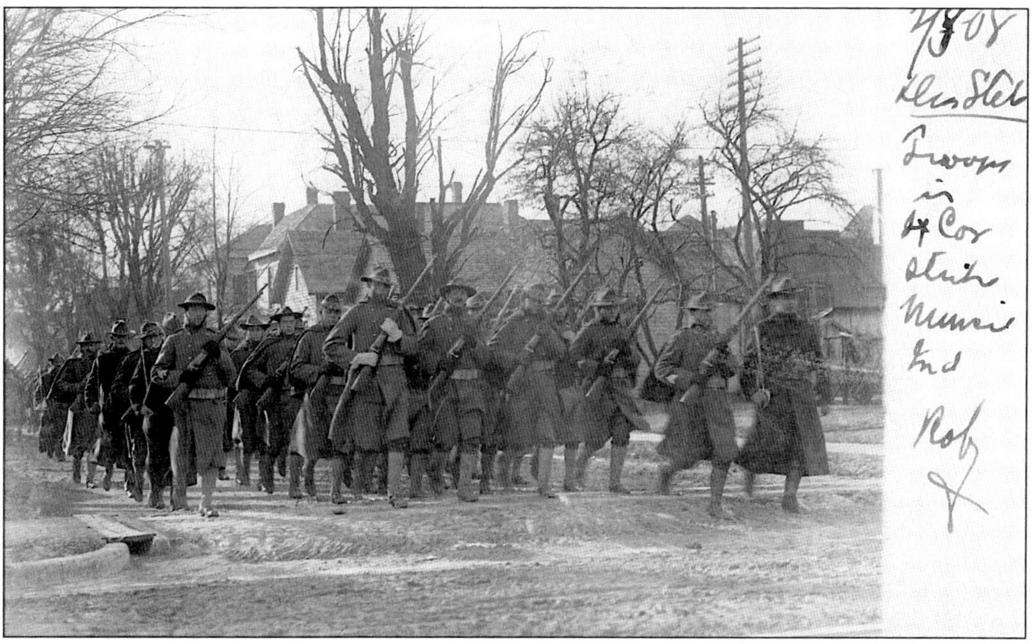

TROOPS MARCHING ON MUNCIE STREET. From January 2 to January 7, 300 troops of the Indianapolis National Guard were called to Muncie by Governor Hanley. The governor declared martial law when violence erupted during a streetcar strike. (Real photo, unidentified photographer.)

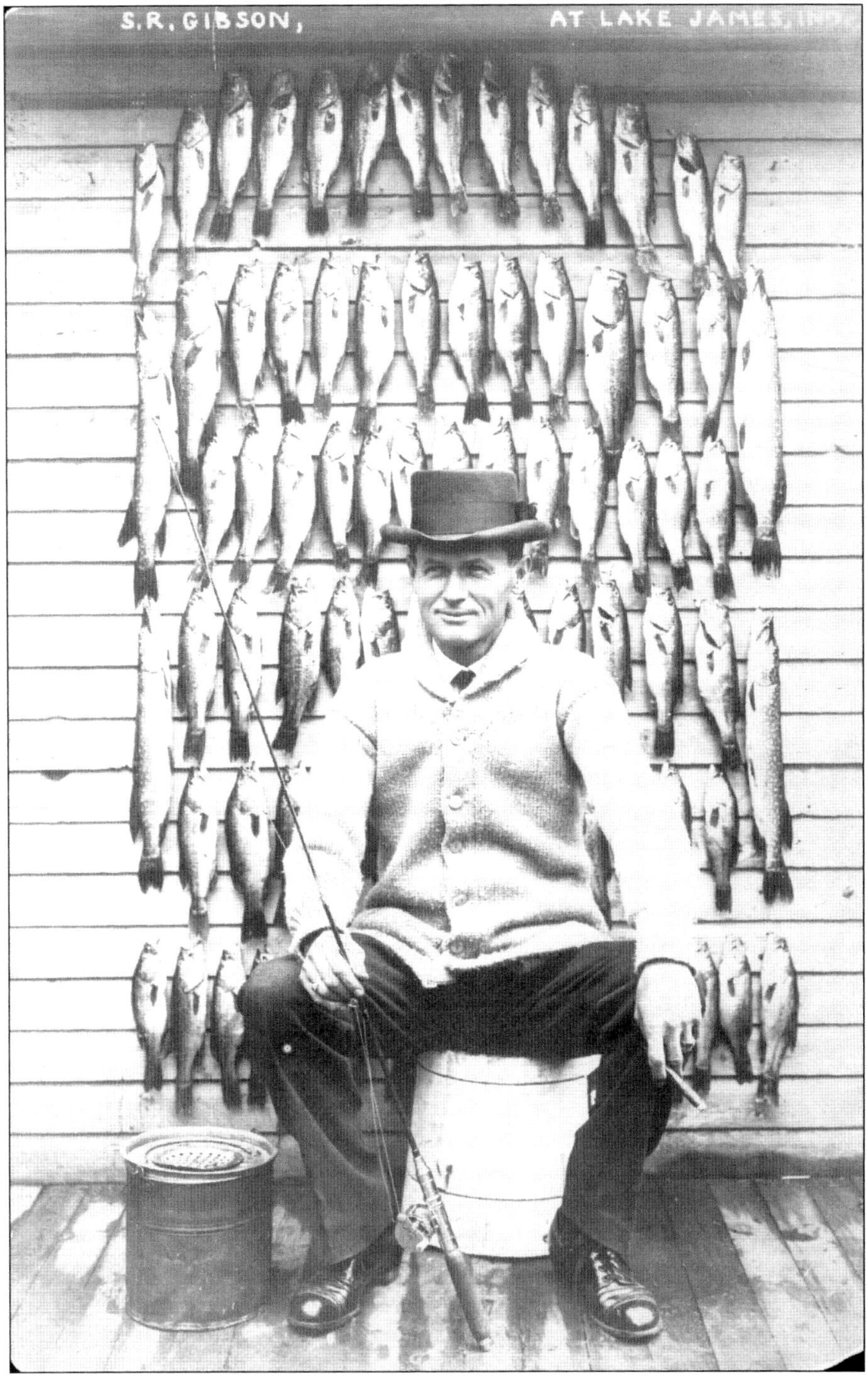

S.R. GIBSON AT LAKE JAMES, IN. Samuel R. Gibson, a resident of Muncie, posed for this photo at Lake James after a fishing outing in northern Indiana. Considering his catch, it is no wonder that he is smiling. Mr. Gibson was part-owner of St. John's Cigar store at 123 East Main Street. His home appears in chapter eight of this book. This photo was taken around 1915. (Real photo, published by J. Inbody, Elkhart, Indiana.)

Three

School Buildings and Education

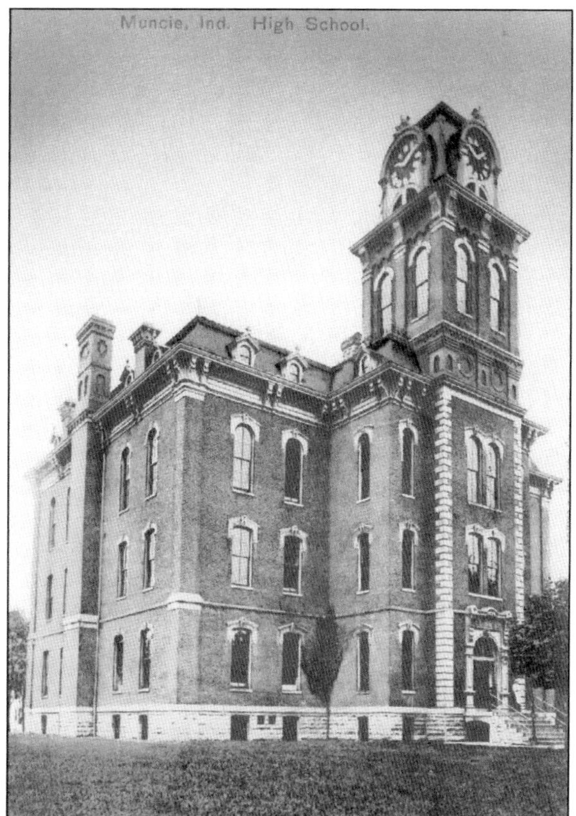

Muncie High School. The Muncie High School was built by local builder John Perry after plans of a school in St. Louis, MO. Completed in 1881, the building was an excellent example of a now rare style of architecture called Second Empire. (Metropolitan News & Pub. Co., for C.A. Penzel.)

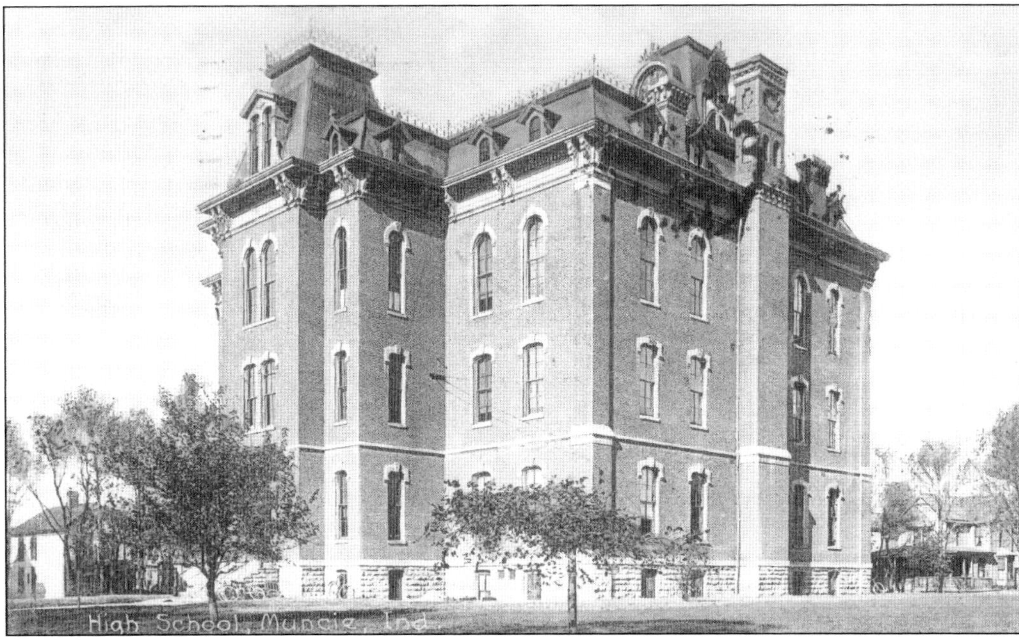

MUNCIE HIGH SCHOOL. The Muncie High School was demolished from 1912 to 1913 to make room for the construction of a new school on the same site. The new school was to be called Central High School. (Kraemer Art Co., for C.A. Penzel.)

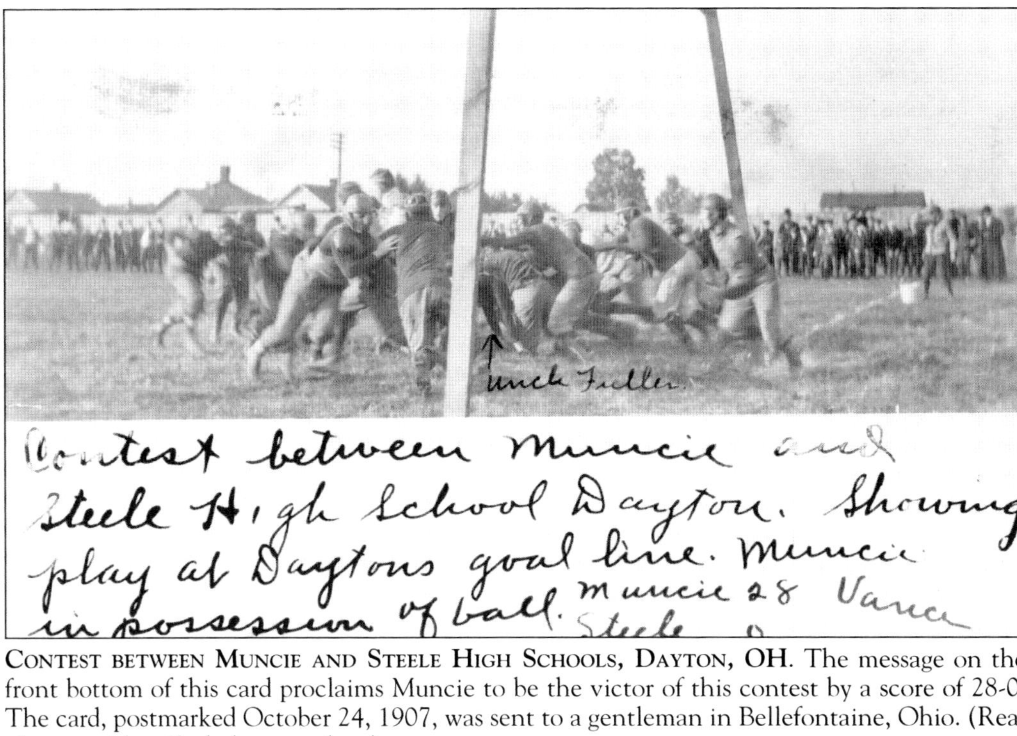

CONTEST BETWEEN MUNCIE AND STEELE HIGH SCHOOLS, DAYTON, OH. The message on the front bottom of this card proclaims Muncie to be the victor of this contest by a score of 28-0. The card, postmarked October 24, 1907, was sent to a gentleman in Bellefontaine, Ohio. (Real photo, unidentified photographer.)

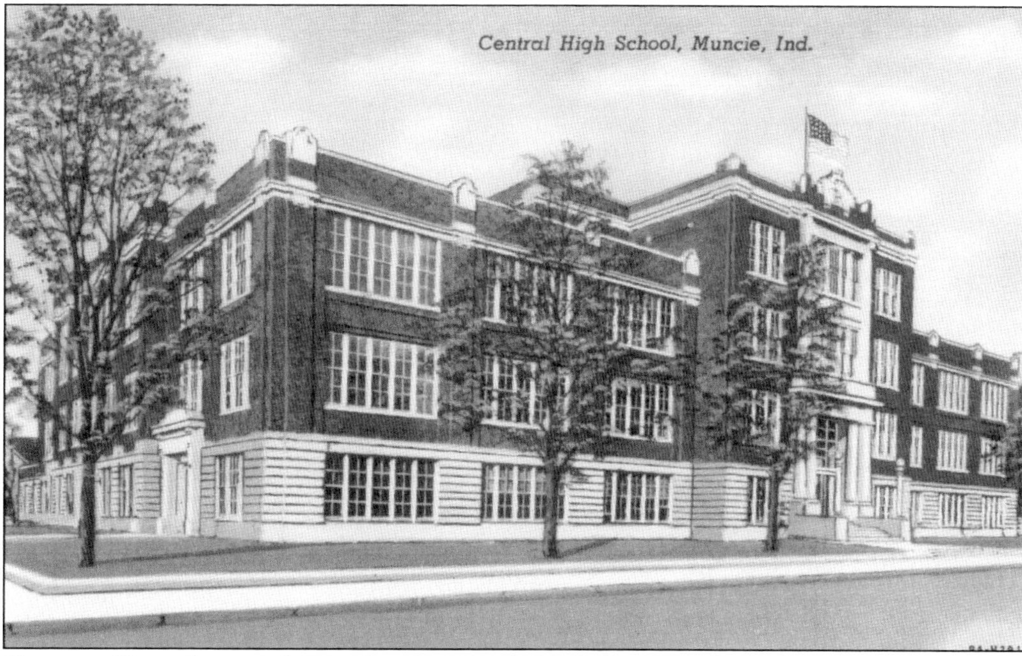

Central High School. Located at 311 South High Street in downtown Muncie, this large building was completed in 1914. The plans for the building were drawn by local architect Cuno Kibele. The building was demolished in 1973 and replaced by the national headquarters of the Ball Corporation. (Curt Teich Co., for Muncie News Co.)

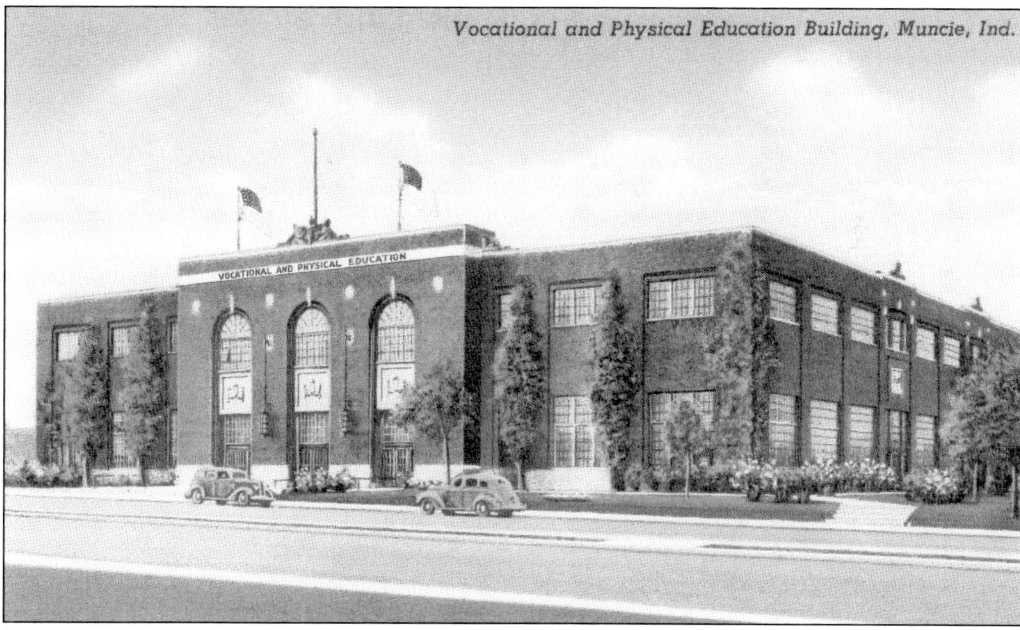

Vocational and Physical Education Building (Muncie Field House). Houck and Smener of Muncie drew the plans for this $160,000 structure that was completed in 1928. A.J. Glaser of Muncie was the contractor for the job. Dedication ceremonies for the building were held December 7, 1928. Many high school basketball tournaments have been played here. (Curt Teich Co., for Muncie News Co.)

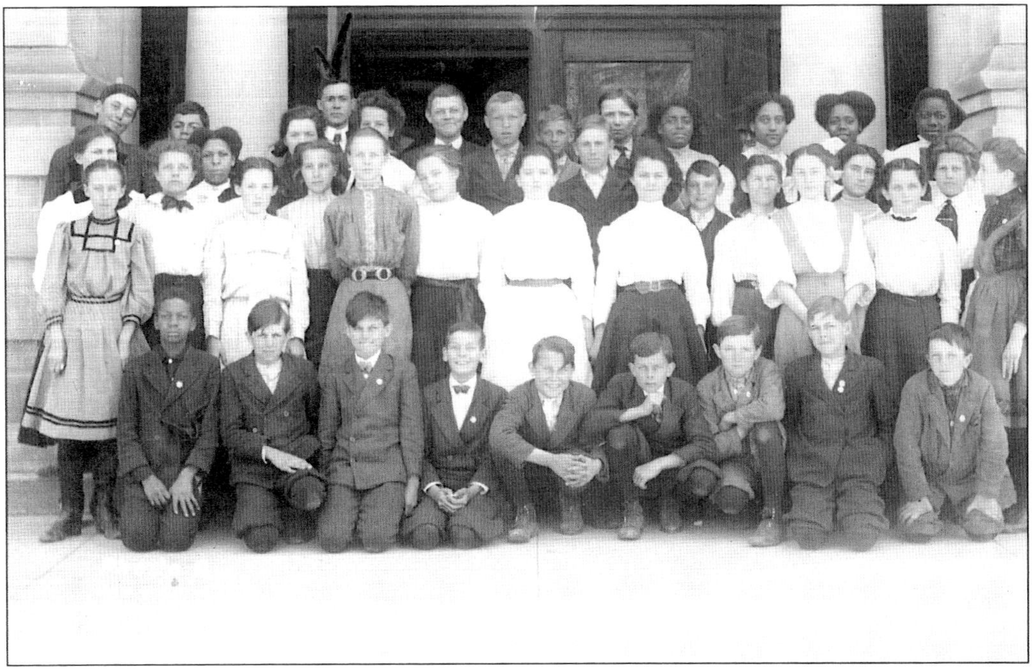

GRADES SIX, SEVEN, AND EIGHT, LONGFELLOW SCHOOL. The penciled writing on the back of this card identifies the name of the school, the grades of the children, and the date of the photograph as being November 29, 1910. The card was never mailed, only identified. (Real photo, published by Mrs. S.H. Burkey of Burkey Bro's Studio.)

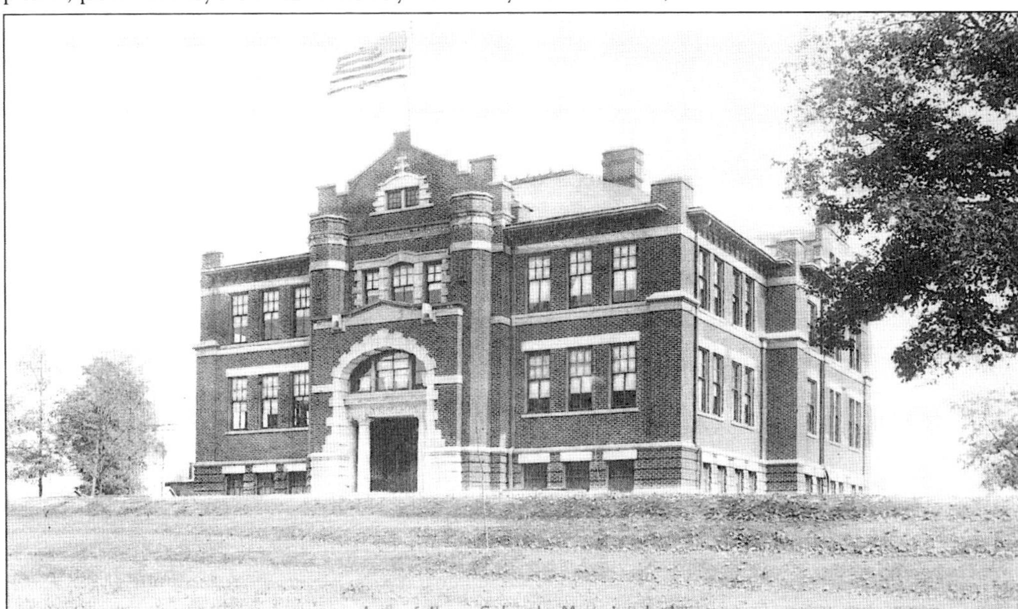

LONGFELLOW SCHOOL. The Longfellow School was located at the top of a slight hill at 1100 North Broadway Street. It was designed by the Fort Wayne architectural firm of Wing & Mahurin and completed in 1905. In 1953, a new Longfellow School was constructed on East Centennial Avenue. (Kraemer Art Co., for C.A. Penzel.)

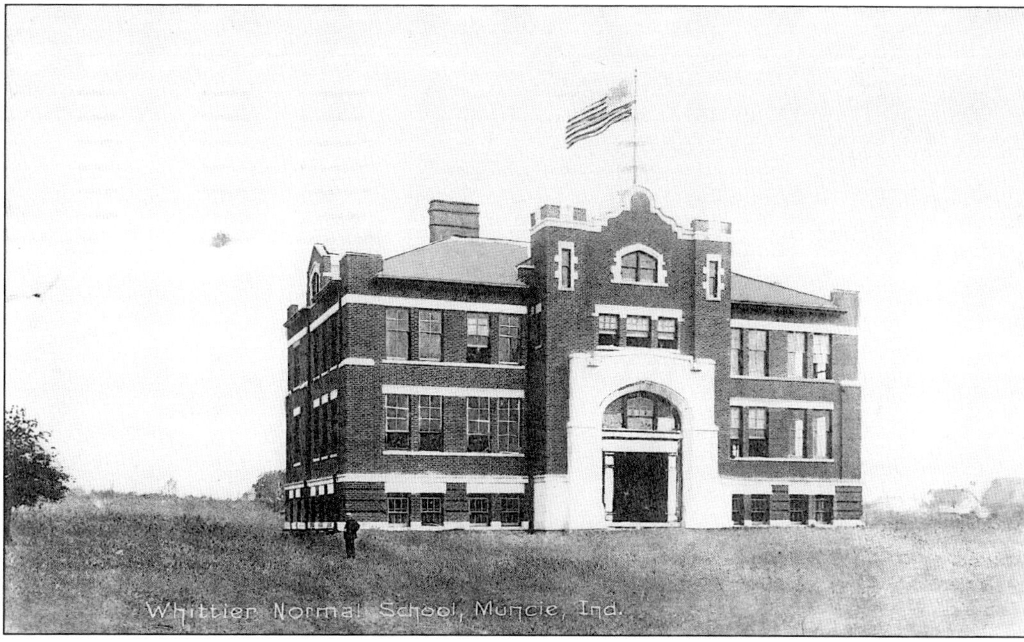

Whittier Normal School. Construction was completed on this school at 100 North College Avenue in 1908. It was dedicated on December 14, 1908. In its final years, it was used as a Sunday school by the College Avenue Methodist Church. In 1956 and 1957, the school was demolished to expand the church. (Kraemer Art Co., for C.A. Penzel.)

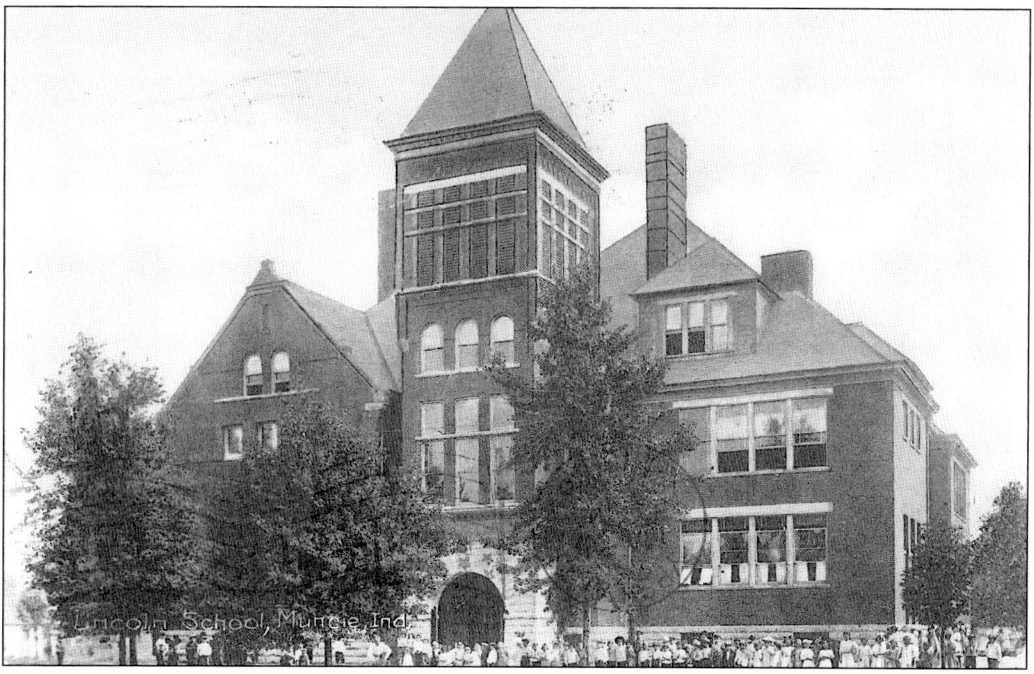

Lincoln School. Like several of the early Muncie school buildings, the Lincoln school was designed by Cuno Kibele. Opened in 1895, it was located in the 1200 block of West Memorial Drive. In 1925 and 1965, additions were made to Lincoln, and in 1980, the building was closed as a school. (Kraemer Art Co., for C.A. Penzel.)

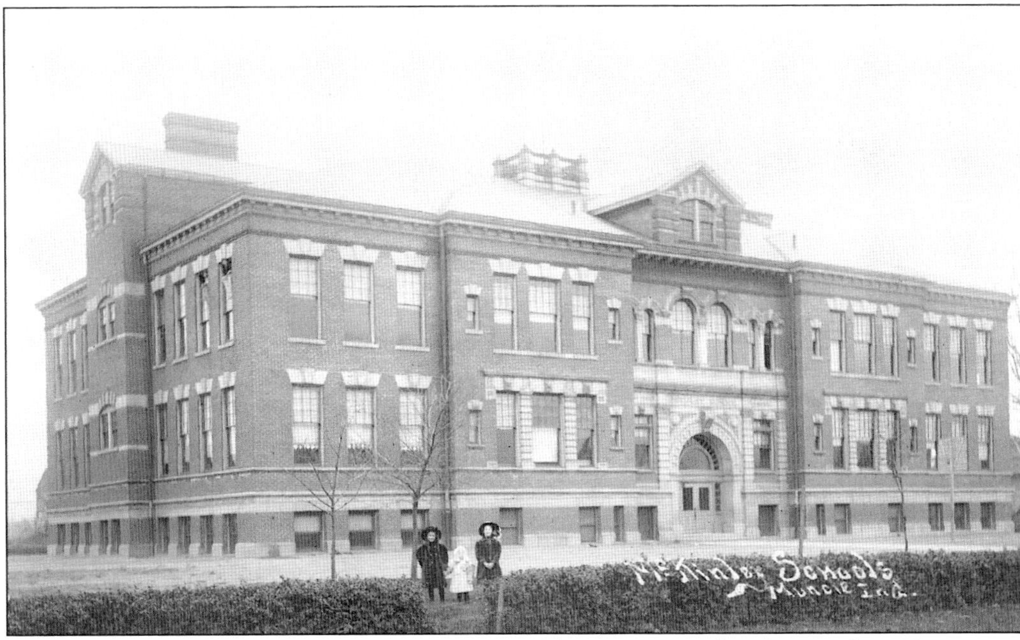

McKinley School. This elementary school building was completed around 1905 at a cost of $40,000 from plans drawn by architects Grindle & Keelor of Fort Wayne, Indiana. It was located at 601 North Jefferson Street. Demolition of the building took place in 1972. (Real photo, unidentified photographer.)

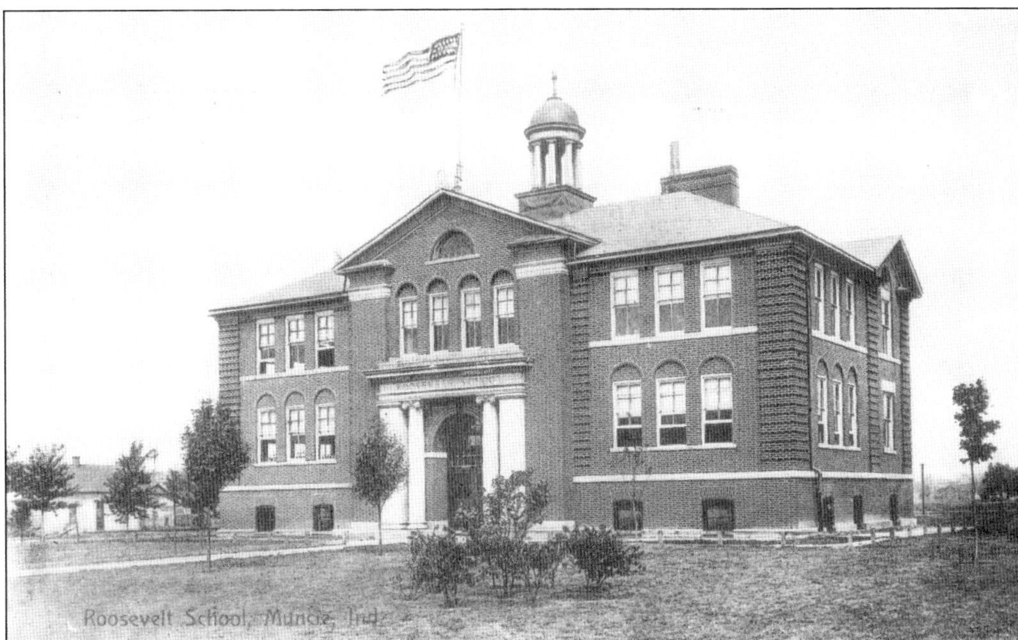

Roosevelt School. Roosevelt School was located at 300 East Twenty-first Street on the northeast corner with Jefferson Street. The building shown here was opened in 1902, added on to in 1922 and 1937, and abandoned in 1980. (Kraemer Art Co., for C.A. Penzel.)

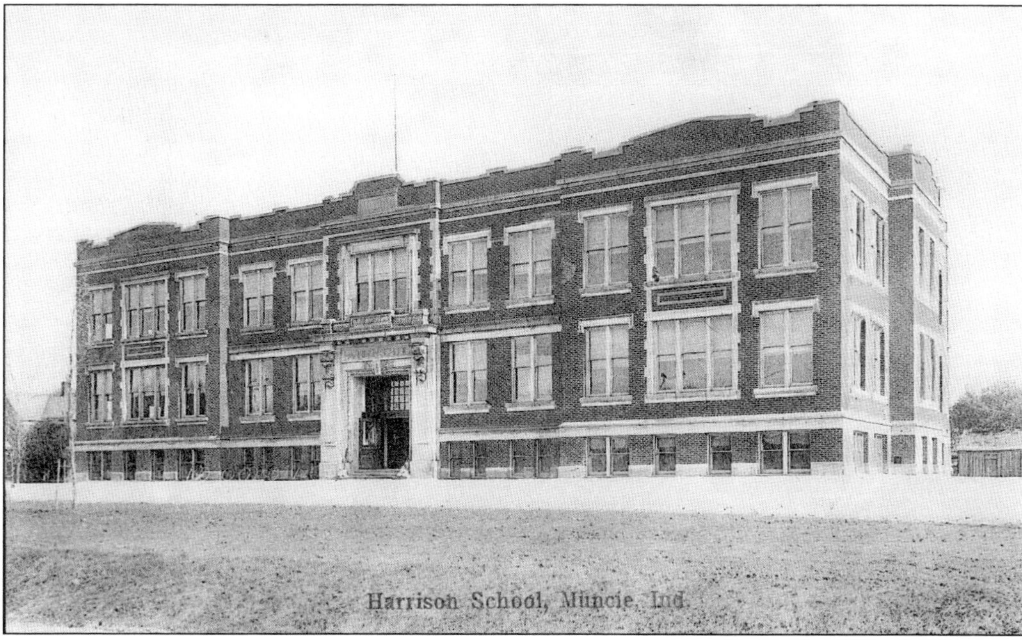

HARRISON SCHOOL. Avis Pittenger was a longtime principal of this school located at 1300 South Liberty Street. It was constructed in 1909 from plans drawn by Cuno Kibele. General contractor for the job was Glass & Humphreys of Muncie for $40,000. (Kraemer Art Co., for C.A. Penzel.)

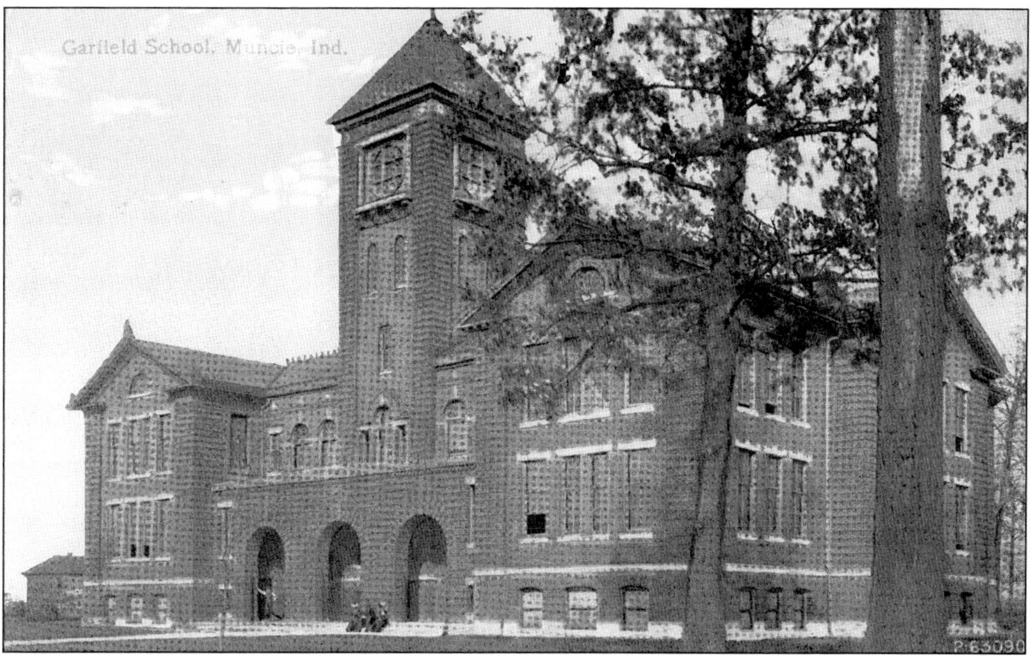

GARFIELD SCHOOL. The address for this elementary school building was 1600 South Madison Street. First constructed in 1901, the building was destroyed by a major fire in 1947 and was rebuilt in 1950 from plans drawn by McGuire and Shook & Associates. A 1977 building now replaces the structure. (Superior Post Card Company [S.P.C.Co.])

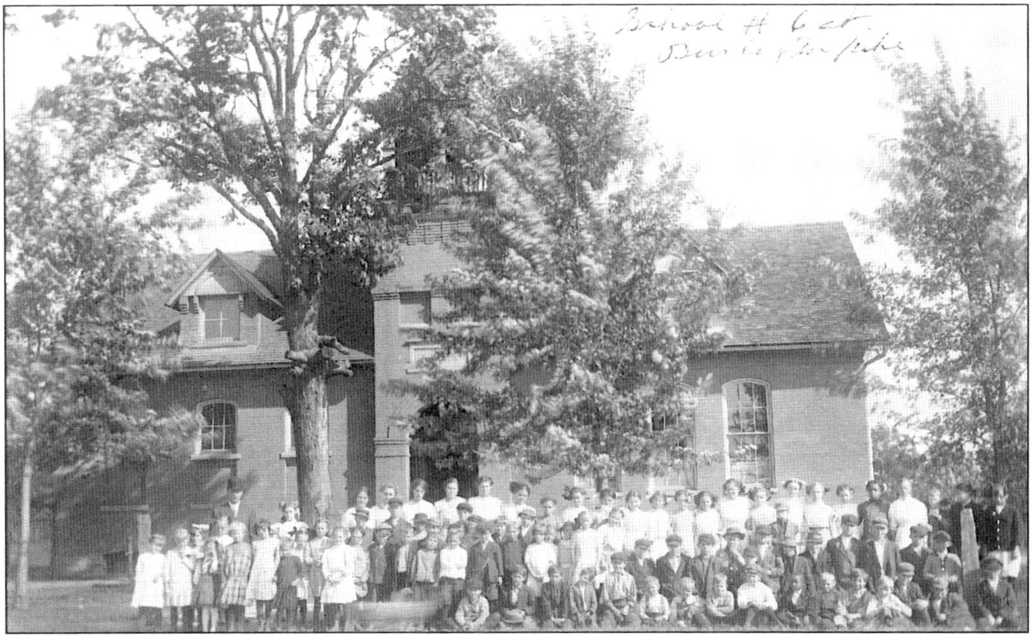

SCHOOL NUMBER SIX. When constructed, this building located on Burlington Pike was not actually in the city of Muncie. It was originally in the county school system and located south of the city. (Real photo, unidentified photographer.)

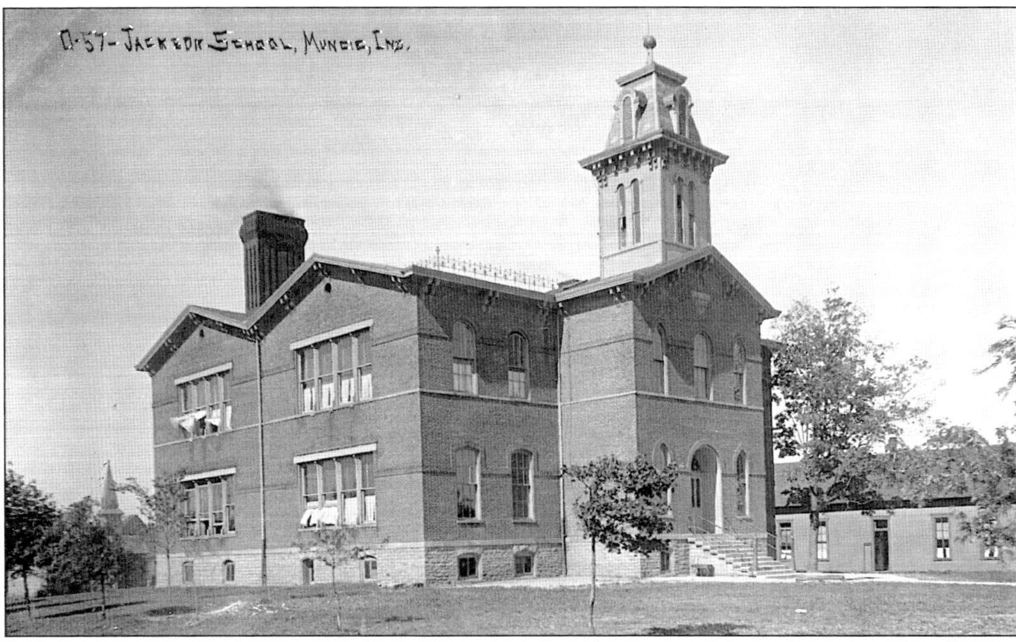

JACKSON SCHOOL. Jackson School was located on Madison Street between Second and Third Streets. This was one of the earliest school buildings in Muncie. It was closed in 1927, sold in 1928, and later replaced with a park named after the school. (Real photo, published by Galion View Co.)

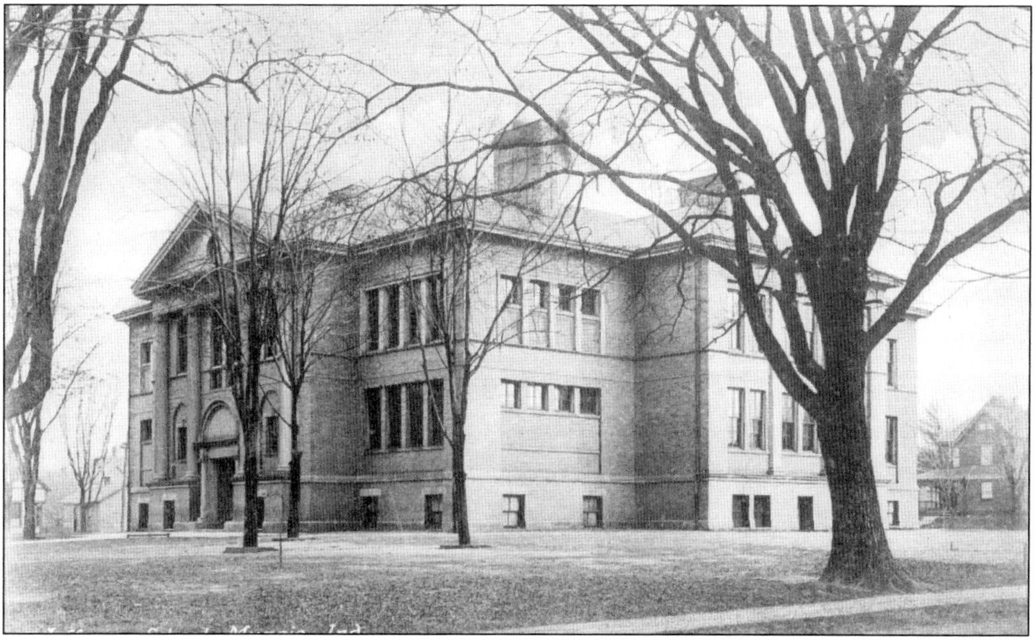

Jefferson School. Completed in 1898, the Jefferson School was located at 701 West Jackson Street on the site now occupied by Gillespie Towers Apartments. The school was closed in 1974 and razed the next year. (IPC Co. [trademark], for C.A. Penzel.)

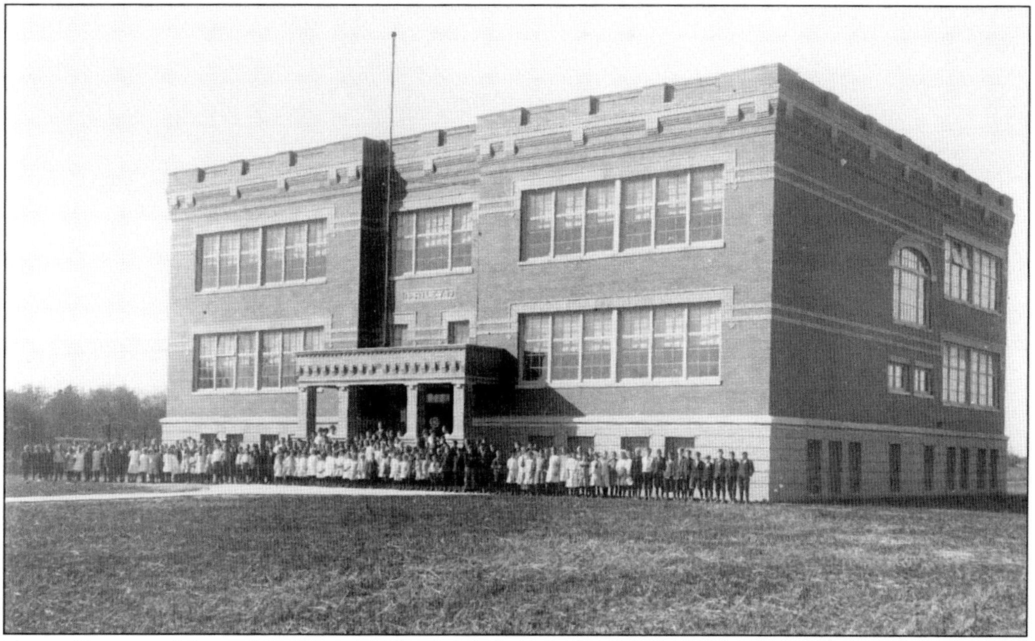

Riley School. Named for James Whitcomb Riley, the famous Indiana poet, this building was constructed from 1913 until 1914. It was located at 1601 North Walnut Street. Opening day for the $28,000 building was February 23, 1914. A 1956 addition rendered this building obsolete. The picture shown here is not a postcard. (Real photo, from the Sellers collection in the Ball State University Archives.)

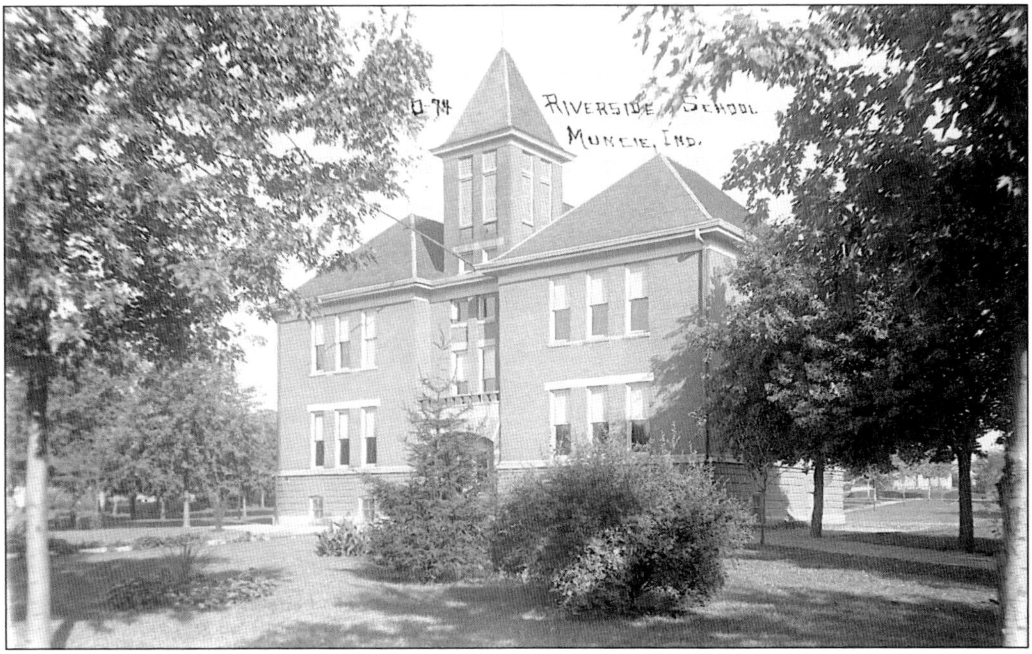

Riverside School. Built in 1899 and razed in 1923, this school was replaced by Emerson School. It was located in the block bounded by Beechwood Avenue, Pauline Avenue, Linden Street, and Ashland Street. This view looks to the northwest. (Real Photo, published by Galion View Co.)

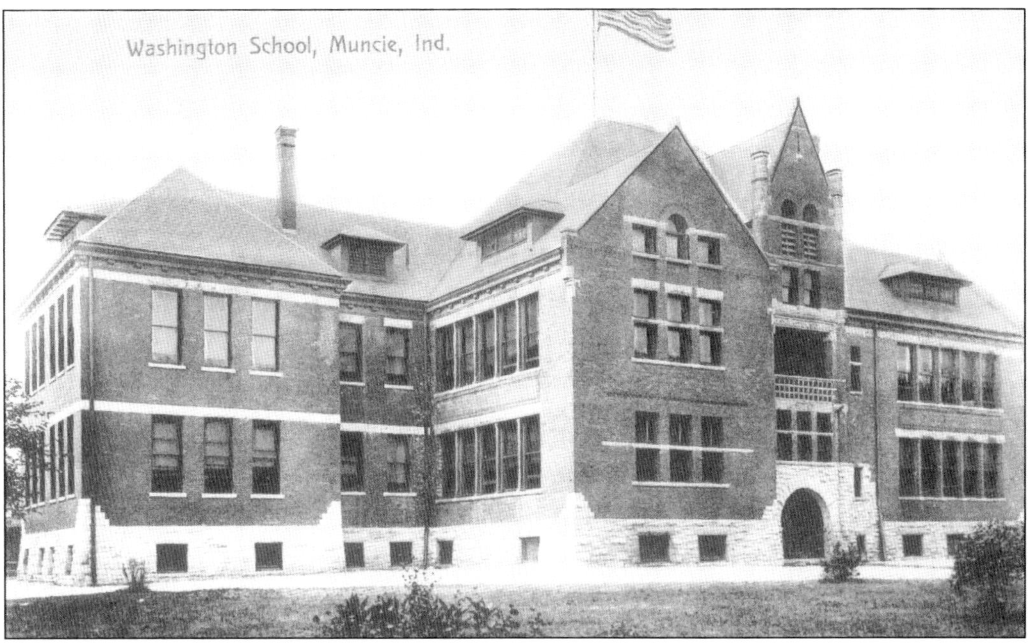

Washington School. One of the older school buildings existing in Muncie during the postcard era, this building was constructed in 1889. It was located at 701 East Adams Street on the southeast corner with South Vine Street. The building contained 20,000 square feet of space. (Kraemer Art Co., for C.A. Penzel.)

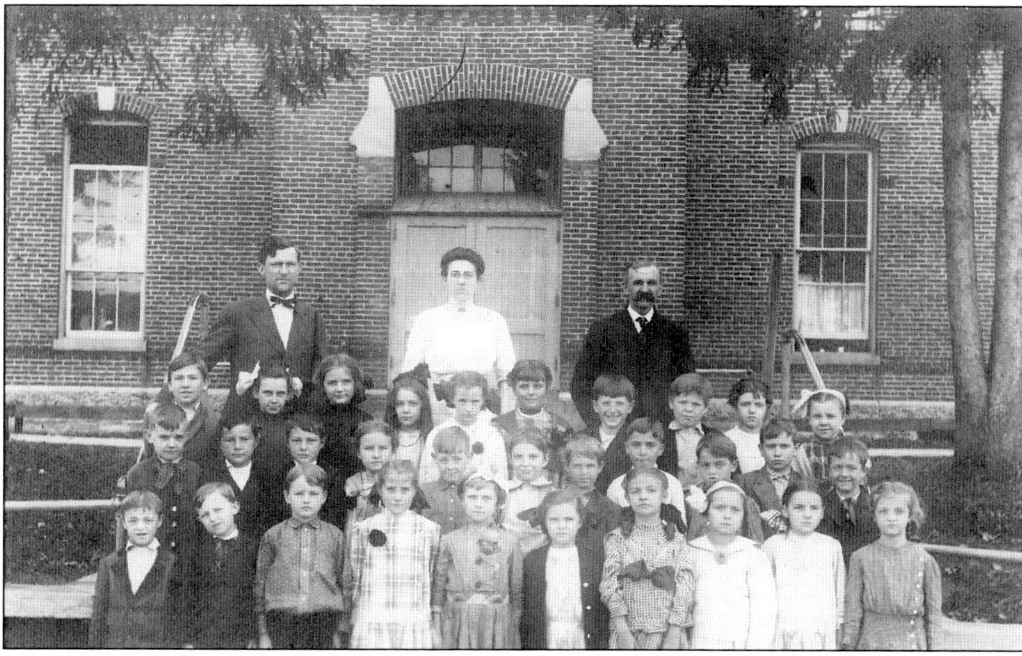

UNIDENTIFIED SCHOOL GROUP. Burkey Brothers took many photos of school groups. Unfortunately, most of them were not identified by the photographer. This picture may have even been located outside the city. (Real photo, published by Burkey Bro's Studio.)

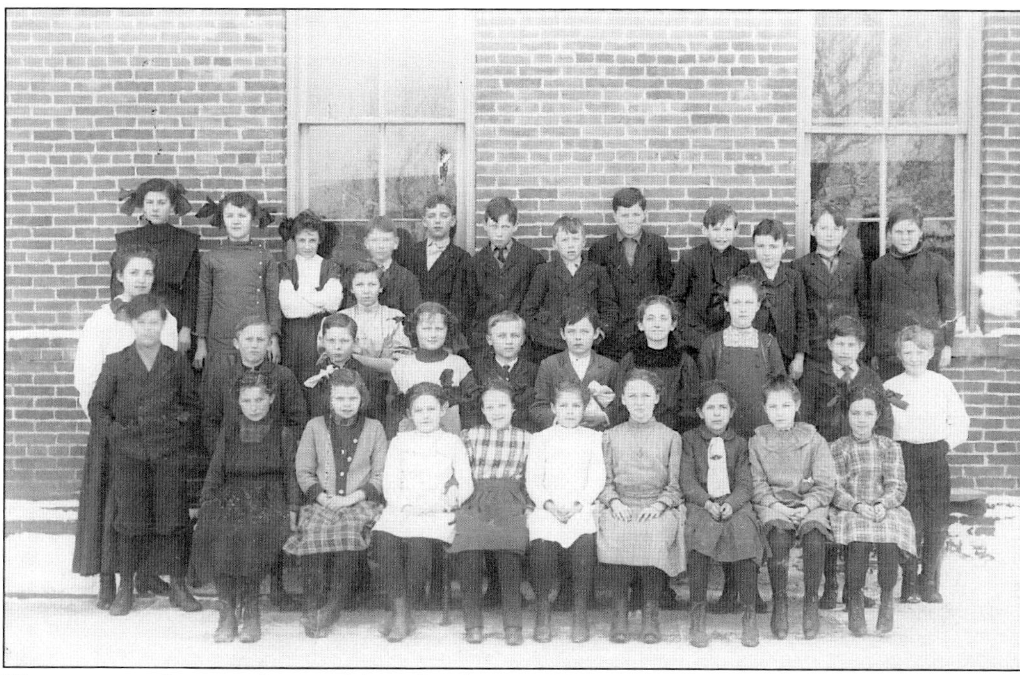

UNIDENTIFIED SCHOOL GROUP. This school group, like the one above, may not actually be from the city of Muncie. The photographer's mark on the back is the only identification, and the picture does not show enough of the building to make an accurate identification. (Real photo, published by Burkey Bro's Studio.)

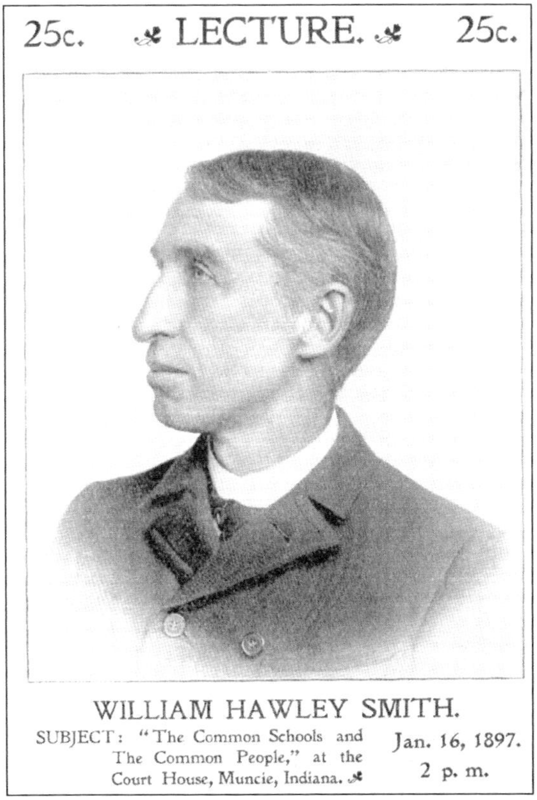

LECTURE BY WILLIAM HAWLEY SMITH. This promotional card for Marion Stewart, a druggist and bookseller, announces an upcoming lecture by writer and speaker William Hawley Smith on January 16, 1897. This card is not truly a postcard, but simply an announcement card. The back of the card declares that "any teacher purchasing a copy of William Hawley Smith's works who, after reading same, is not fully satisfied, may return it and the price will be refunded."(Unidentified printer, for Marion Stewart.)

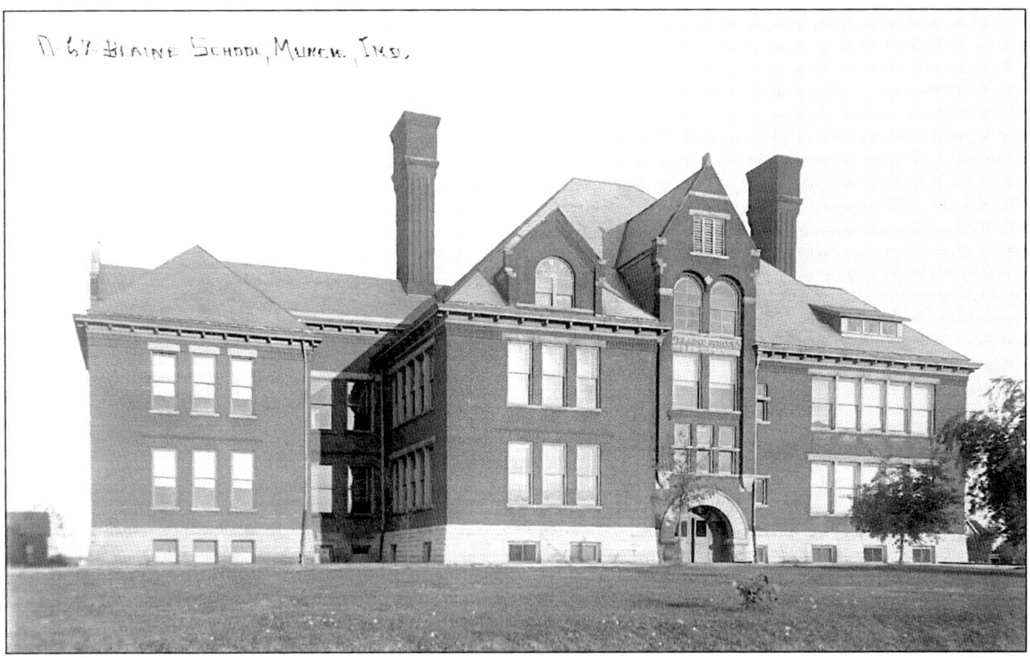

BLAINE SCHOOL. Designed by Muncie architect Cuno Kibele, this elementary school building was opened in 1893. It was located at the corner of Seventh and Shipley Streets on the southeast side of the city. In 1978, the school was closed. (Real Photo, published by Galion View Co.)

Four

STREET SCENES AND BIRDS-EYE VIEWS

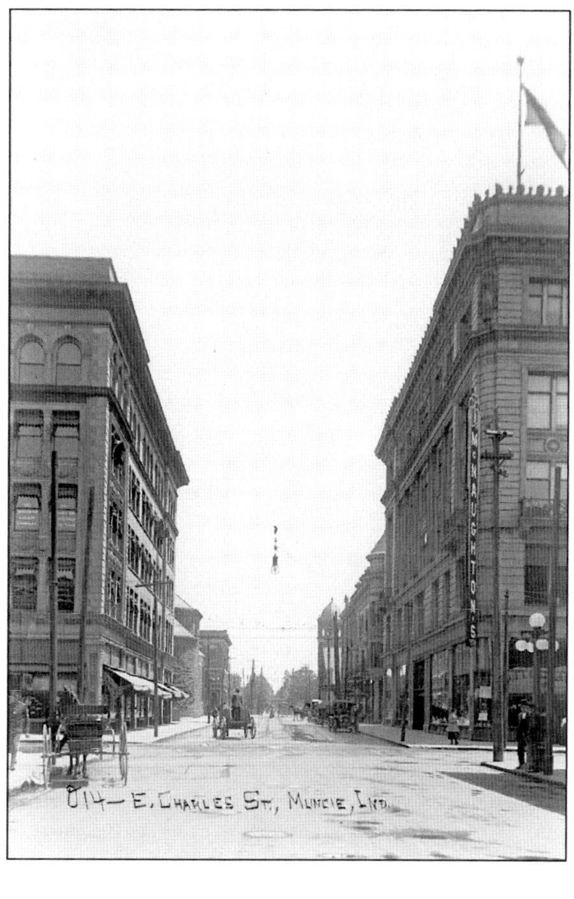

EAST CHARLES STREET. This real photo card was published by the Galion View Company around 1910. It shows East Charles Street looking east from the 100 block of West Charles Street. The McNaughton Department Store and the Johnson block can be seen at the intersection with Walnut Street. Galion View Company produced one of the highest quality series of postcards ever made for Muncie. They provided close to 90 different postcards of Muncie that were simply outstanding in photographic quality. This is view number 14. (Real photo, published by Galion View Co.)

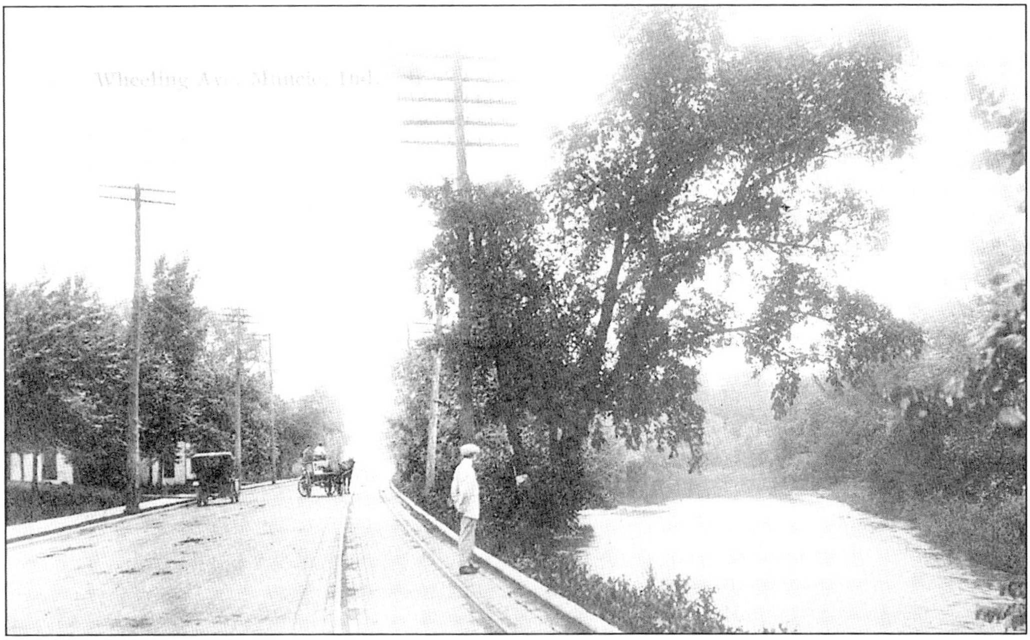

WHEELING AVENUE. Looking north and a bit to the west, this view shows Wheeling Avenue where it runs alongside White River. Streetcars ran along Wheeling Avenue. The tracks for the trolley cars can be seen near the right side of the road, between the road and the river bank. (Kraemer Art Co., for C.A. Penzel.)

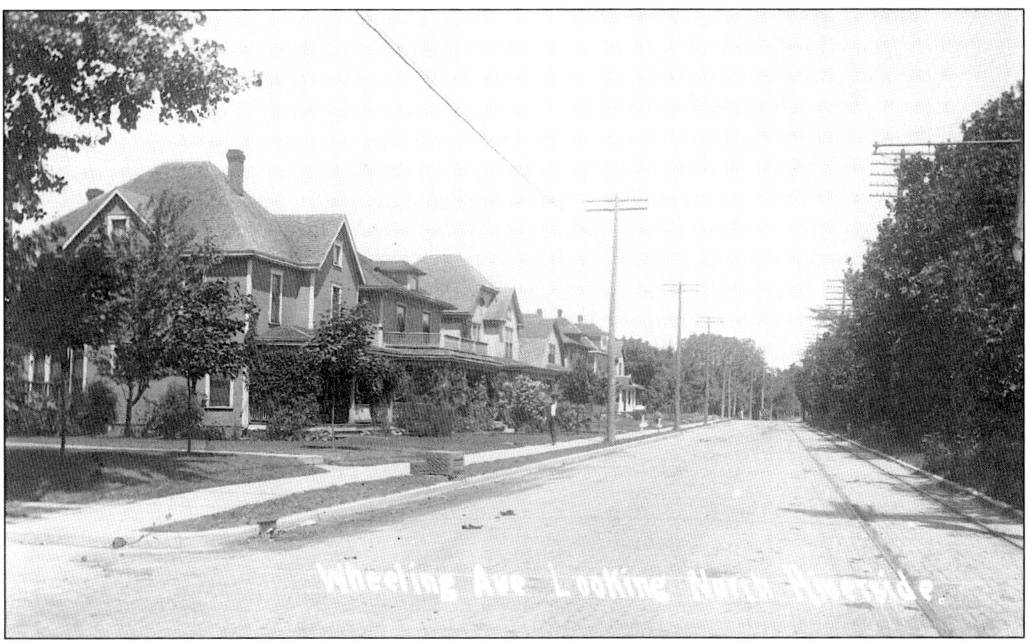

LOOKING NORTH FROM WHEELING AVENUE, RIVERSIDE. This real photo postcard is looking north on Wheeling Avenue in the neighborhood that once was known as Riverside. Note the brick pavement. (Real photo, unidentified photographer.)

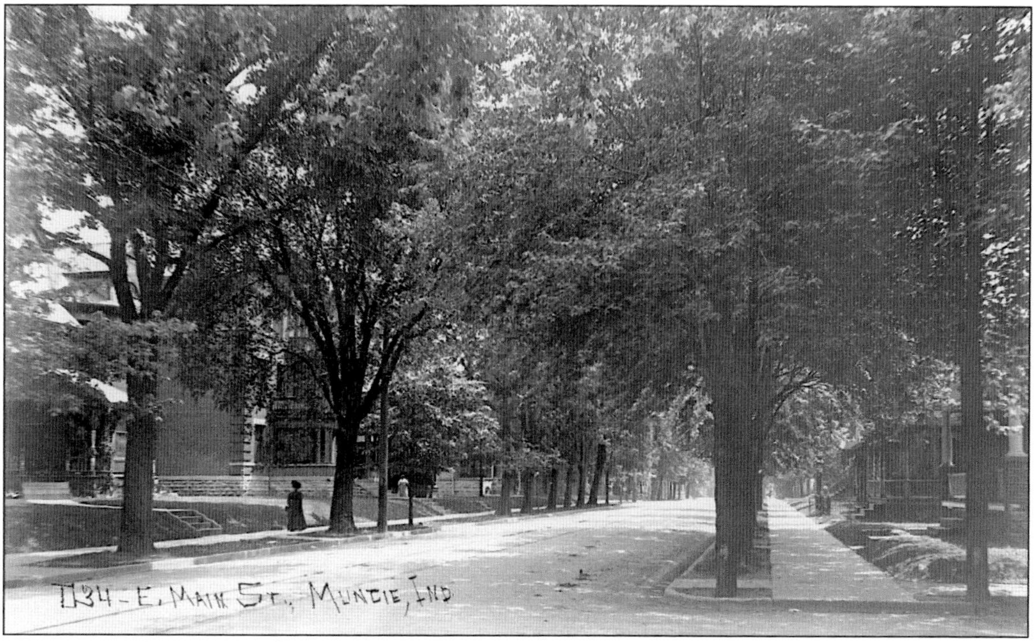

East Main Street. At the time of this photograph, East Main Street was home to numerous prominent citizens and marvelous homes. Most of the homes are still standing today, with some still in excellent condition. (Real photo, published by Galion View Co.)

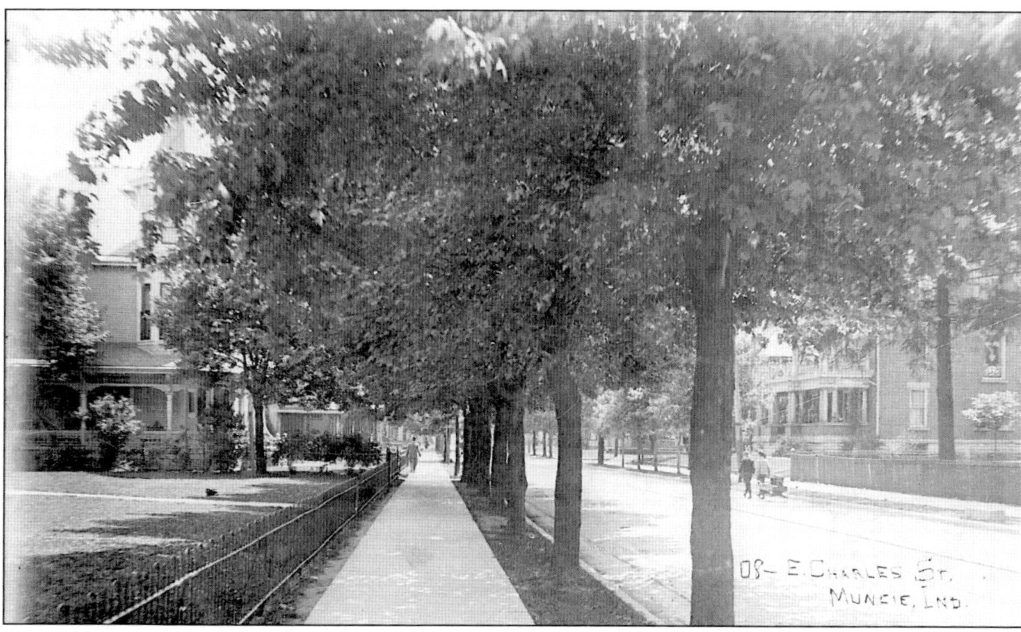

East Charles Street. This postcard, number eight in the series published by Galion View Company, depicts life along East Charles Street around 1910. Like many streets east of the downtown area, wealthy citizens lived in these large and beautiful homes. (Real photo, published by Galion View Co.)

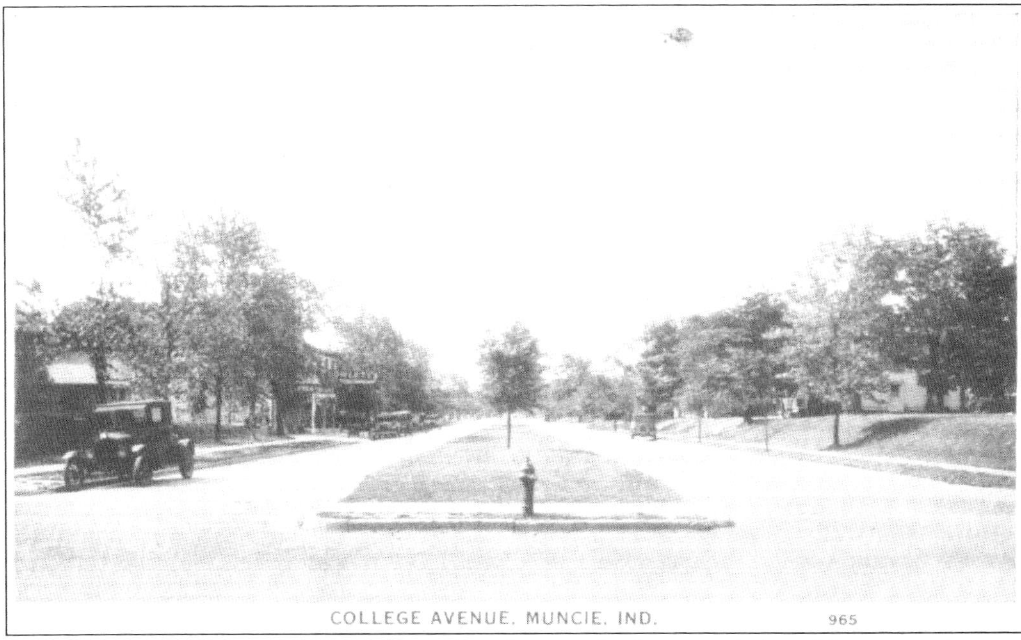

College Avenue. The image here is College Avenue, looking south from University Avenue. The photo was taken in the early 1930s. When the Pittenger Student Center expansion was started in 1956, there was no longer access to College Avenue from University Avenue. (The S.L. Co., Sturgis, MI, for Muncie News Co.)

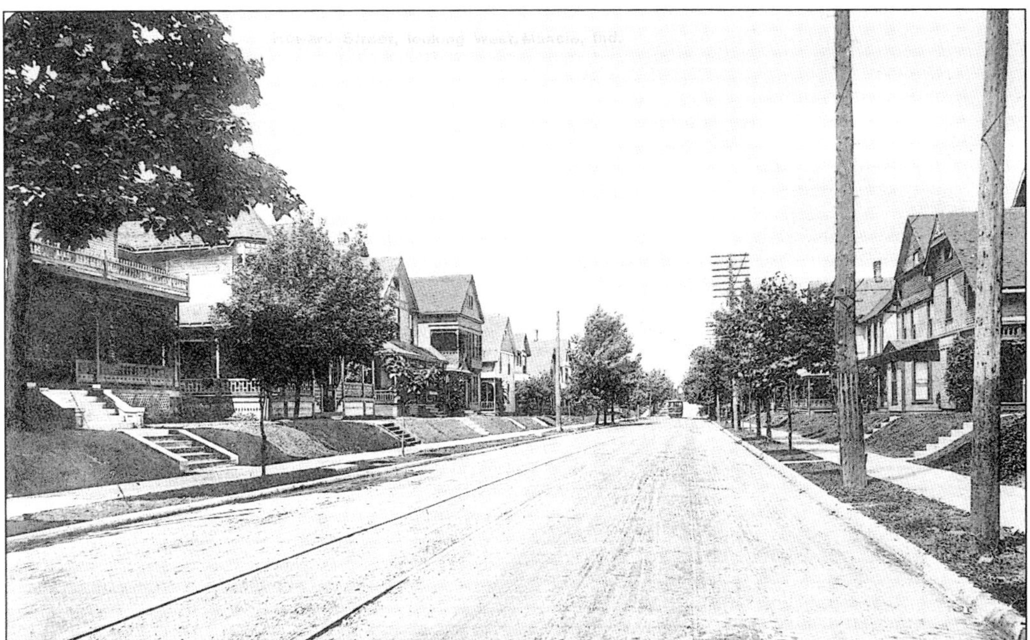

Howard Street Looking West. This *c.* 1915 postcard shows the tracks that carried the city trolleys on their Avondale line and the interurban cars on their way to Anderson and Indianapolis. Local streetcar service ended in 1931, but the "inter-urban" lines ran until 1941. (Newvo-chrome card, published by Watson, Muncie, IN.)

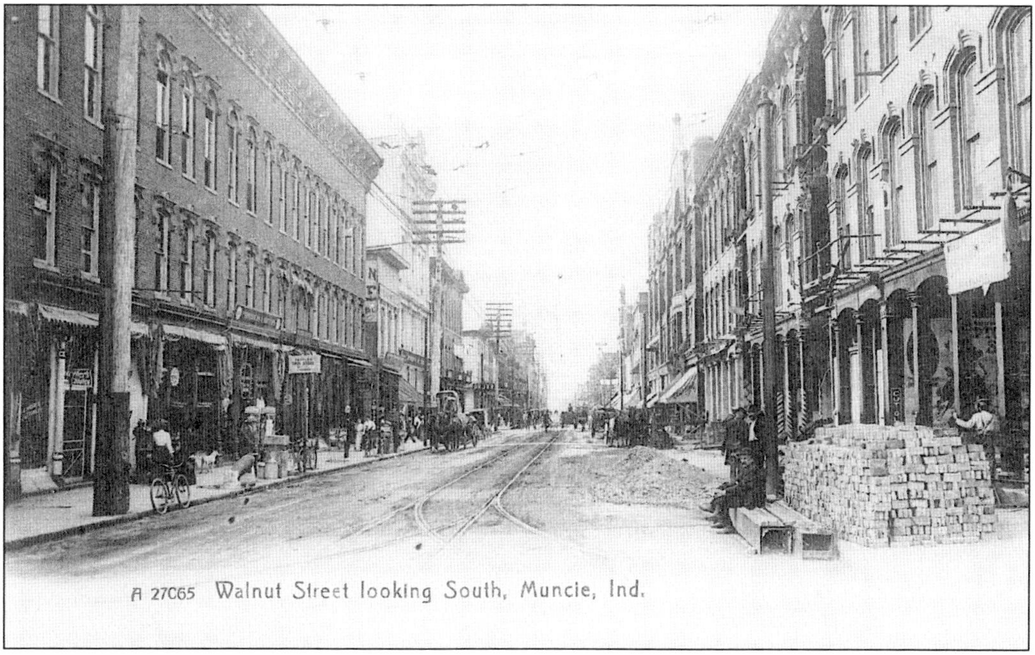

WALNUT STREET LOOKING SOUTH. Looking south from Main Street, this view shows Walnut Street with stacks of bricks that were to be used for the expansion of Jacob H. Wysor's office building. The building at the left edge of the picture is the Patterson block. (The Rotograph Co.)

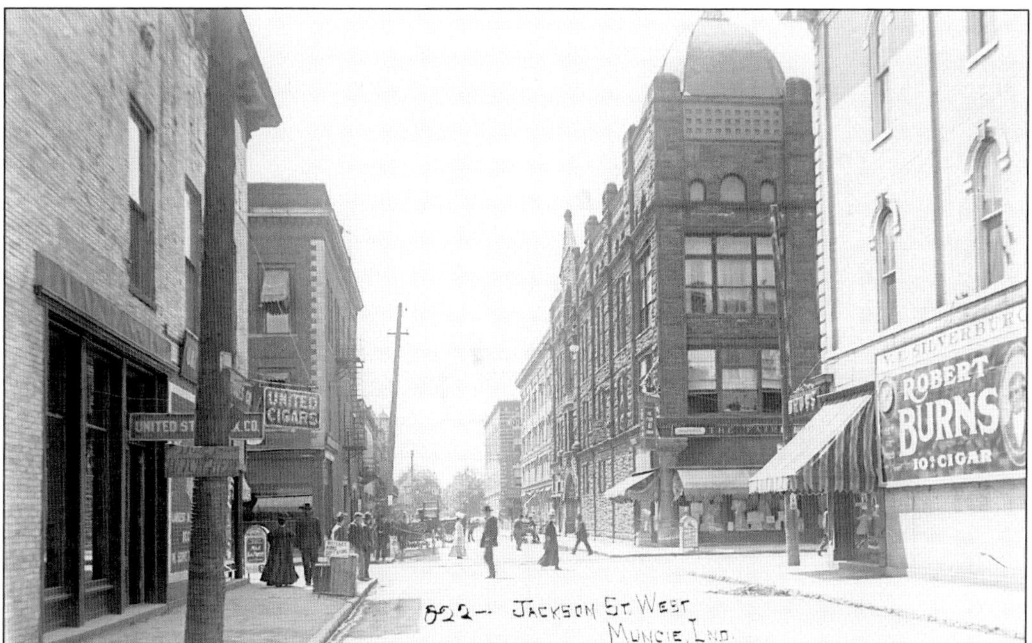

JACKSON STREET. This photographer stood between Walnut and Mulberry Streets and pointed his camera west on Jackson Street to take this photo. The Anthony block, built in 1888, can be seen right of center at the northwest corner. (Real photo, published by Galion View Co.)

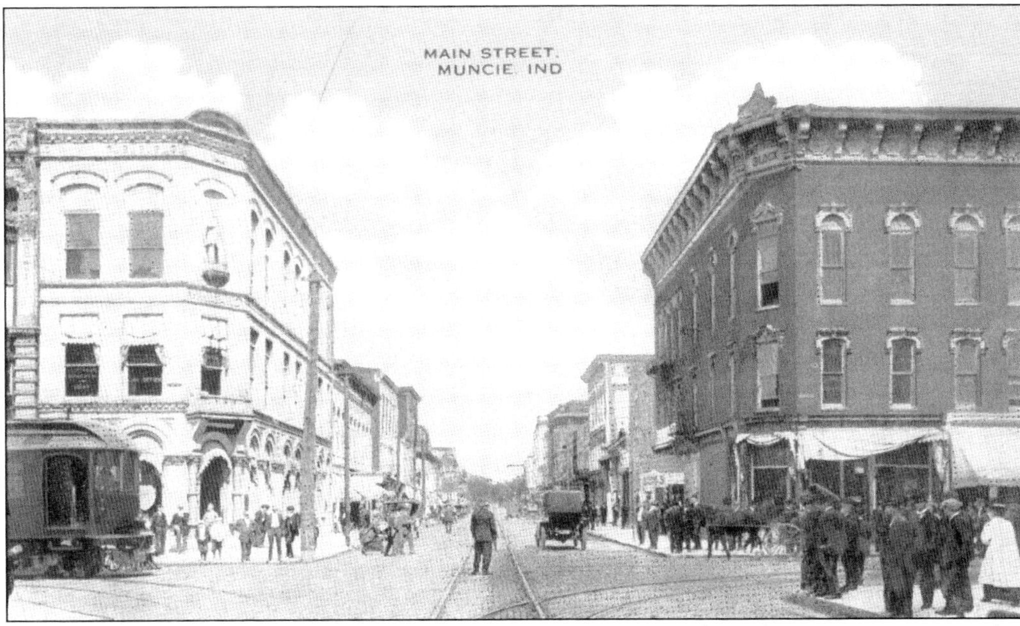

Main Street. The Patterson and Willard blocks are presented in this pre-1910 postcard of Main Street that looks east from Walnut Street. The Willard block, on the left, was built in 1886 and housed the Delaware County National Bank. The Patterson block on the right was built in 1876. (Commercial-chrome trademark.)

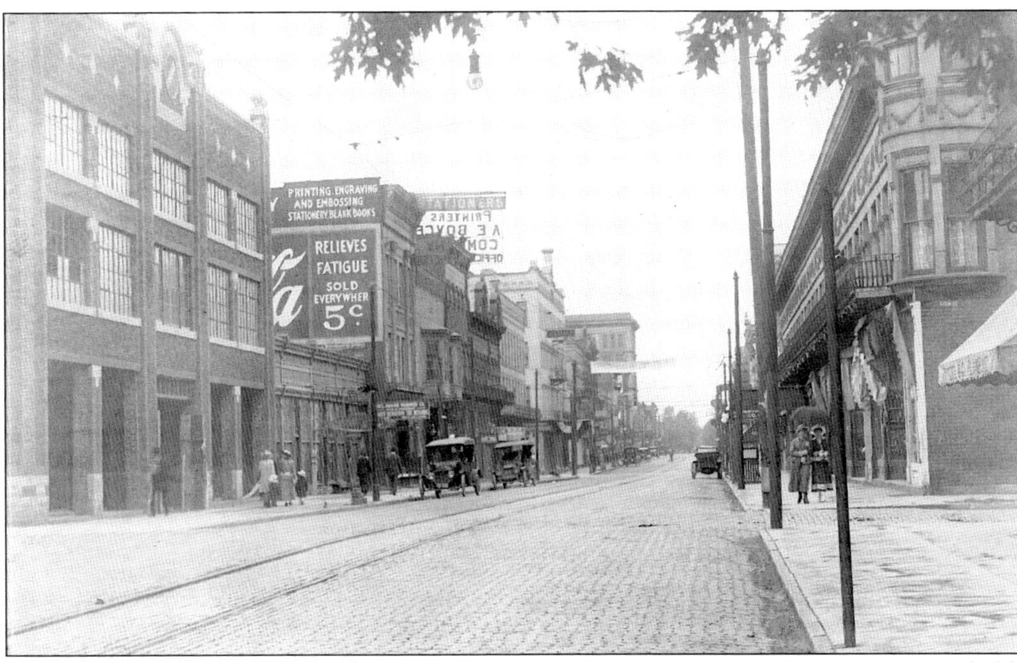

Main Street Looking West. This view shows Main Street paved with bricks. It was probably photographed shortly after WW I. The prominent building on the left housed Clark's Service Station for several decades. Mr. Lindley H. Clark was the owner and president. (Real photo, unidentified photographer.)

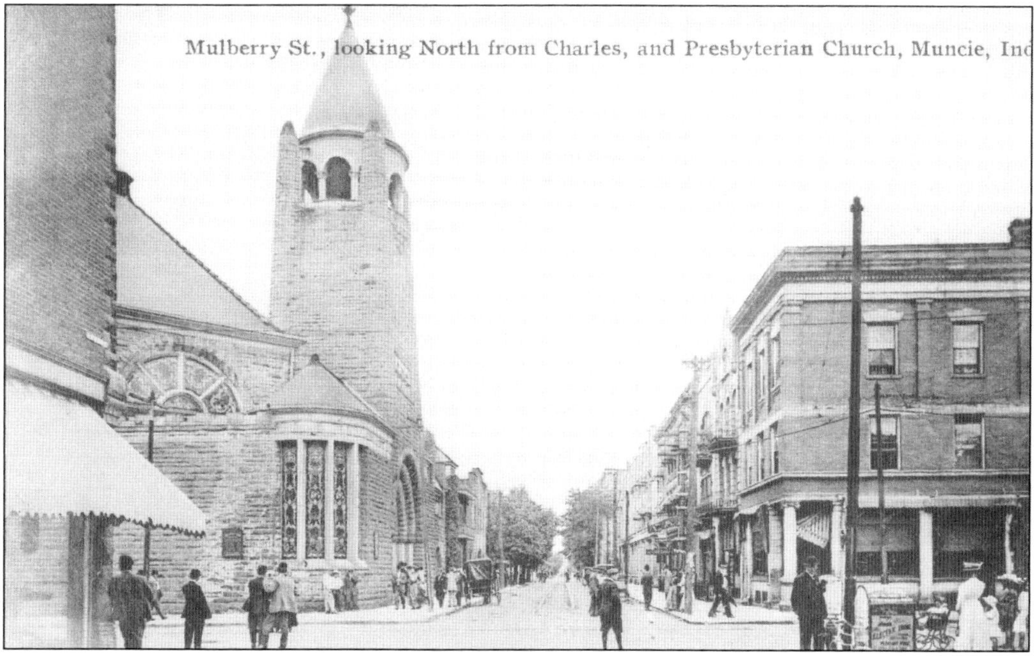

MULBERRY STREET, LOOKING NORTH FROM CHARLES STREET, AND THE PRESBYTERIAN CHURCH. This intersection was the busiest in the county for streetcars and interurban traffic. The Electric Terminal Station, located at the southeast corner, was at one time the third busiest traction terminal in the country. (Dexter-Fawley Co.)

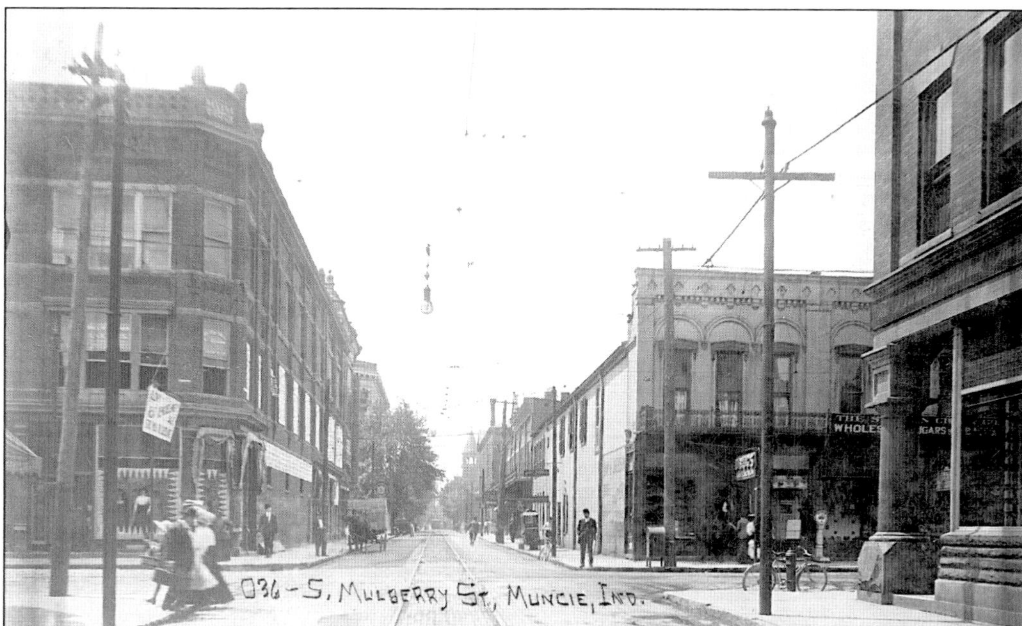

SOUTH MULBERRY STREET. The photographer for this view was standing adjacent to the Merchants National Bank in the middle of Mulberry Street and looking south. Later, the bank relocated to the northeast corner of Mulberry and Jackson Streets. The three-story Little Block is seen on the left. (Real photo, published by Galion View Co.)

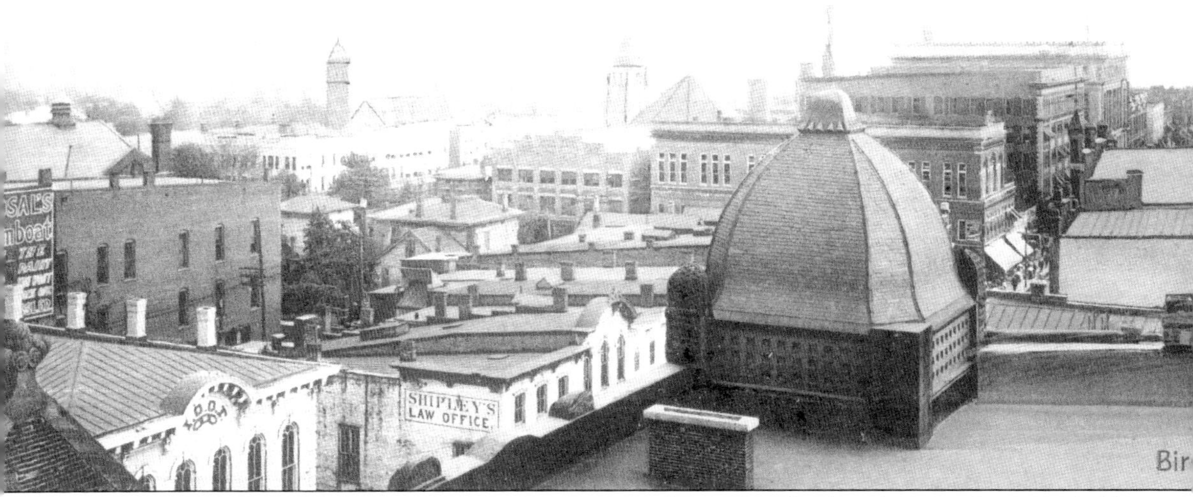

Birds-Eye View of Muncie from Wysor Building (Left Half). This photograph was probably taken just after the Wysor building was completed in 1906. Prominent buildings in the left-half portion of the picture include the IOOF Building (foreground), First Baptist Church steeple,

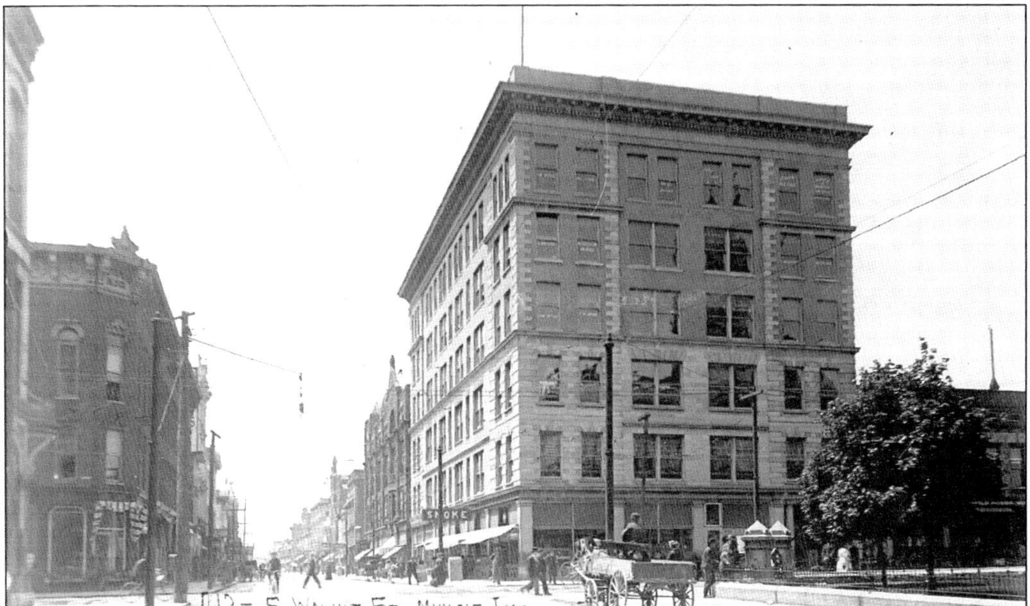

South Walnut Street. The prominent building in this picture is the six-story Wysor Building. During the construction of the fourth courthouse in the 1960s, a number of county offices were housed in the Wysor building. The building has since been demolished. (Real Photo, published by Galion View Co.)

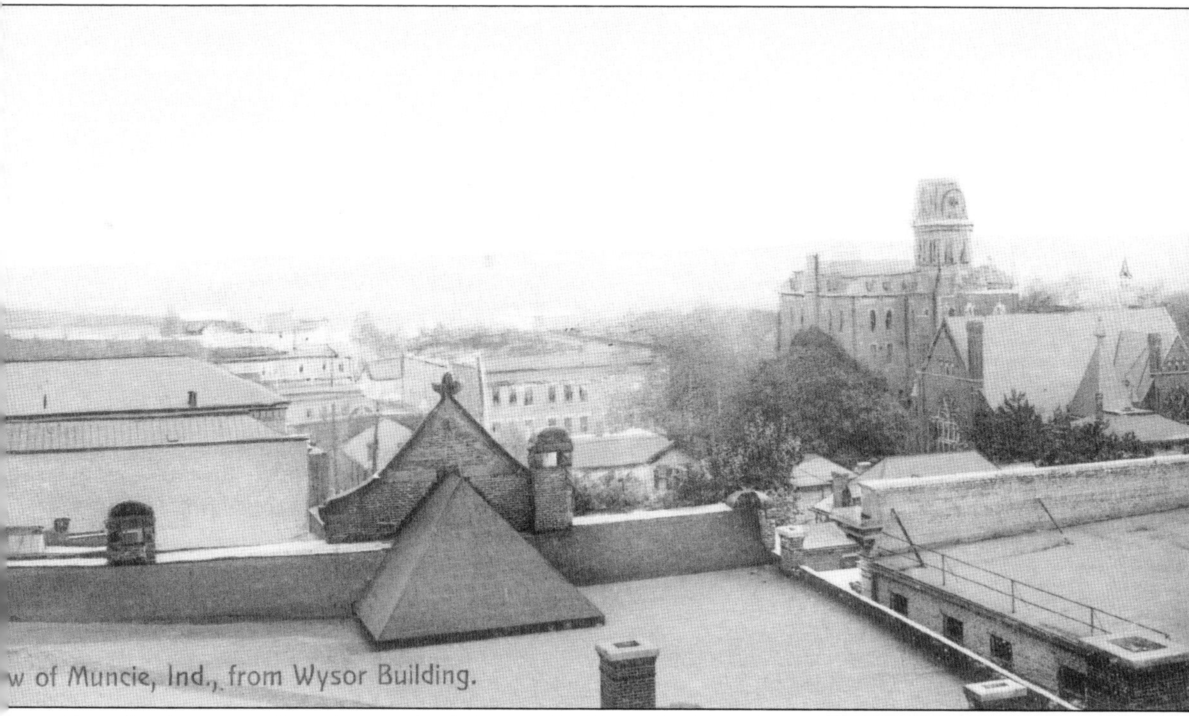

First Presbyterian Church steeple, Johnson Building, McNaughton Building, and the roof of the Anthony Building. On the right-half, one finds Muncie High School and the Methodist Episcopal Church. (Kraemer Art Co., for C.A. Penzel.)

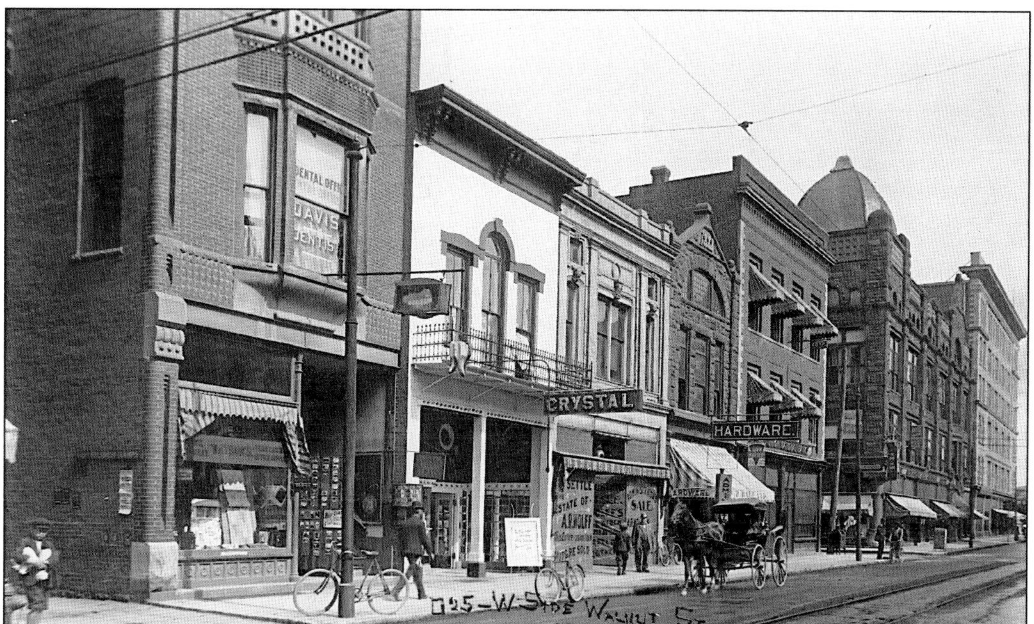

West Side, Walnut Street. The Crystal Theatre occupied the second building on the left in this *c.* 1911 real photo postcard. The buildings in this photo are on the west side of Walnut Street in a block often referred to as "rats' row." (Real photo, Galion View Co.)

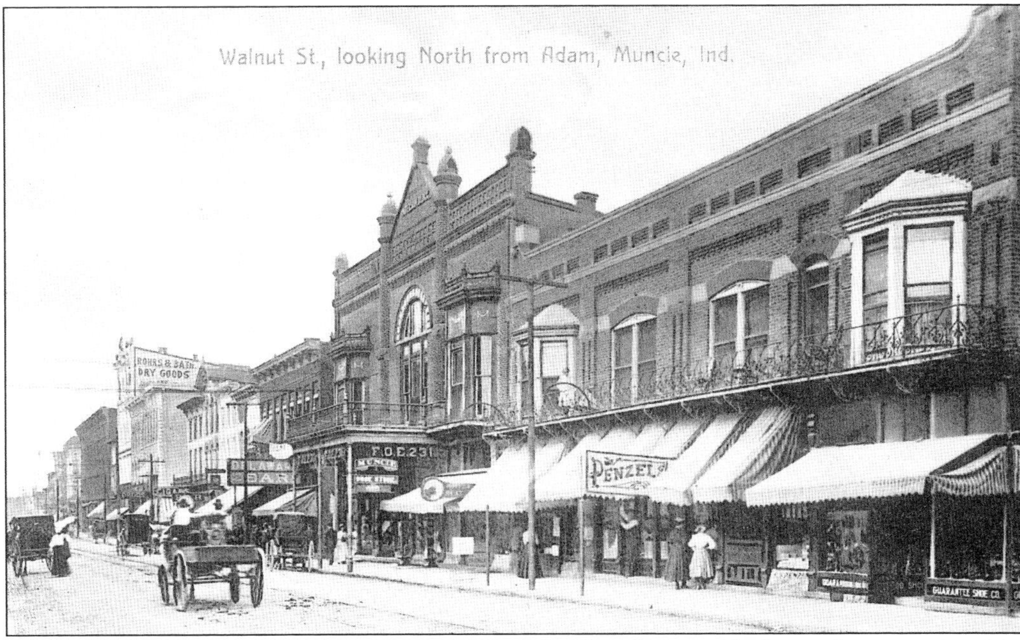

Walnut Street, Looking North from Adam[s]. This photograph shows the east side of the 200 block of South Walnut Street. Visible businesses include Penzel's Bookstore, the Delaware Bar, and a dry goods store called Rohrs and Bath. The Eagles' Lodge is visible in the center of the block. (Kraemer Art Co., for C.A. Penzel.)

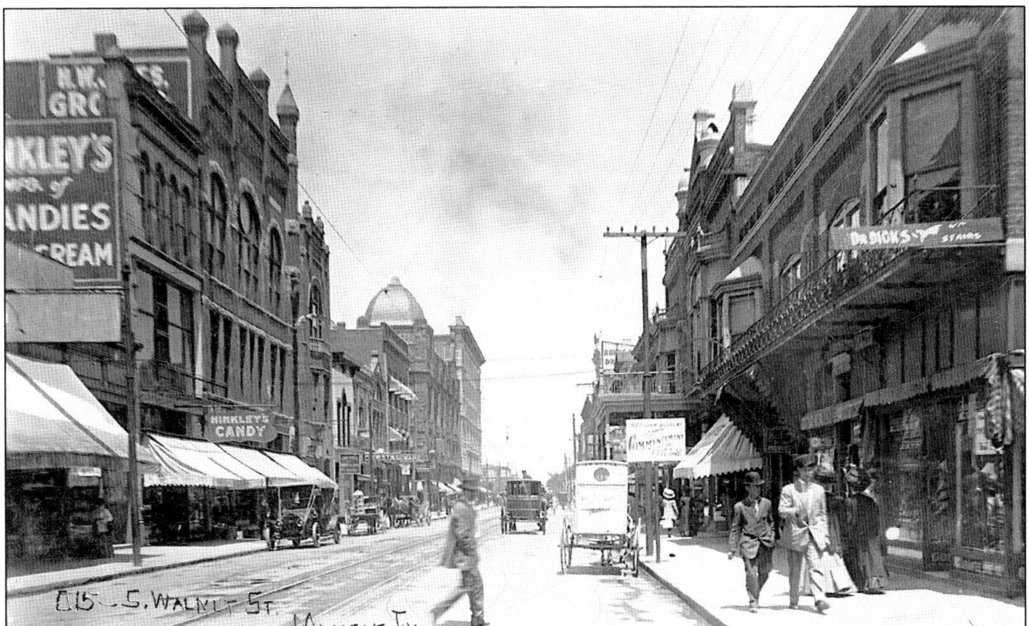

South Walnut Street. At the time this postcard was published, c. 1910, automobiles were not common in the streets of Muncie. Most of the vehicular traffic was either still horse-drawn or powered by electric lines. (Real photo, published by Galion View Co.)

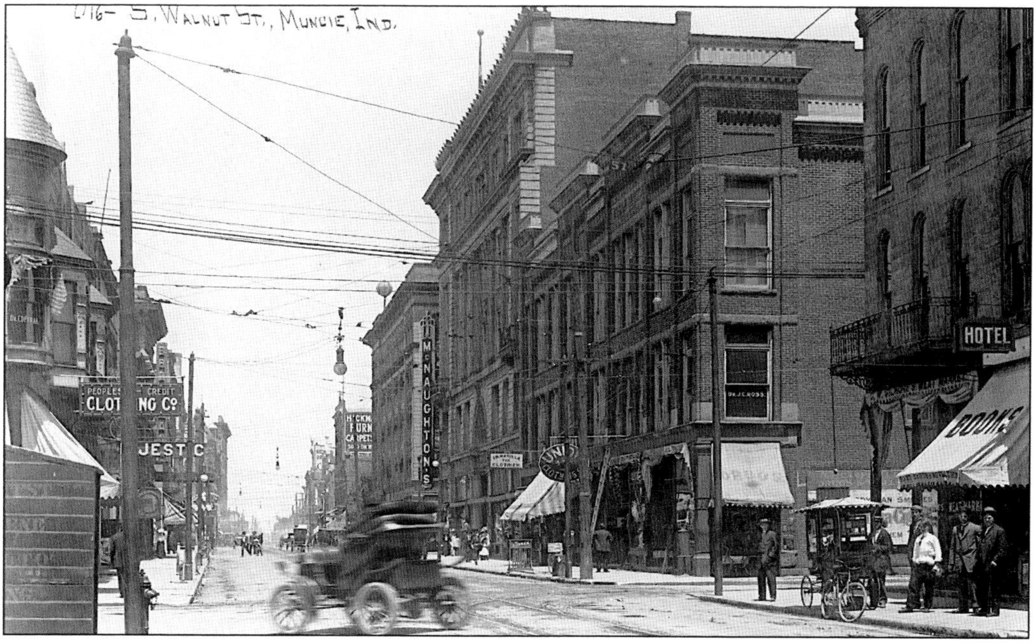

SOUTH WALNUT STREET. This real photograph shows what most of the hand-tinted postcards of the time did not: electric lines for the trolley cars, electric light bulbs dangling from the lines, and refuse left from the horses that pulled carriages and wagons. (Real photo, published by Galion View Co.)

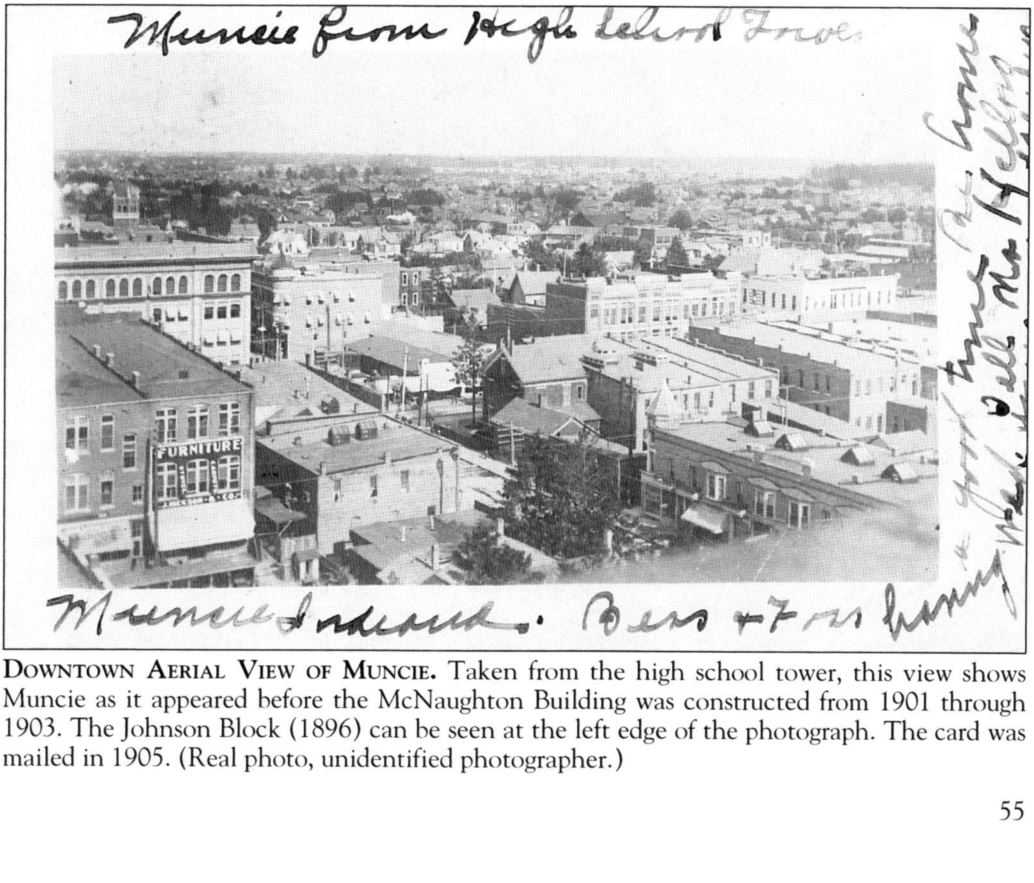

DOWNTOWN AERIAL VIEW OF MUNCIE. Taken from the high school tower, this view shows Muncie as it appeared before the McNaughton Building was constructed from 1901 through 1903. The Johnson Block (1896) can be seen at the left edge of the photograph. The card was mailed in 1905. (Real photo, unidentified photographer.)

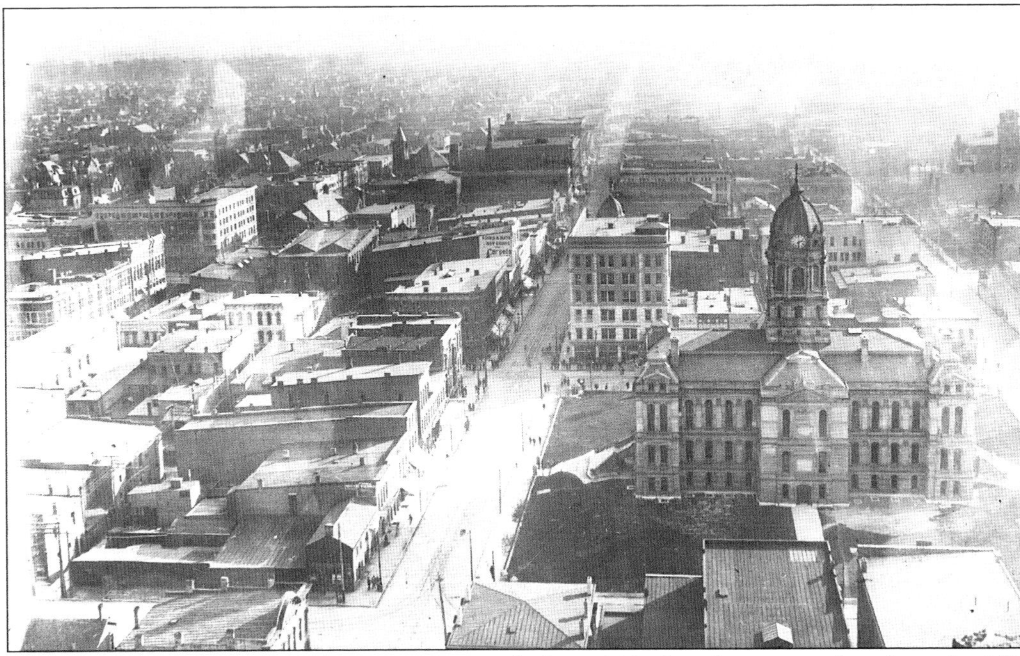

AERIAL VIEW OF DOWNTOWN MUNCIE. Postmarked in 1910, this photo was taken from the 250-foot smokestack of the Muncie Electric Company. The third Delaware County Court House can be seen in the right foreground. (Real photo, unidentified photographer.)

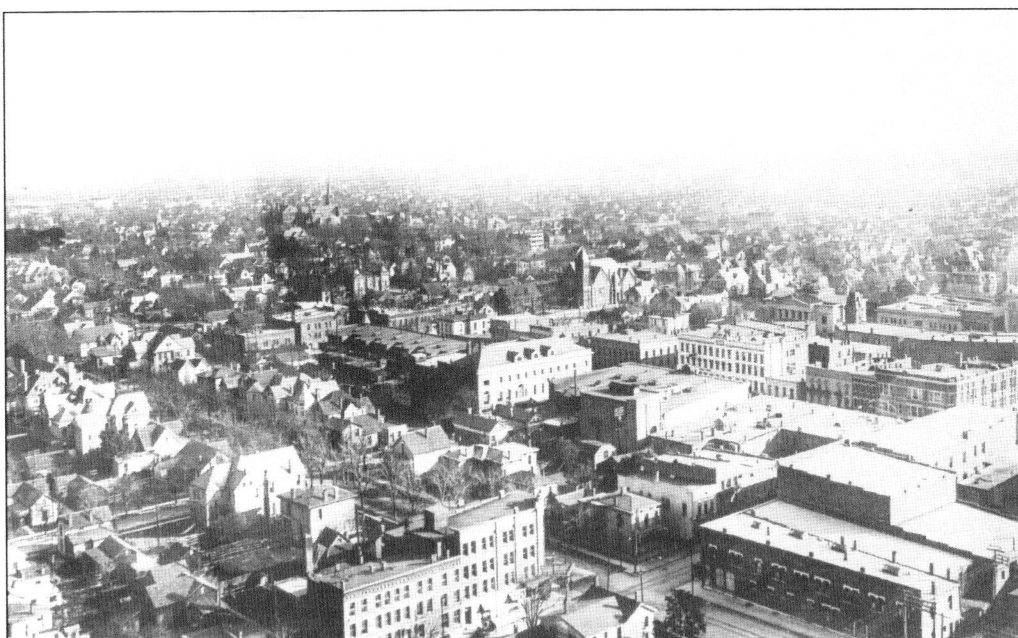

AERIAL VIEW OF DOWNTOWN MUNCIE. Like the card on the top of the page, this one also bears a 1910 postmark and was taken from the stack of the Muncie Electric Company. This view looks to the southeast. The Braun House is in the near foreground. (Real photo, unidentified photographer.)

Five

Church Buildings and Religion

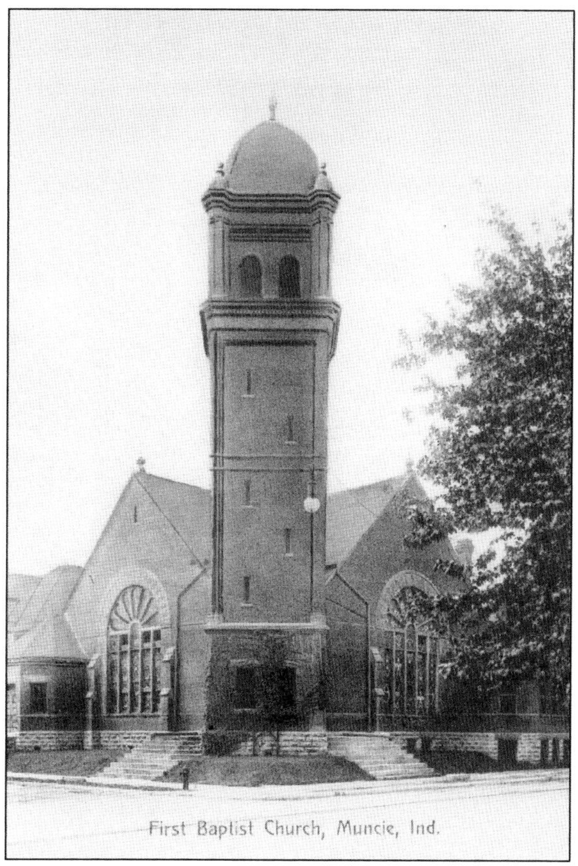

First Baptist Church. Located on the northwest corner of Charles and Jefferson Streets, the First Baptist Church cornerstone was laid on October 5, 1889, with Reverend S.A. Northrup, of Fort Wayne, Indiana, delivering the address. It was dedicated on July 20, 1890. Its cost, including grounds, was $27,000. In 1900, the church added an institutional annex to the building at a cost of $18,000 that included a gymnasium and four other rooms. (Kraemer Art Co., for C.A. Penzel.)

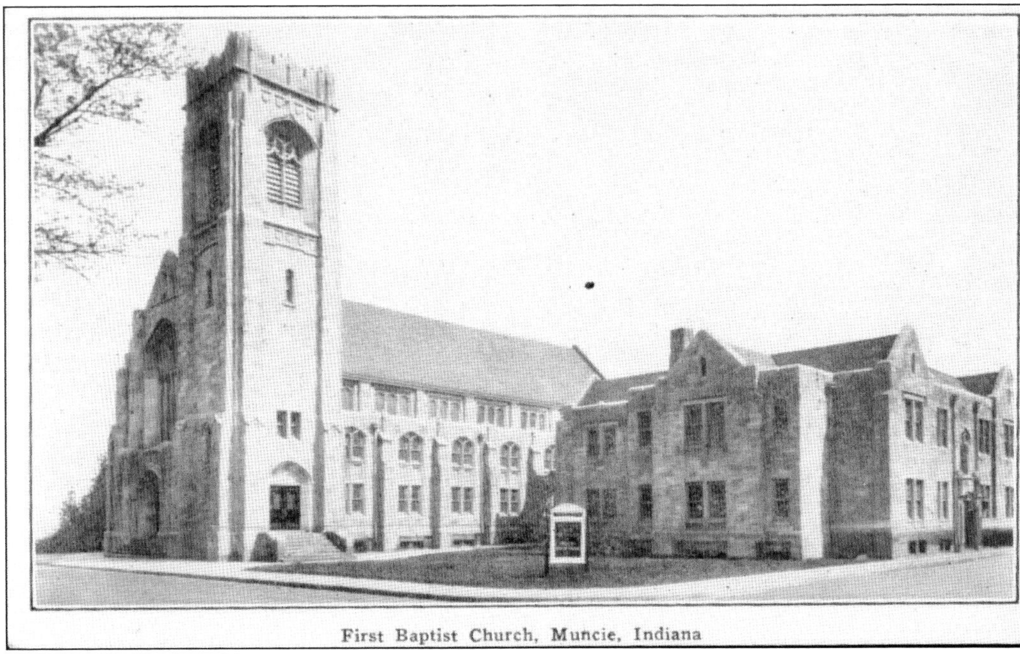

FIRST BAPTIST CHURCH. Samuel W. Hannaford & Son of Cincinnati were the architects for this $338,000 Gothic structure. The building was completed in 1929 and dedicated on May 19 of that year. The structure is still used today. (Unidentified printer, unidentified publisher.)

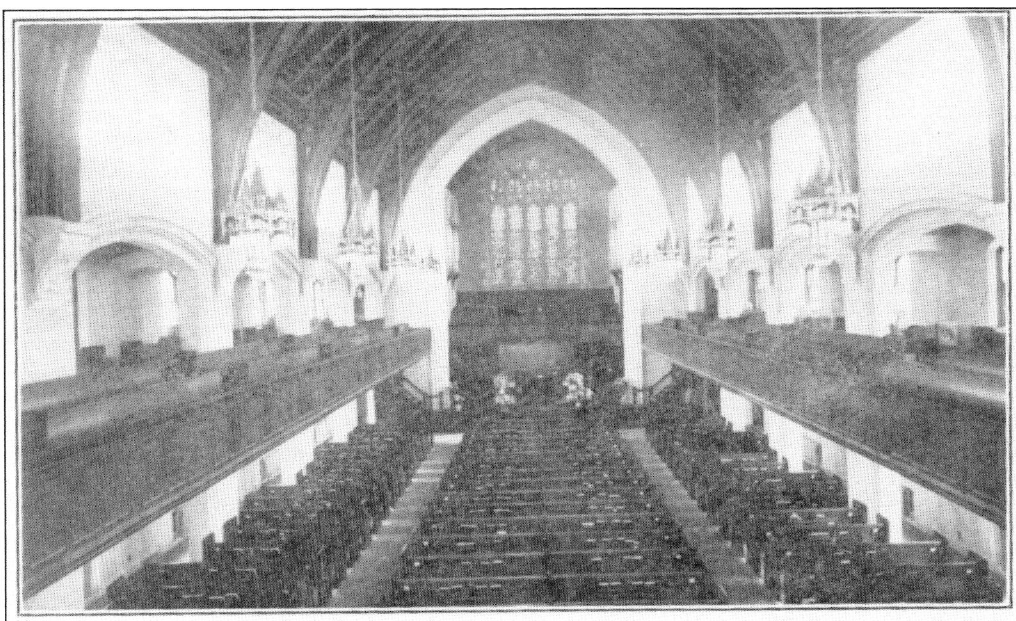

AUDITORIUM, FIRST BAPTIST CHURCH. The first service to be held in this auditorium was on May 12, 1929. The 10:30 a.m. service was attended by 1,258 members and conducted by Reverend Wm. G. Everson. (Unidentified printer, unidentified publisher.)

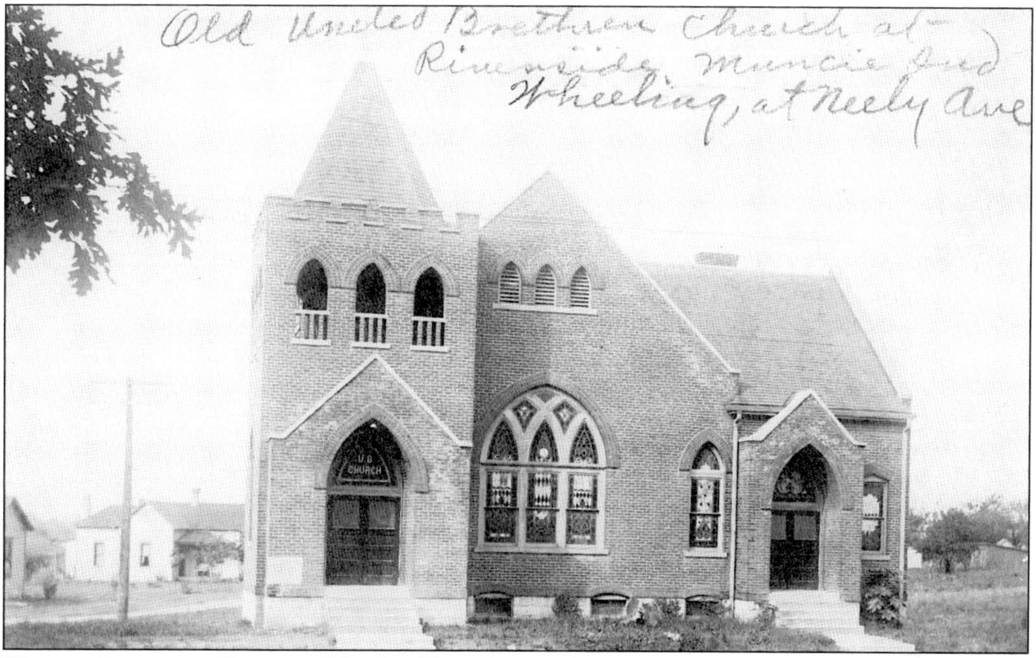

United Brethren Church. The building shown above was replaced at the same site by the building shown below. (Real photo, unidentified photographer.)

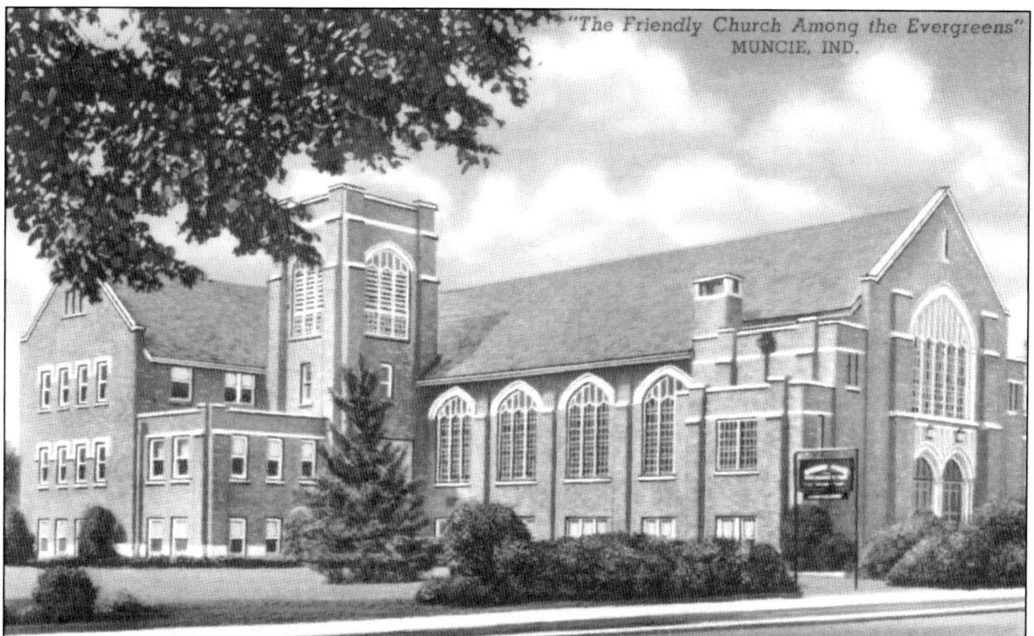

Riverside United Brethren Church, Wheeling Avenue at Neely. This church is still in use at 1201 North Wheeling Avenue. A groundbreaking ceremony was held in May of 1929, and construction was completed in 1930. A substantial addition was made to the building in 1965. (Curt Teich & Co., unidentified publisher.)

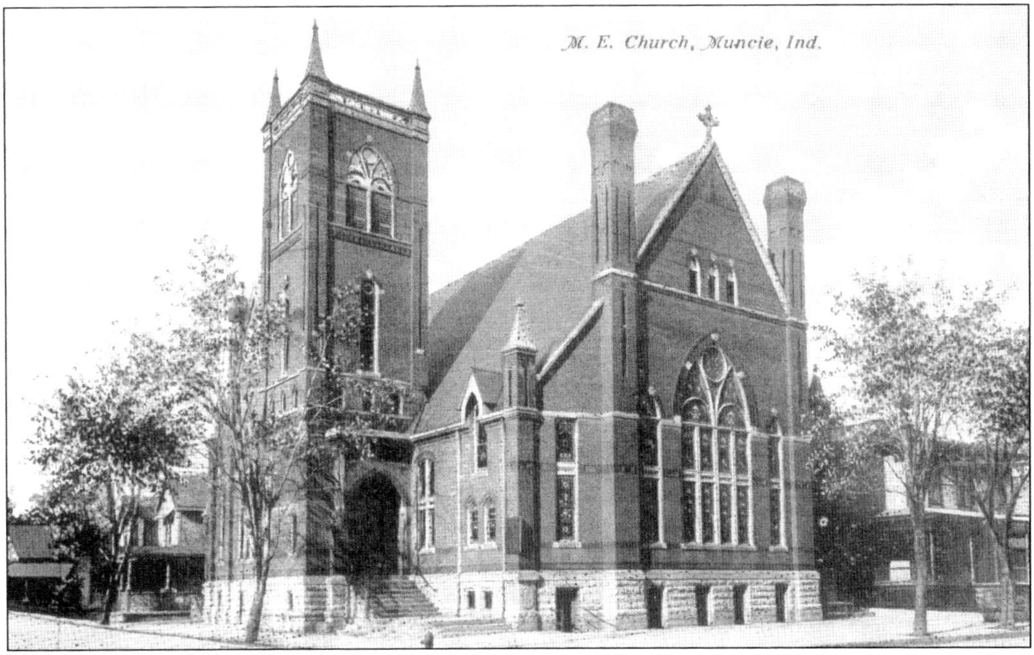

M.E. Church. Methodists built this church building in Muncie on South High Street from 1888 until 1889 at a cost of $40,000. C.H. Hoffman was the contractor. The building was dedicated on June 2, 1889, and torn down c. 1928 to make room for a new structure (see below). (S.H. Knox & Co.)

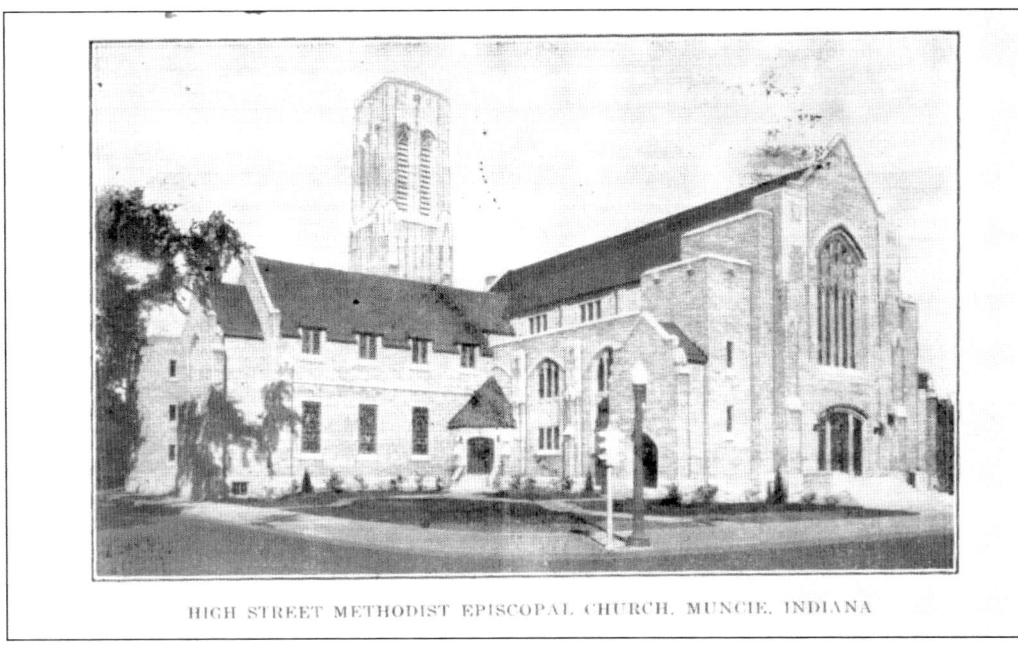

High Street Methodist Episcopal Church. The address of this building, designed by Houck & Smenner of Muncie, is 219 South High Street. It was built at a cost of $400,000 under the pastorate of Dr. Claude H. King. A major fire on January 27, 1978, caused the need for extensive repairs to be made. (Unidentified printer, unidentified publisher.)

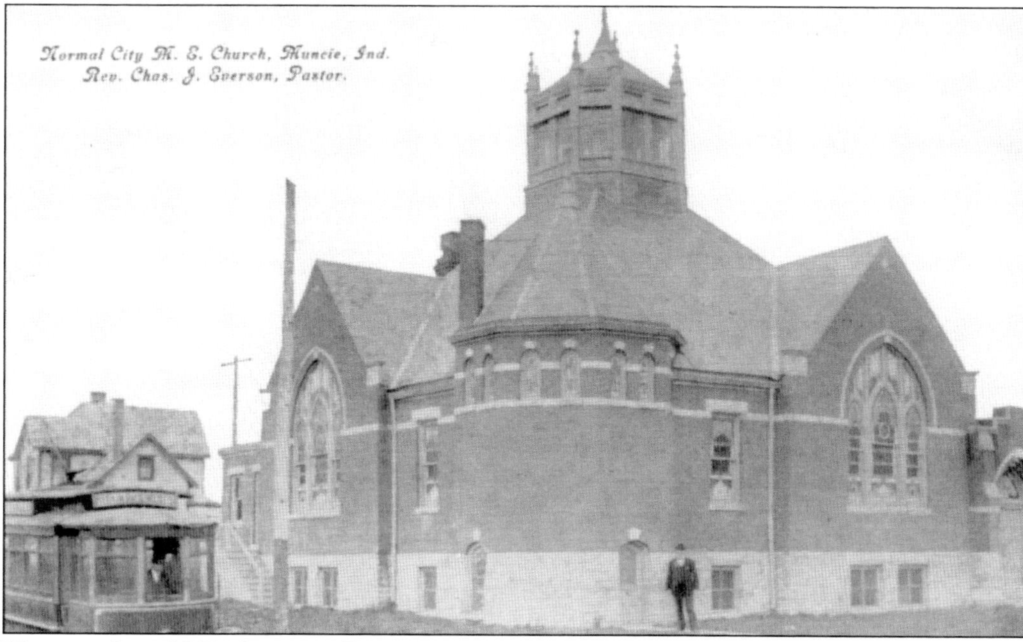

NORMAL CITY M.E. CHURCH, REV. CHAS. J. EVERSON, PASTOR. Muncie architect Herbert F. Smenner designed this building at 1711 West Jackson Street. J.B. Snyder & Son contracted the construction of the building at $6,000. (Unidentified printer, unidentified publisher.)

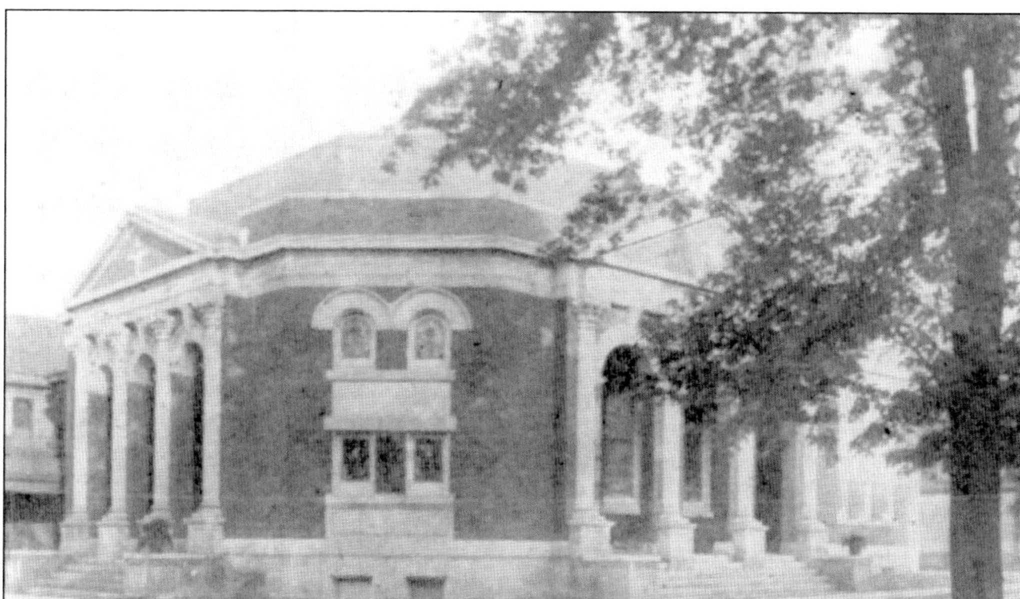

FIRST METHODIST PROTESTANT CHURCH. Located at Main and Pershing Streets, the First Methodist Protestant Church was erected in 1912. The Neo-Classical design of this building was planned by the Muncie architect Charles H. Houck. In 1939, the name of the church was changed to Main Street United Methodist Church. (Unidentified printer, unidentified publisher.)

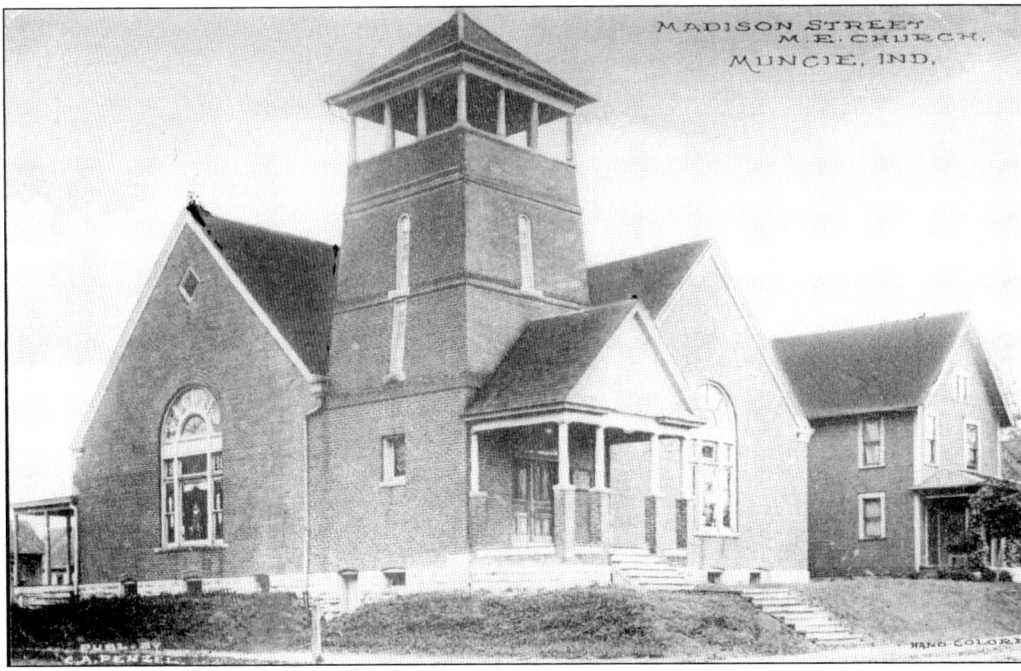

MADISON STREET M.E. CHURCH. Built on the east side of south Madison Street, the cornerstone for this $5,000 building was laid on September 11, 1899. The building was condemned in 1922 and replaced in 1925 by the church shown below. (The Albertype Co., for C.A. Penzel.)

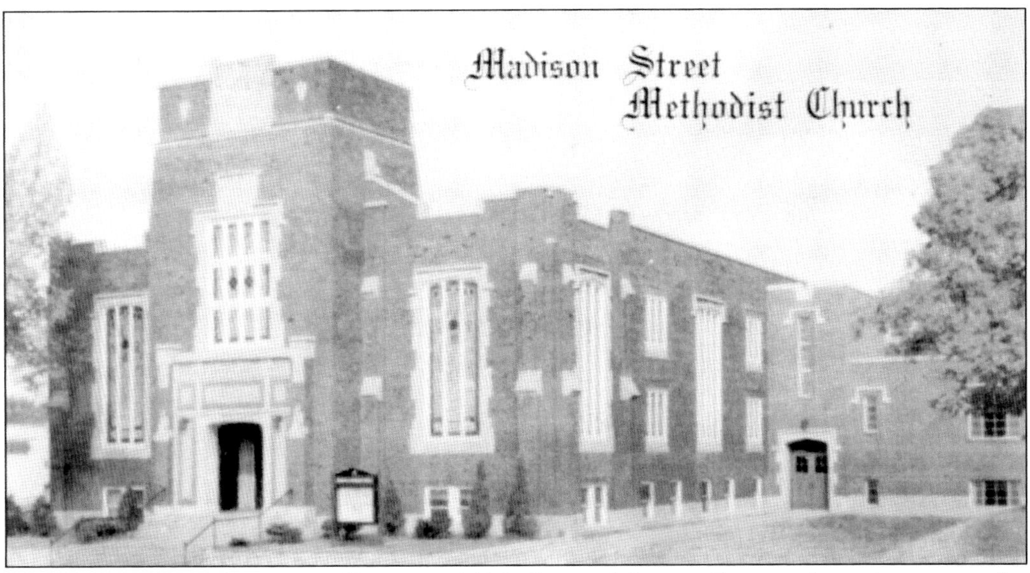

MADISON STREET METHODIST CHURCH, 1400 SOUTH MUNCIE STREET. Later known as the Madison Street Methodist Episcopal Church, this structure was constructed in 1925 in the Jacobean Revival style of architecture. (Unidentified printer, unidentified publisher.)

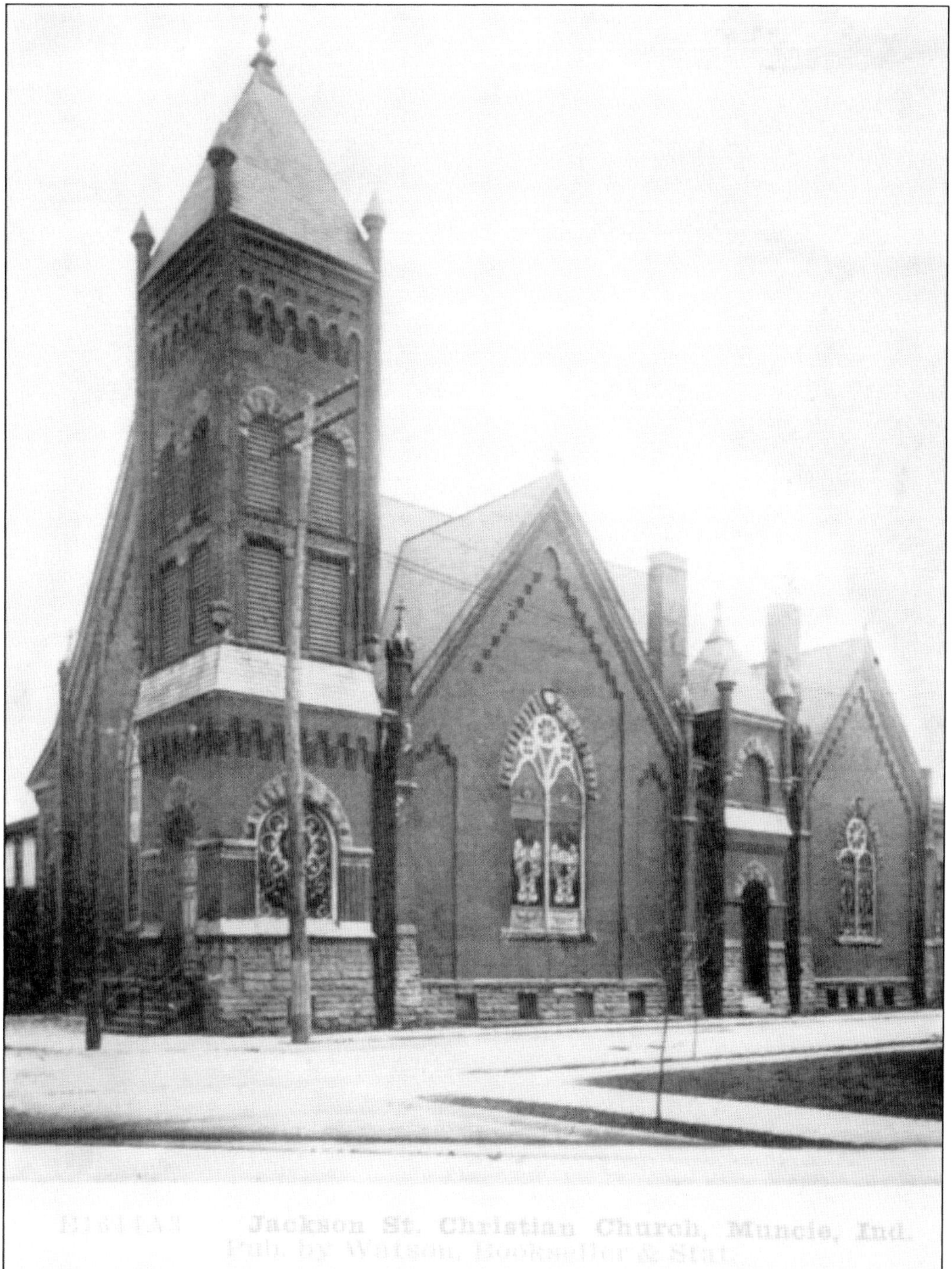

JACKSON STREET CHRISTIAN CHURCH. The Jackson Street Christian Church was located at 401 East Jackson Street. It was completed in 1894 at a cost of $30,000, including the lot and furnishings. The dedication ceremony was held March 12, 1895. After the Hazelwood Christian Church was completed on the old Kitselman estate, this building was razed. (H.G. Zimmerman & Co., for Watson, Bookseller & Stationer.)

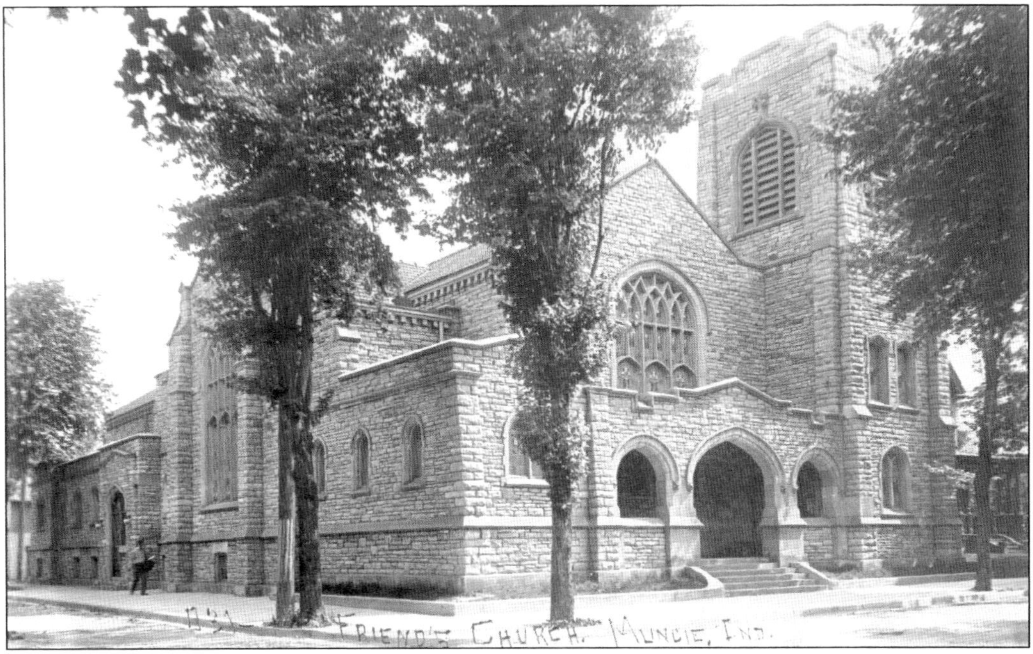

FRIENDS CHURCH. Built to replace an earlier church building at the corner of Seymour and Mulberry Streets, this structure at 418 West Adams Street was designed by Fort Wayne architects Wing and Mahurin. The Gothic Revival-style building was constructed from 1906 until 1908. In 1965, it was enlarged to the east according to the plans drawn by local architects Hamilton and Graham. (Real photo, published by Galion View Co.)

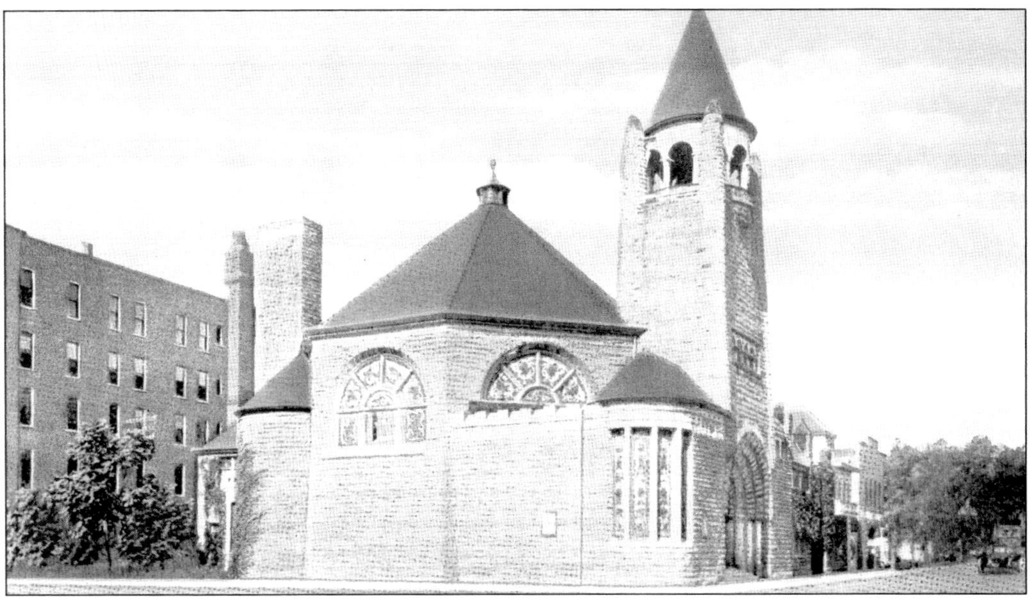

FIRST PRESBYTERIAN CHURCH. Elah Terrell, of Columbus, Ohio, was the architect of this church located at 321 South Mulberry Street. The Romanesque building was constructed from 1892 until 1894 by Thomas Jones & Co. On June 24, 1894, it was dedicated; in 1955, it was demolished. (Harry H. Hamm.)

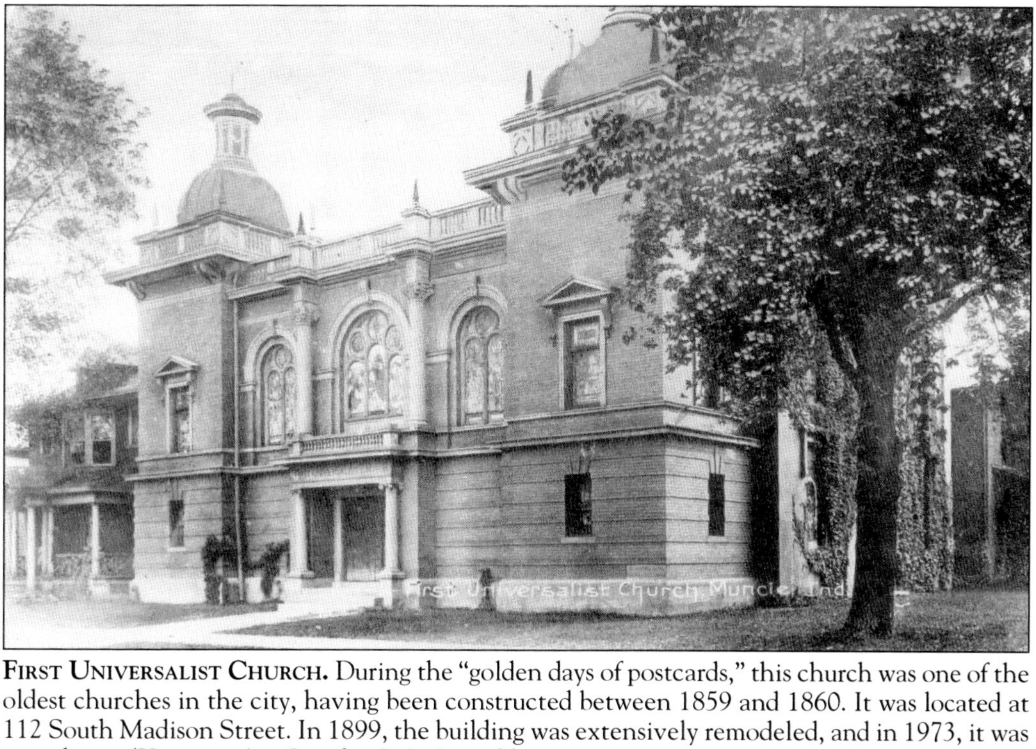

First Universalist Church. During the "golden days of postcards," this church was one of the oldest churches in the city, having been constructed between 1859 and 1860. It was located at 112 South Madison Street. In 1899, the building was extensively remodeled, and in 1973, it was torn down. (Kraemer Art Co., for C.A. Penzel.)

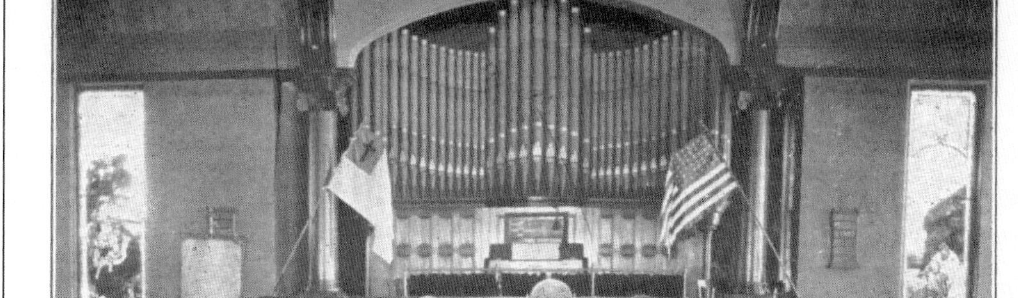

St. John's Universalist Church. This card shows the following: 1) Guthrie Memorial Front, 2) Christian flag, 3) American flag, and 4) St. John's Sunday school banner, dedicated in 1921. The first service in this church was delivered on December 9, 1860. (Unidentified printer, unidentified publisher.)

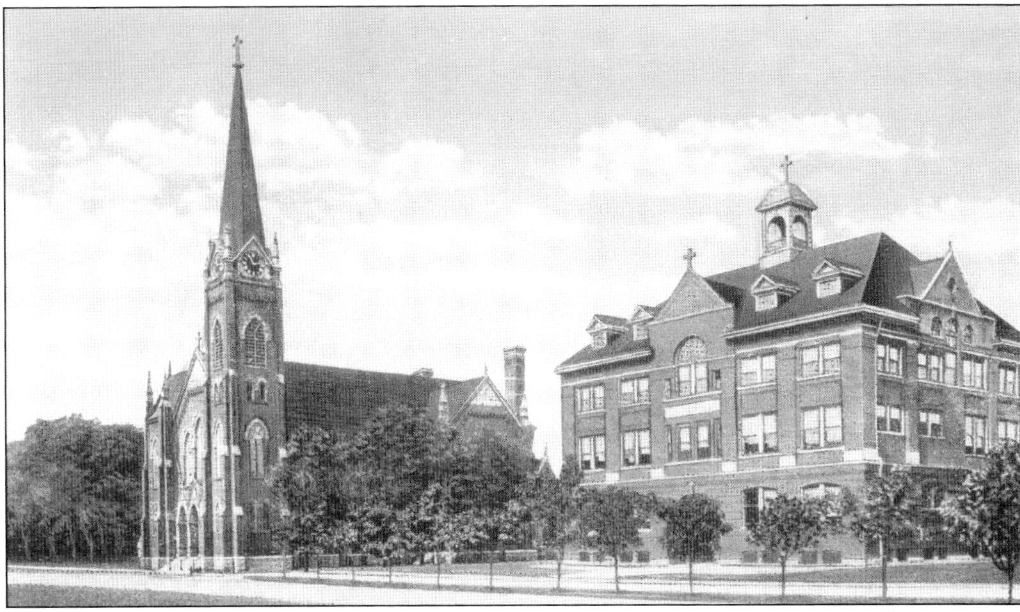

ST. LAWRENCE CATHOLIC CHURCH AND SCHOOL. This imposing Gothic Revival structure at 824 East Charles Street was constructed from 1893 to 1895. The cornerstone on the building is dated July 4, 1893. The school building adjacent to the church was completed and opened in 1900. Both buildings are still in use. (Harry H. Hamm.)

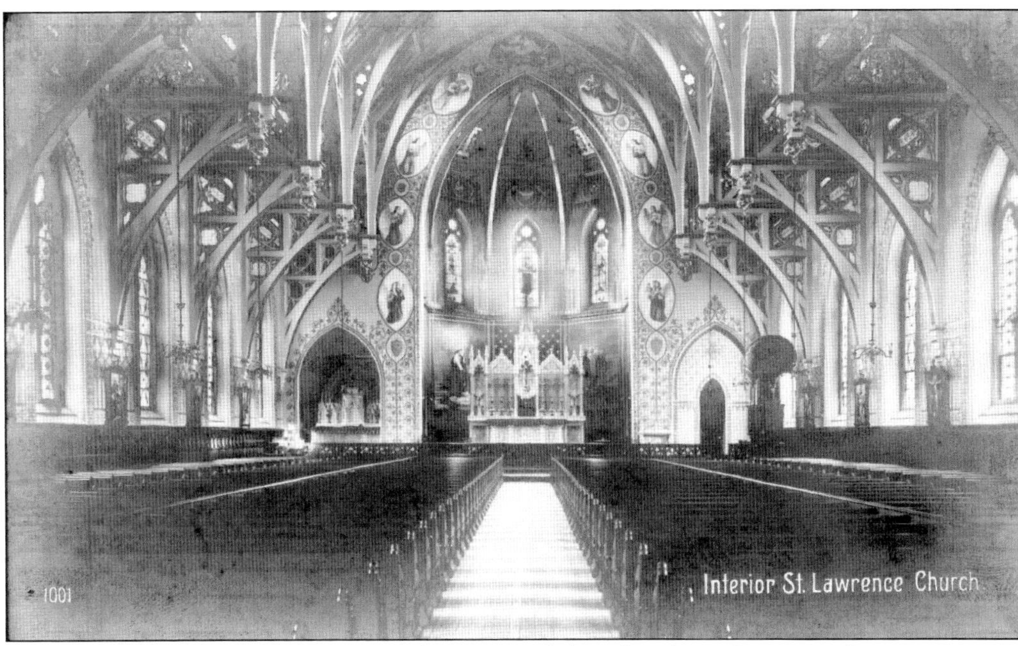

INTERIOR, ST. LAWRENCE CHURCH. The pastor of this church at the time of construction of this church building was Reverend William G. Schmidt, a native of Germany. (Real photo, published by H.S. Hutchinson & Co., New Bedford, MA.)

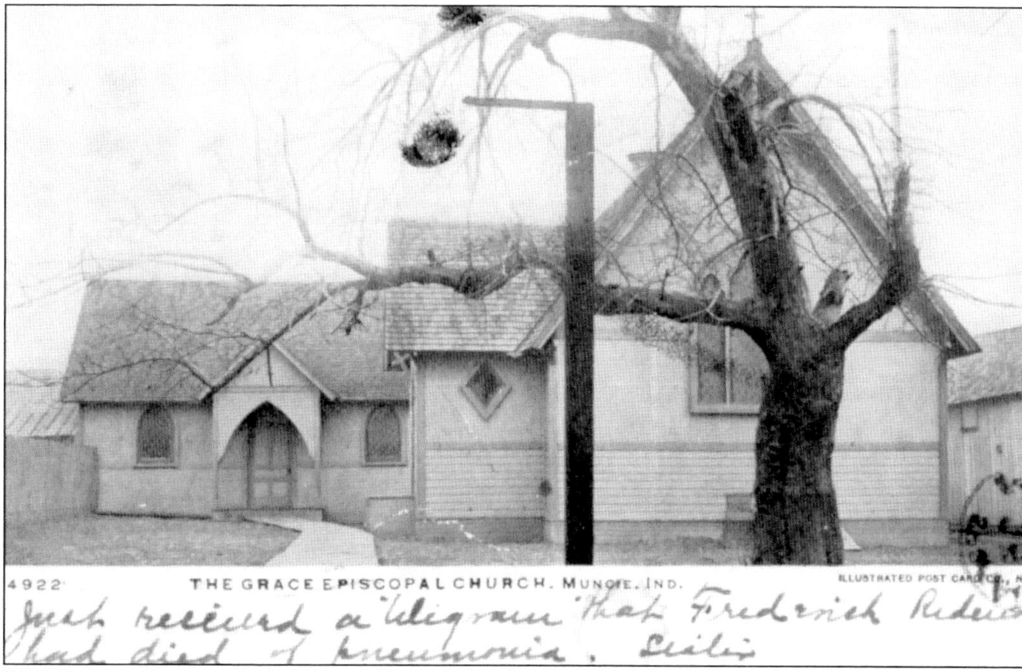

THE GRACE EPISCOPAL CHURCH. This photo shows the Grace Episcopal Church before it was remodeled into the Tudor Revival style of architecture. Original construction of this building at 209 North Walnut Street was completed in 1872. In 1923, the church was relocated to 300 South Madison Street, where it was remodeled and expanded to its current style and size. (Illustrated Post Card Co.)

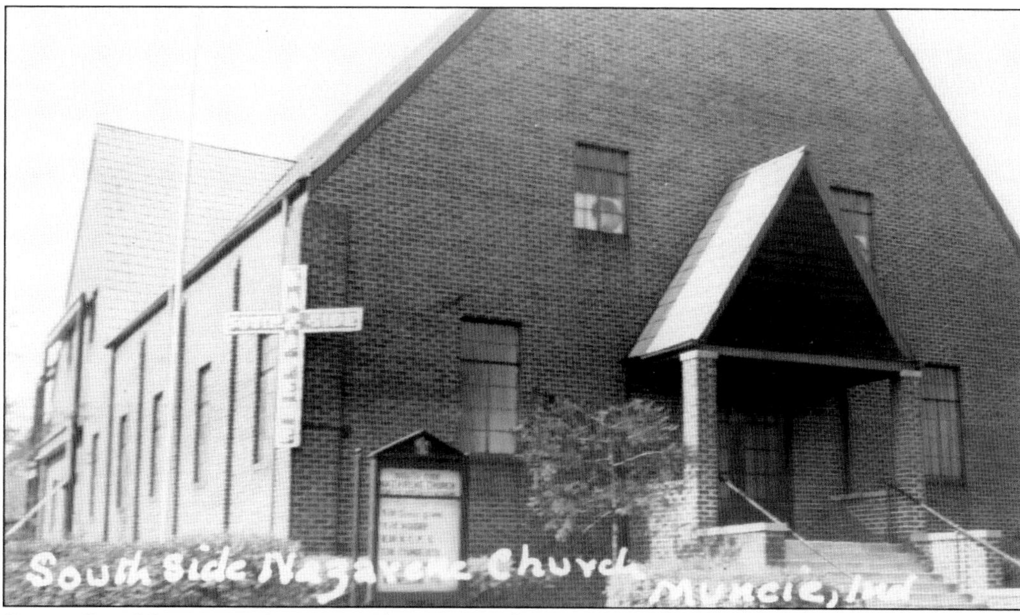

SOUTH SIDE NAZARENE CHURCH. The Reverend H.W. Cornelius was probably the pastor of this church when this postcard was made. The church is located on the northwest corner of Seventh and High Streets. The Nazarene church at this location dates back to the early 1920s. (Real photo, unidentified photographer.)

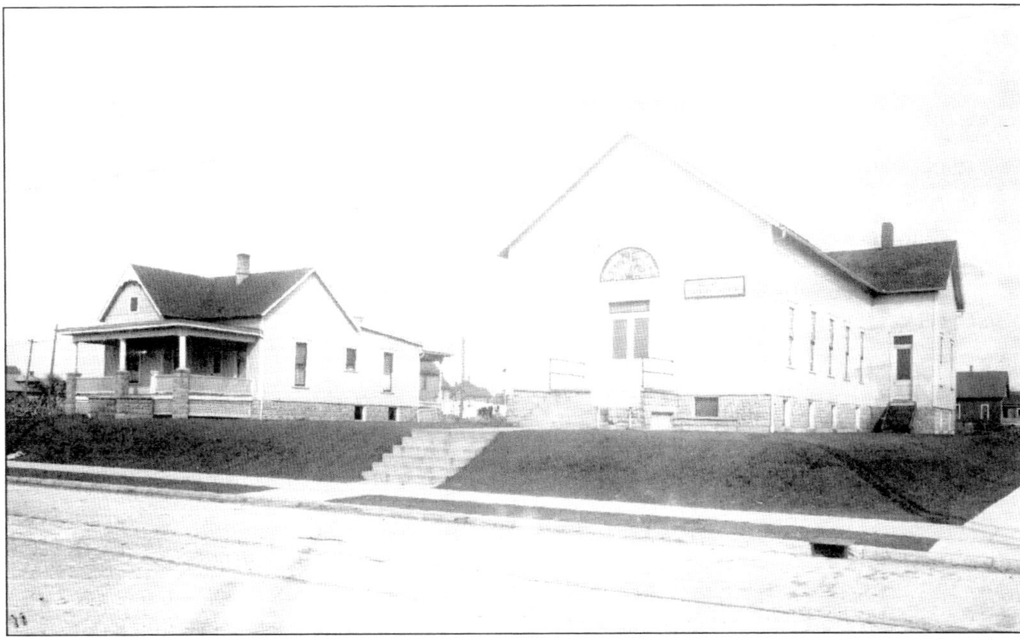

WALNUT STREET BAPTIST CHURCH. This building, located on the northeast corner of Walnut Street and Memorial Drive, was built in the first decade of the 1900s. In the early 1970s, the building was sold by the Baptists and became Gesthemaine Apostolic Church. (Real photo, unidentified photographer.)

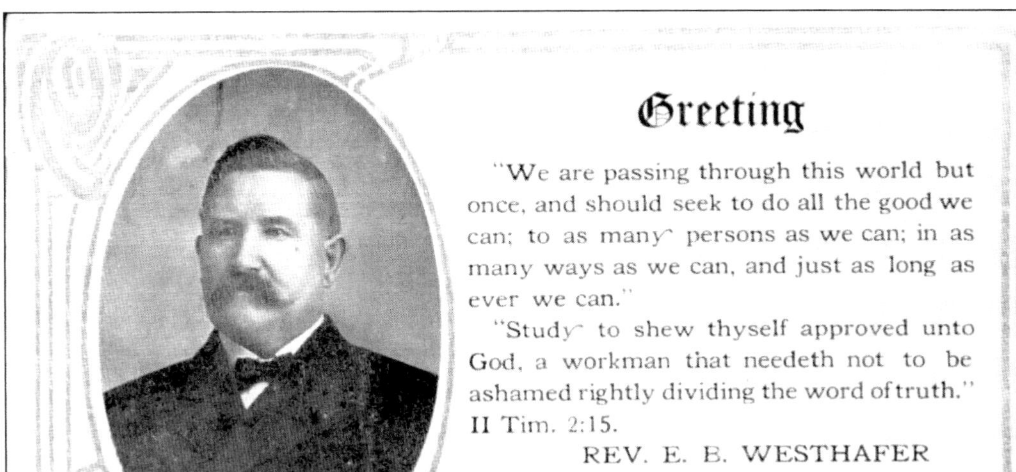

CARD ANNOUNCING REV. E.B. WESTHAFER, EVANGELIST. No additional information could be found regarding the announcement made on this card. (North Indiana Conference.)

Six

FACTORIES

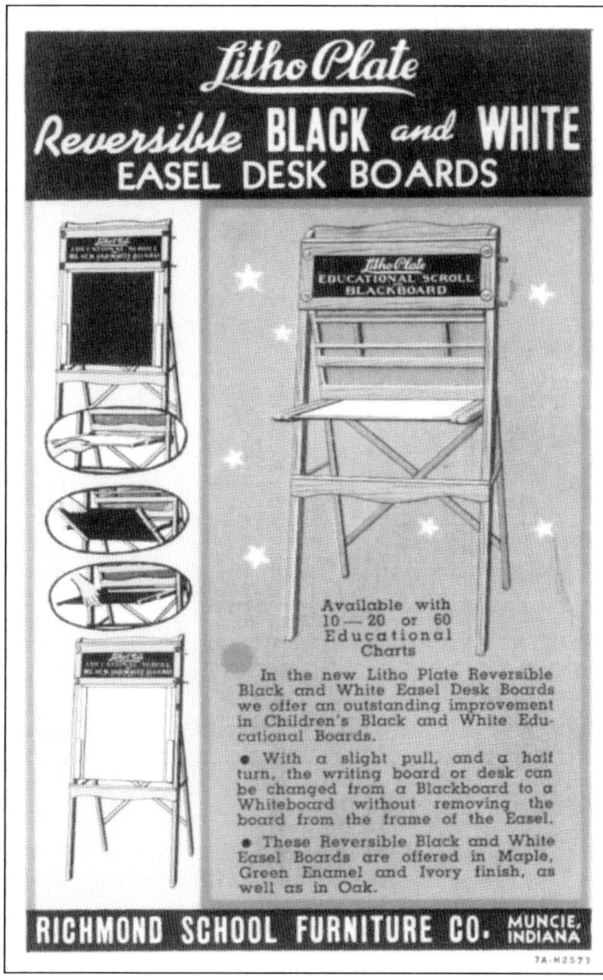

RICHMOND SCHOOL FURNITURE CO. This advertising postcard for the Richmond Furniture Company touted the benefits of their "Reversible Black and White Easel Desk Boards." The factory, located at Monroe and Eighteenth Streets for many years, made children's blackboards and other articles such as school desks, handmade cabinets, post office furniture, and other miscellaneous wood products. The Monroe and Eighteenth Street location was also the home to the American Lawn Mower Company, which manufactured 127 varieties of lawn mowers, which were sold in the United States and 37 different countries. (Advertising card by Curt Teich Co.)

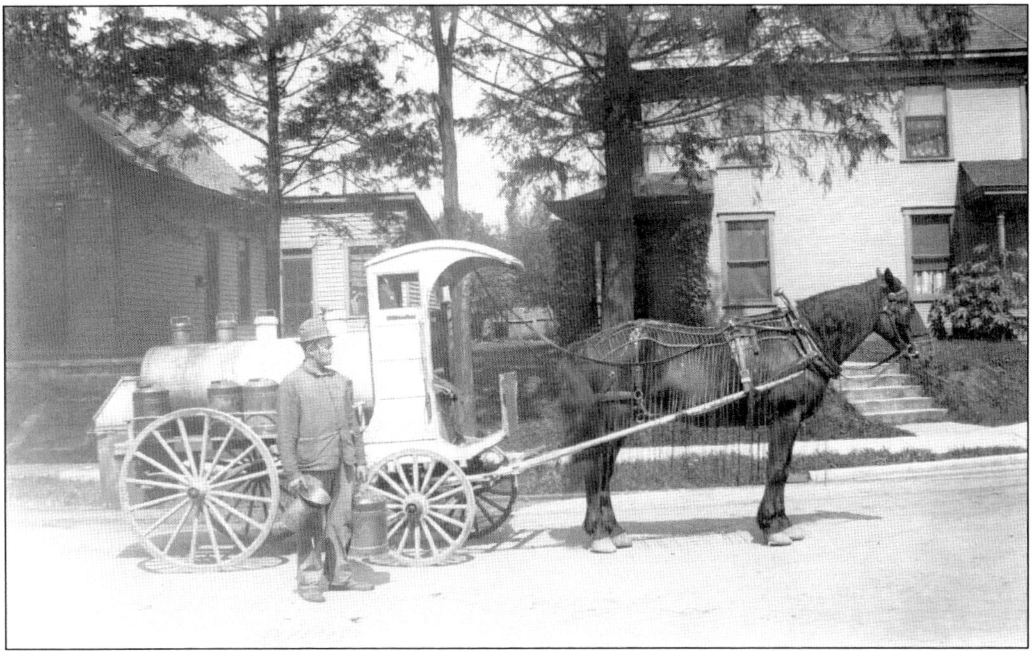

MUNCIE OIL & COAL CO. An employee of the Muncie Oil & Coal Company was captured on film delivering his goods in the early part of the century. The business, located at 425 West Ninth Street, was a dealer in oil, gasoline, coal, and feed. A.A. Bibler was the manager of this business that prospered for a number of years. (Real photo, unidentified photographer.)

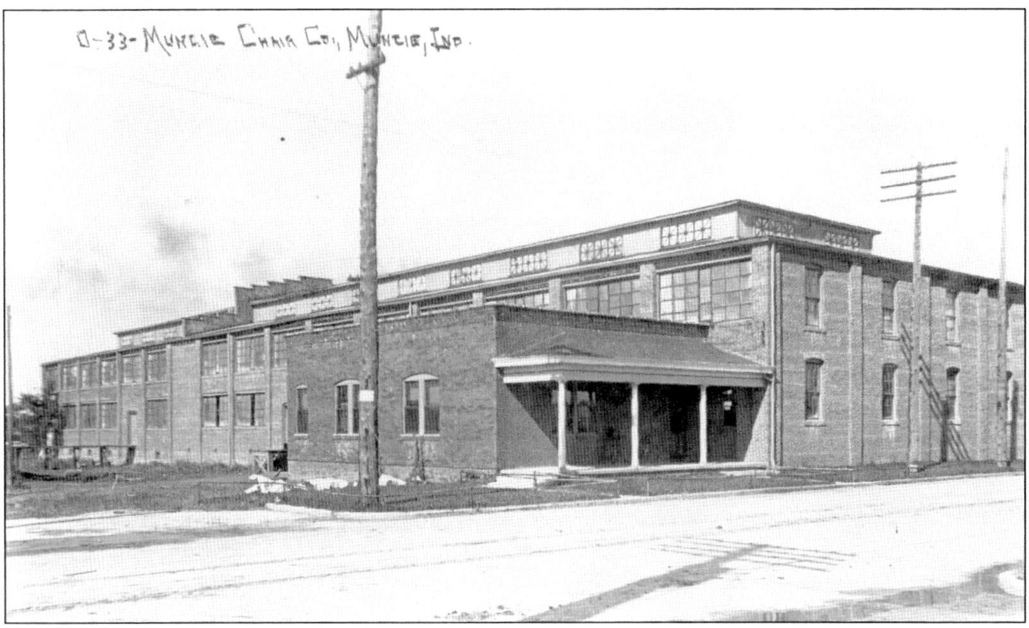

MUNCIE CHAIR CO. Upon searching for this company in the available city directories, no listing could be found. The 1911 Sanborn Fire Map for Muncie, however, indicates that the company was located on the northwest corner of South Walnut and Twentieth Streets. This space would later be occupied by the Excel Electric Company. (Real photo, published by Galion View Co.)

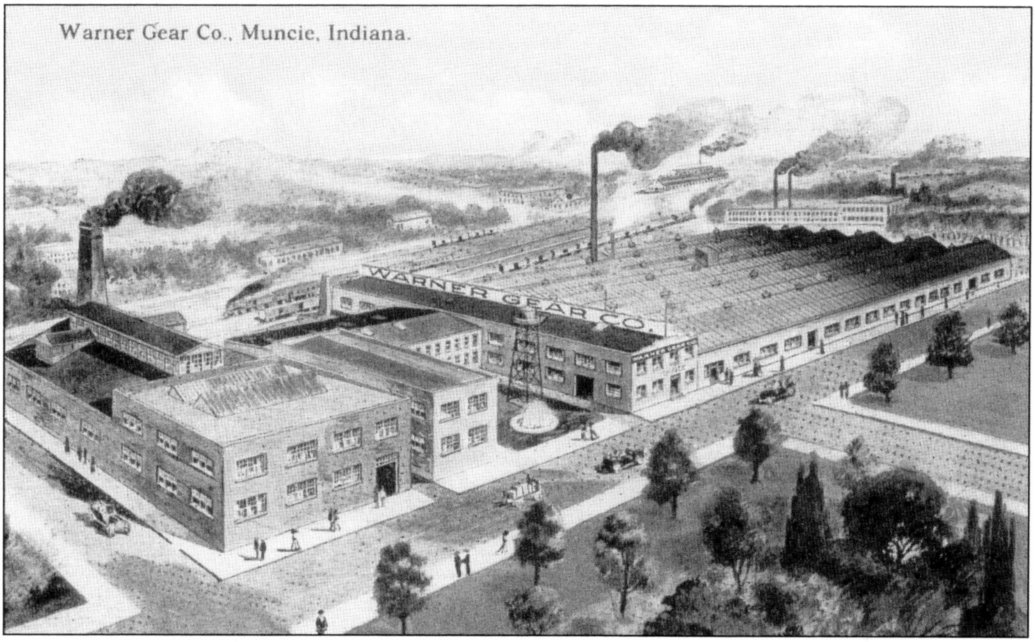

WARNER GEAR CO. The Warner Gear Plant was established on a small scale in 1901. In 1909, at about the time this picture was taken, the plant was located between Grant and Blaine Streets. They manufactured rear-axle differentials and other parts for automobiles. (S.H. Knox & Co.)

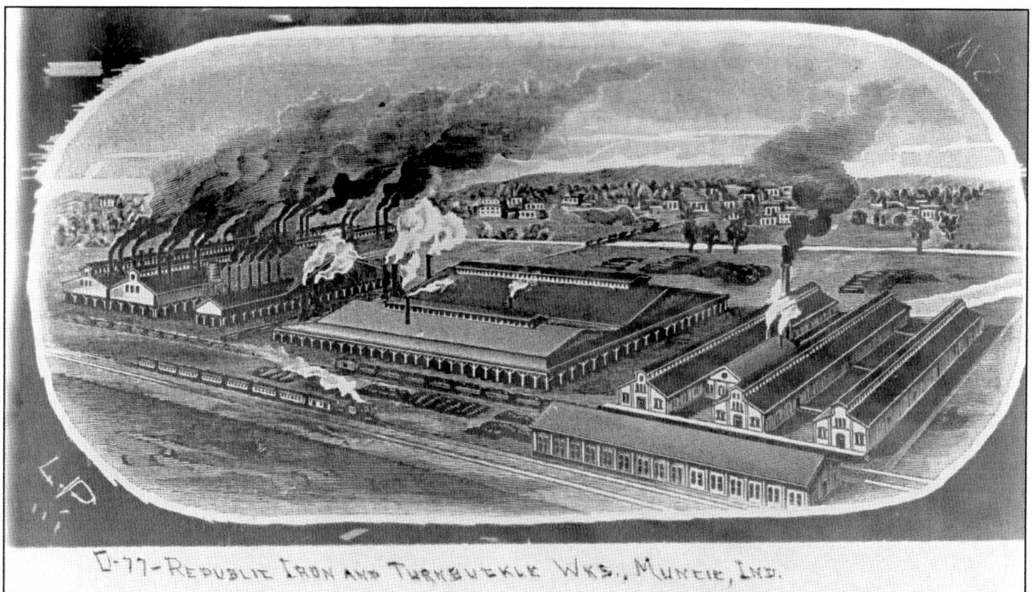

REPUBLIC IRON & TURNBUCKLE WORKS. This factory, better known as the Indiana Works of the Republic Iron & Steel Co., was located on the corner of Monroe and Eighteenth Streets. (Real photo, published by Galion View Co.)

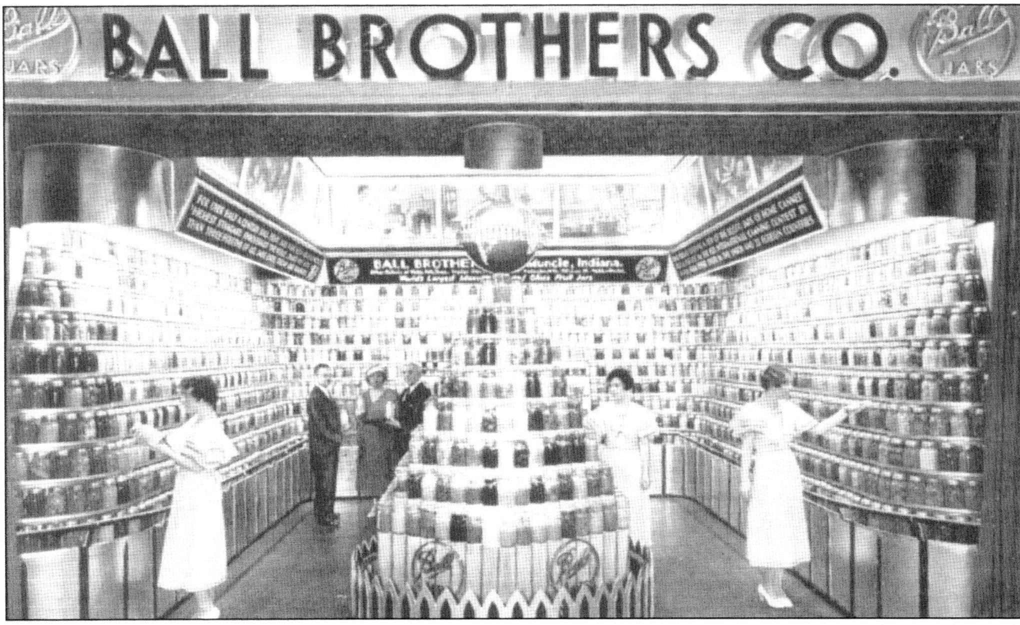

BALL BROTHERS CO. AT A CENTURY OF PROGRESS, CHICAGO, 1933. This view shows the Ball Brothers Co. display in the Foods and Agriculture Building at the 1933 Chicago Century of Progress Exhibition. (Unidentified printer and publisher.)

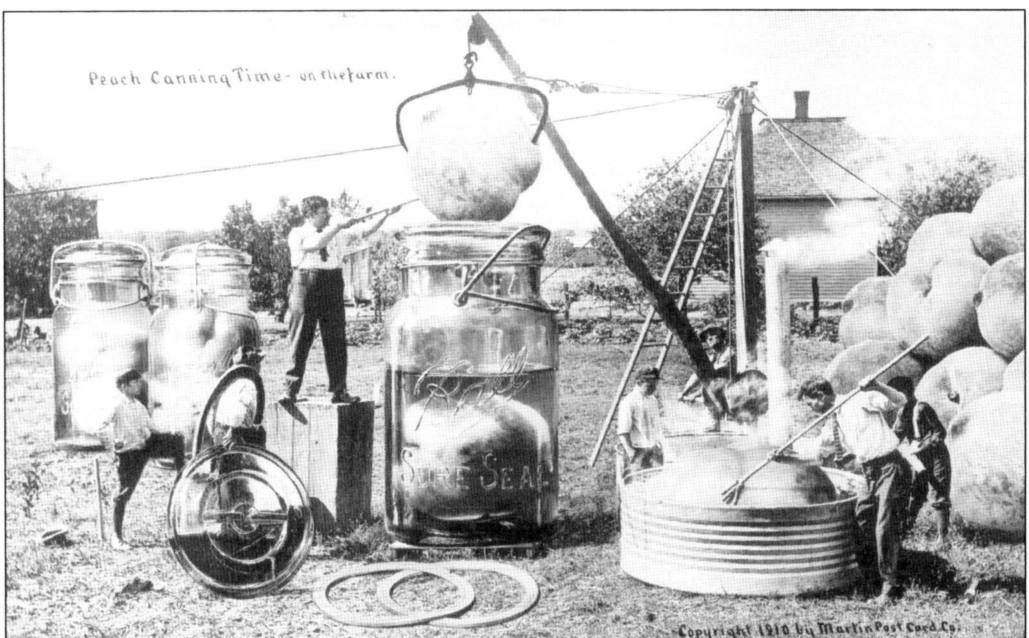

PEACH CANNING TIME—ON THE FARM. This exaggerated postcard is not actually of Muncie. It is included here because it features a Muncie industrial product—a Ball Brothers Co. "Sure Seal" canning jar. (Real Photo, published 1910 by the Martin Post Card Co.)

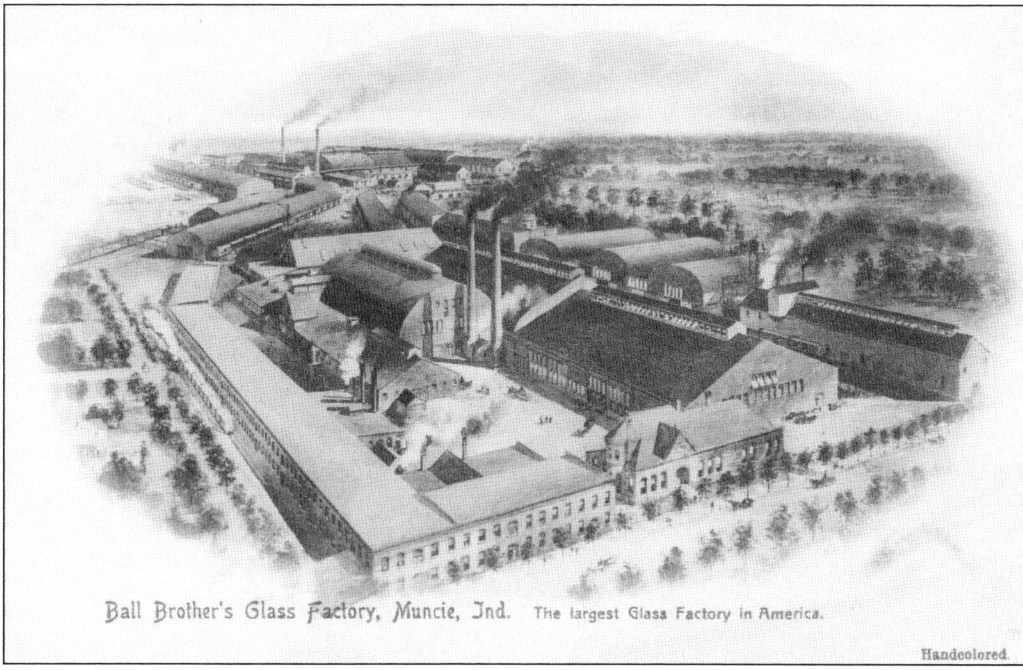

Ball Brothers Glass Factory—The Largest Glass Factory in America. The Ball Brothers Glass Factory moved to Muncie from Buffalo, New York, after the discovery of natural gas in eastern Indiana. After the gas reserves failed in the late 1890s, both Muncie and the Ball Brothers Glass Company continued to prosper and grow. (Marion Stewart.)

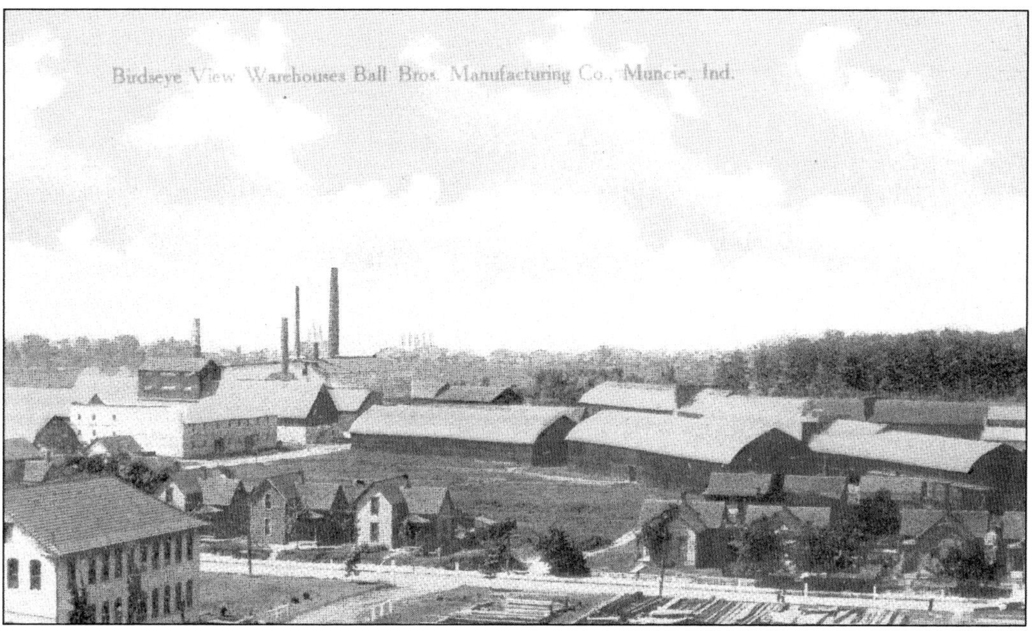

Birds-Eye View of Warehouses for the Ball Bros. Manufacturing Co. Officers of the company in 1909 were Frank C. Ball, president; Edmund B. Ball, vice-president; George A. Ball, treasurer; and William C. Ball, secretary. The principle products manufactured in the early years were fruit jars and glass oil cans. (Unidentified printer and publisher.)

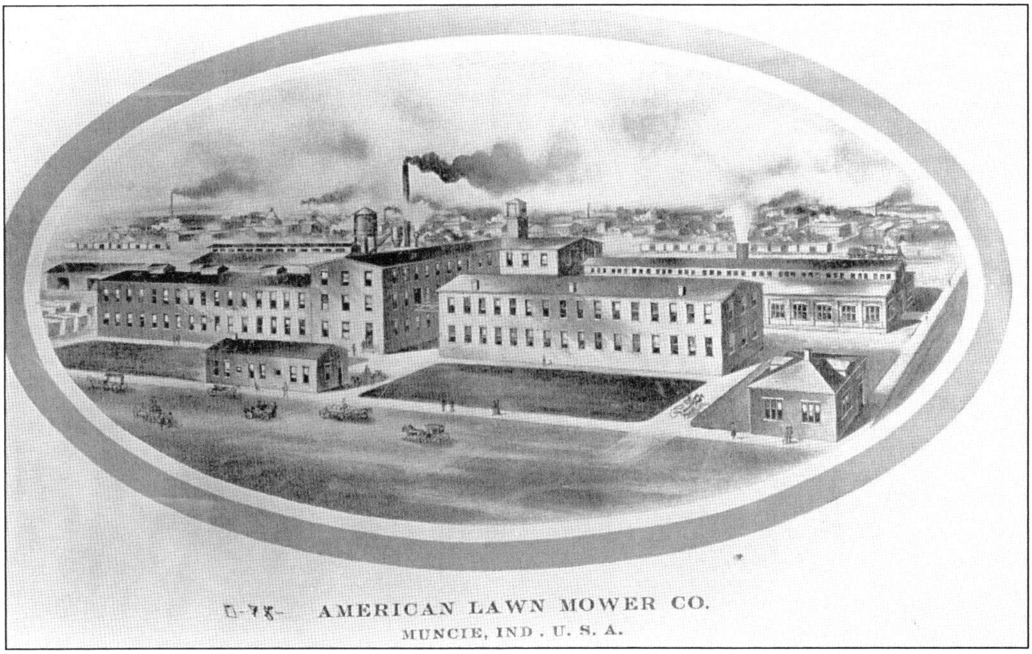

American Lawn Mower Co. The American Lawn Mower Company moved to Muncie from Richmond, Indiana, in the year 1900. Men who were active in the founding and development of the factory were W.F. Spencer, George M. Spencer, Robert B. Kersey, and W.F. Spencer II. (Real photo, published by Galion View Co.)

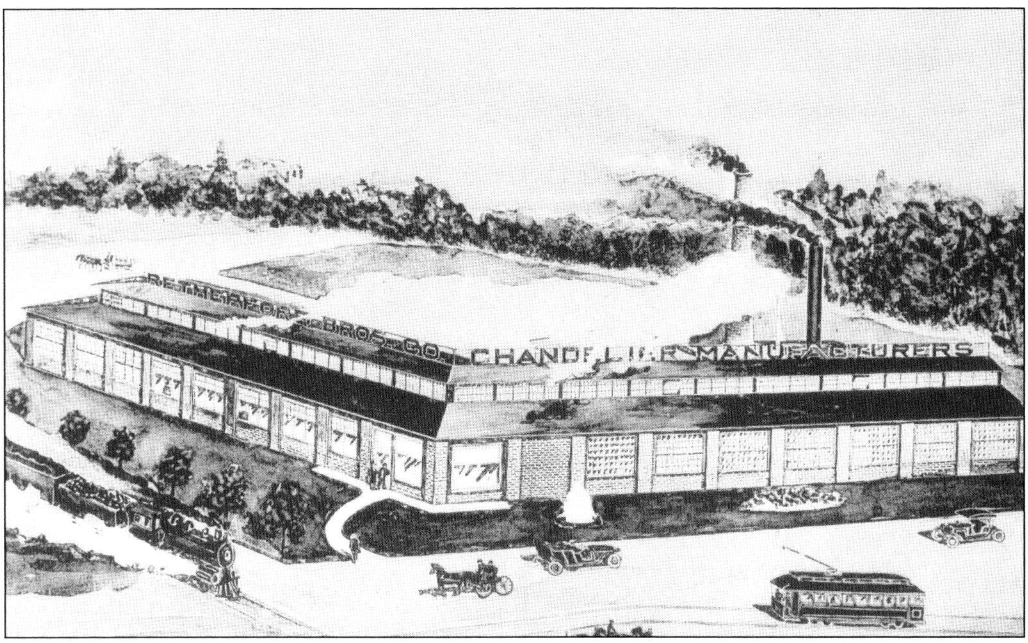

Retherford Brothers, Chandelier Manufacturers. John and R. Milton Retherford owned this plant located on East Main Street. They manufactured chandeliers and incandescent mantels, along with natural gas and electric supplies. (Unidentified printer and publisher.)

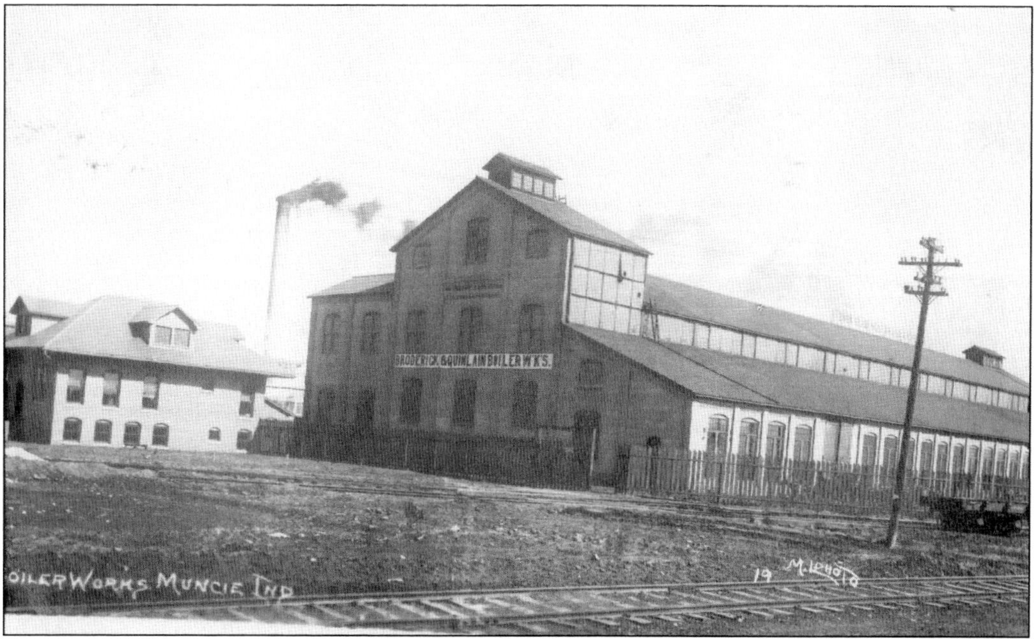

Broderick and Quinlan Boiler Works. This factory, located on Windsor Street at the C.C.C. & St. L Railway tracks, manufactured boilers. The company was later renamed the Broderick Company. The longtime president of the company was Michael H. Broderick. (Real photo, published by M.L. Photo.)

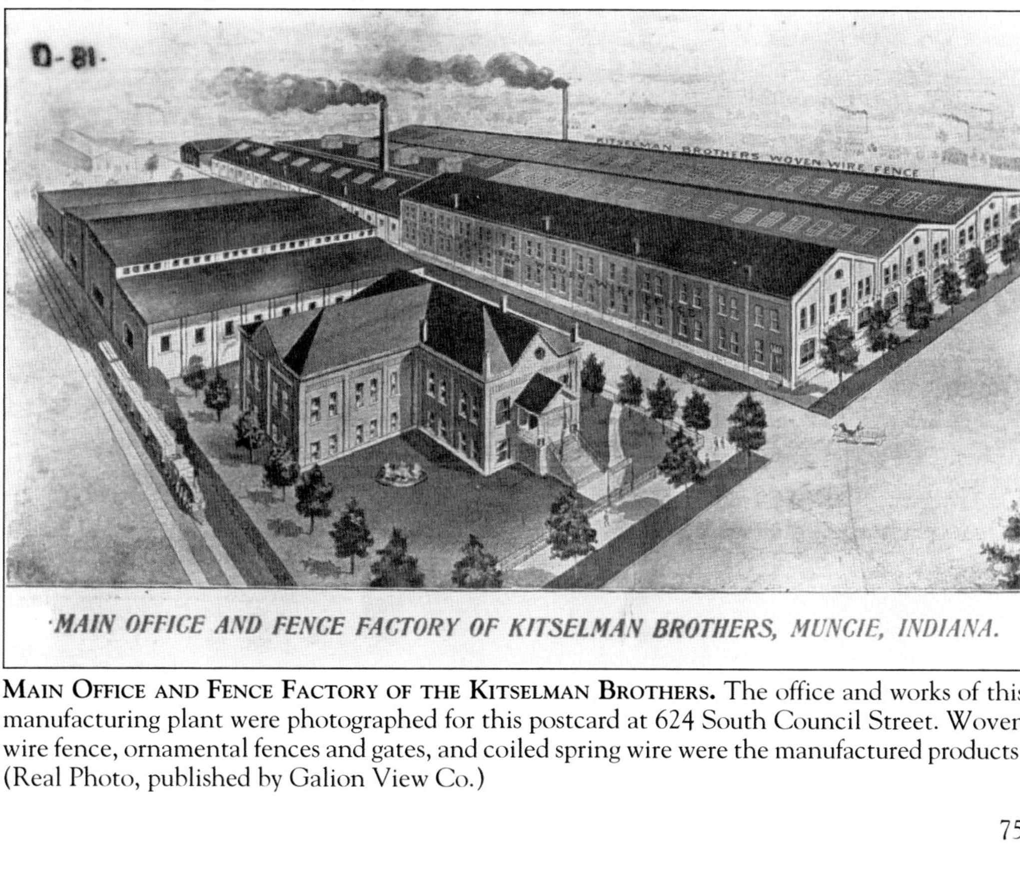

Main Office and Fence Factory of the Kitselman Brothers. The office and works of this manufacturing plant were photographed for this postcard at 624 South Council Street. Woven wire fence, ornamental fences and gates, and coiled spring wire were the manufactured products. (Real Photo, published by Galion View Co.)

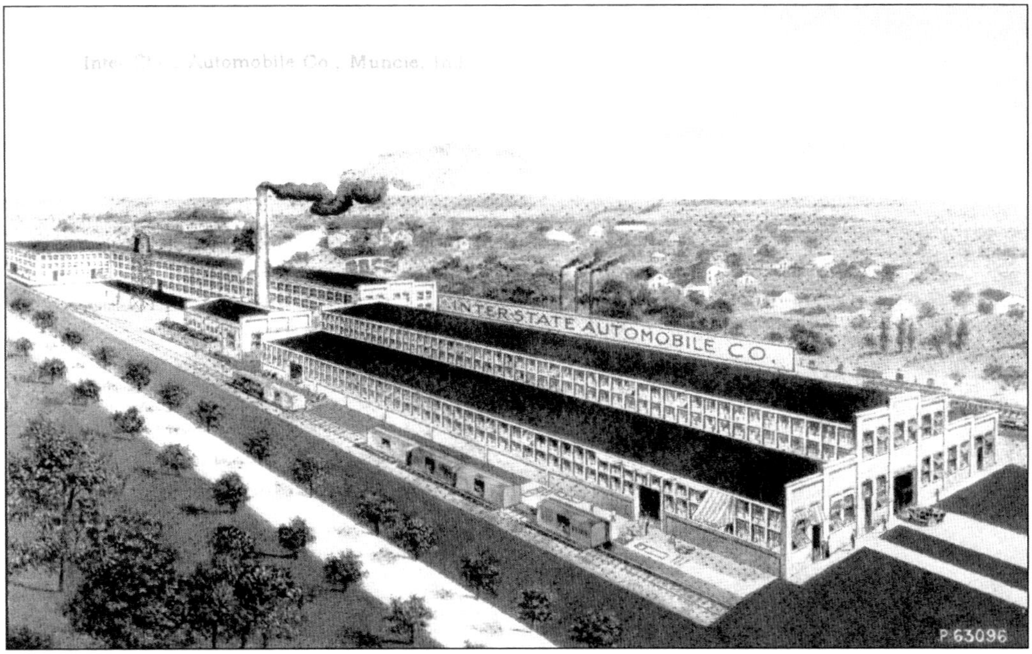

INTER-STATE AUTOMOBILE CO. Leaders of the Inter-State Automobile Company in 1909 were T.F. Hart, president and general manager; J.M. Maring, vice-president and secretary; and, Otto Holden, treasurer. (Superior Post Card Co.)

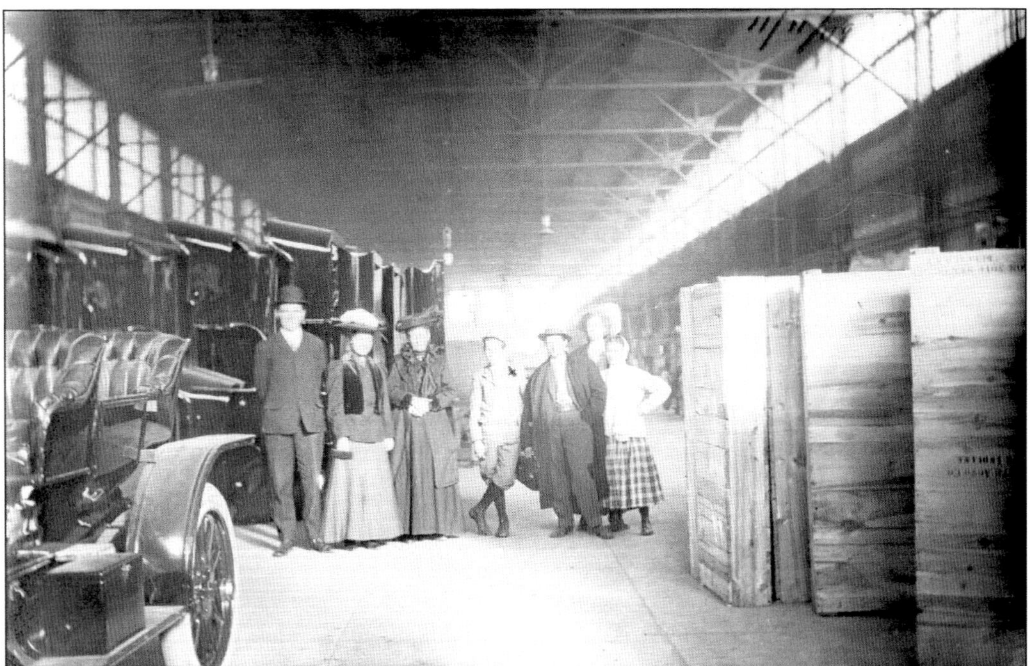

INTER-STATE AUTOMOBILE FACTORY. At one time, this factory was said to be the largest auto works in the state of Indiana. The car on the left in the photo is Inter-State's "Bull Dog 40." (Real photo, unidentified photographer.)

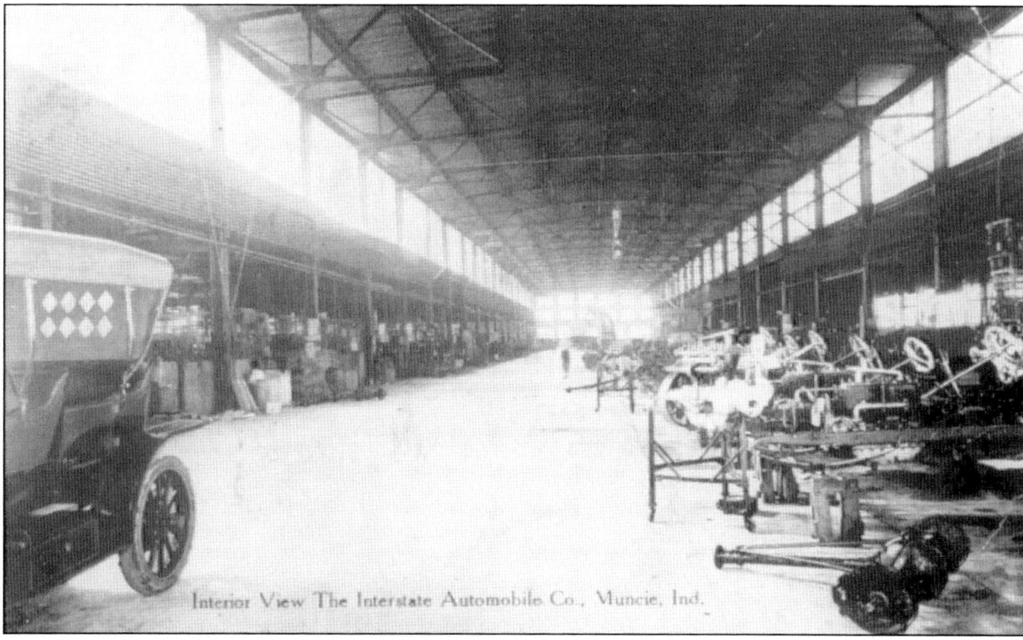

INTERIOR VIEW, INTERSTATE AUTOMOBILE CO. This manufacturing plant was started in 1917 by local citizens, including two of the Ball brothers who moved to Muncie from Buffalo, New York. The plant operated for only a short time before becoming the Durant Motor Co. (Unidentified printer and publisher.)

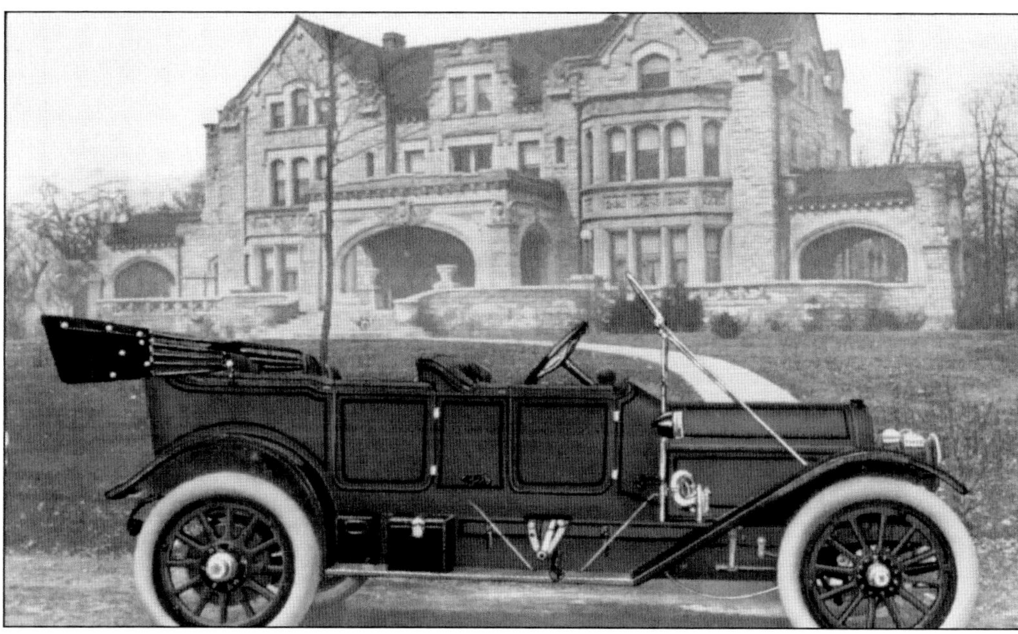

INTER-STATE "BULLDOG" MODEL. The advertisement on the back of the card reads, "35, 50 Horse Power Five or Seven Passenger Torpedo Touring Car, $2700." It also includes, from a new 1911 catalog, a request section to send for eight "40" and "50" models. (Unidentified printer and publisher.)

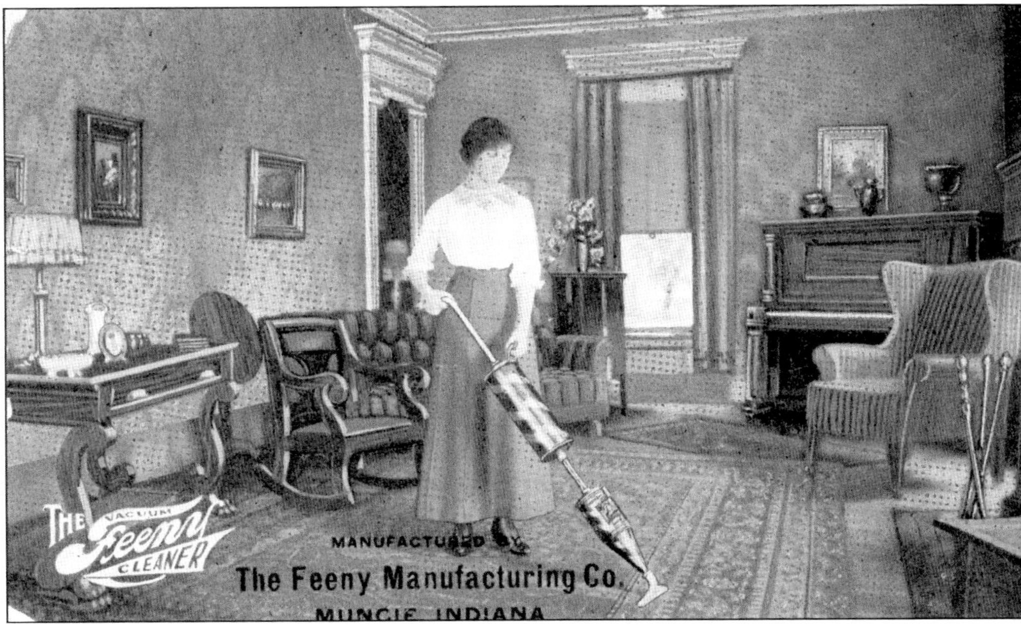

The Feeny Vacuum Cleaner, Manufactured by the Feeny Manufacturing Co. Vacuum cleaners and insecticide dusters were the products produced by this company. It was located on the intersection of Ohio Avenue and Washington Streets. Shown in the advertisement is the cleaner "Model D," selling for $12.50. (Published by Indianapolis Engraving & Electrotyping Co., Indianapolis, Indiana.)

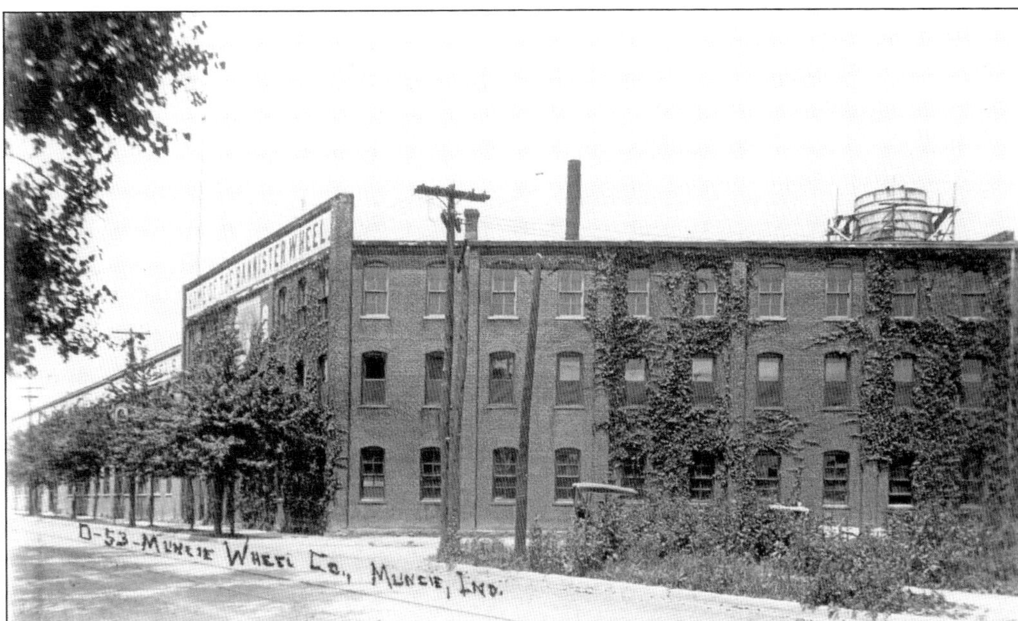

Muncie Wheel Co. The Muncie Wheel Company manufactured wooden wheels for buggies, wagons, and motor vehicles. The factory was located in this three-story building on the southeast corner of Ohio Avenue and the C.C.C. & St. L. (later the Big Four and after that, Conrail) tracks. (Real Photo, published by Galion View Co.)

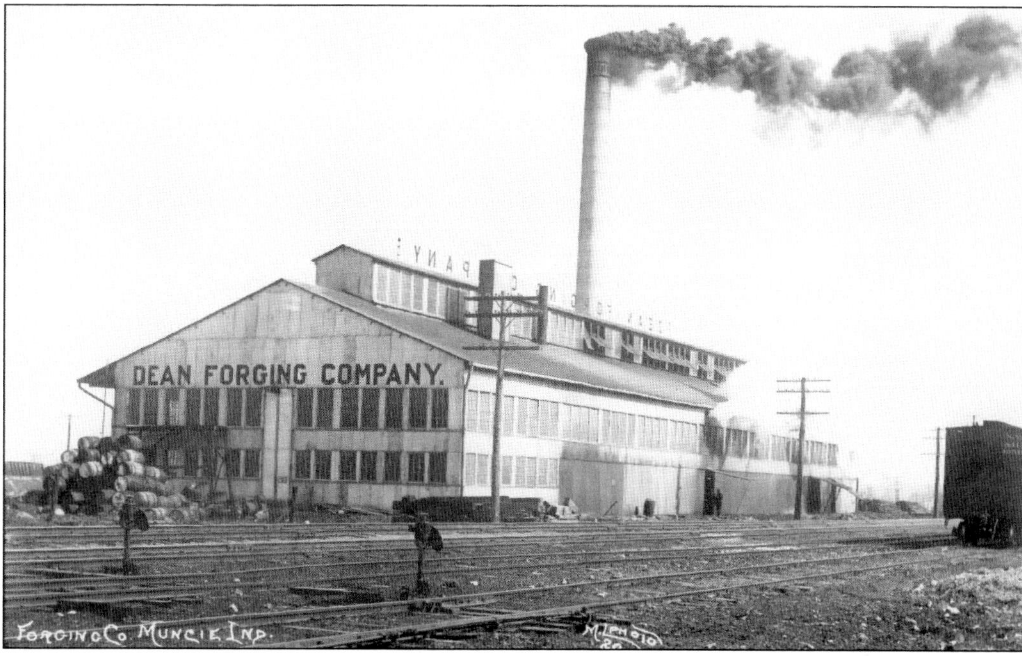

Forging Co. This factory, the Dean Forging Co., was located at 1825 East Jackson Street. Mr. J. Judson Dean was the president, Mr. Wilbur A. Full was secretary, and Mr. W.H. Carpenter was the general manager. (Real Photo, published by M.L. Photo.)

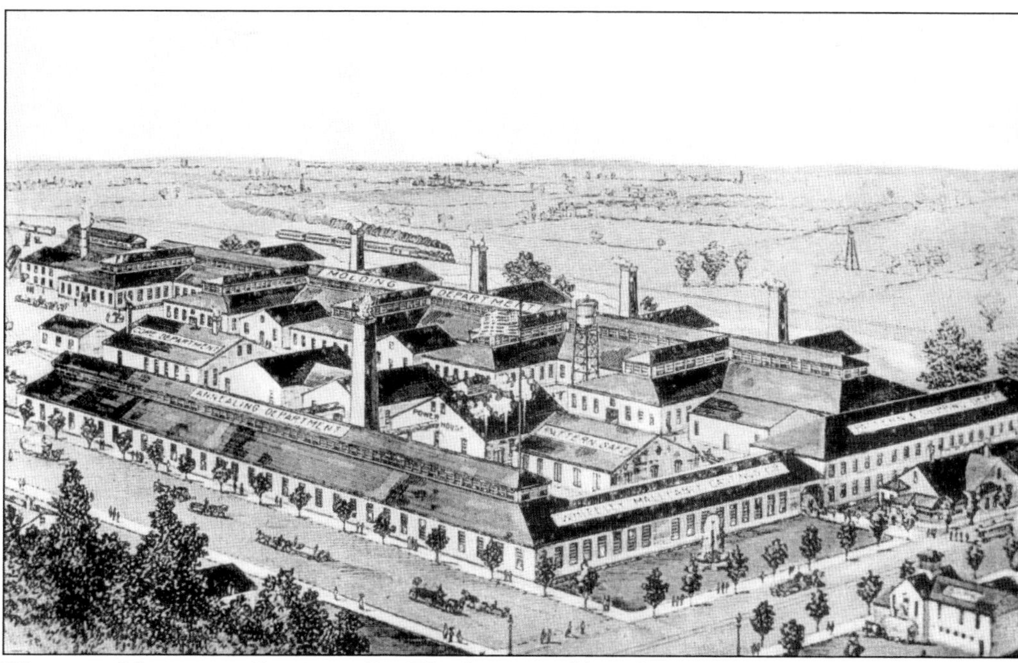

Whiteley Malleable Castings Co. This large, rambling factory was destroyed by fire in 1916. Before the fire, it manufactured castings for the automobile industry. It was operated by the Whiteley family. (Unidentified printer and publisher.)

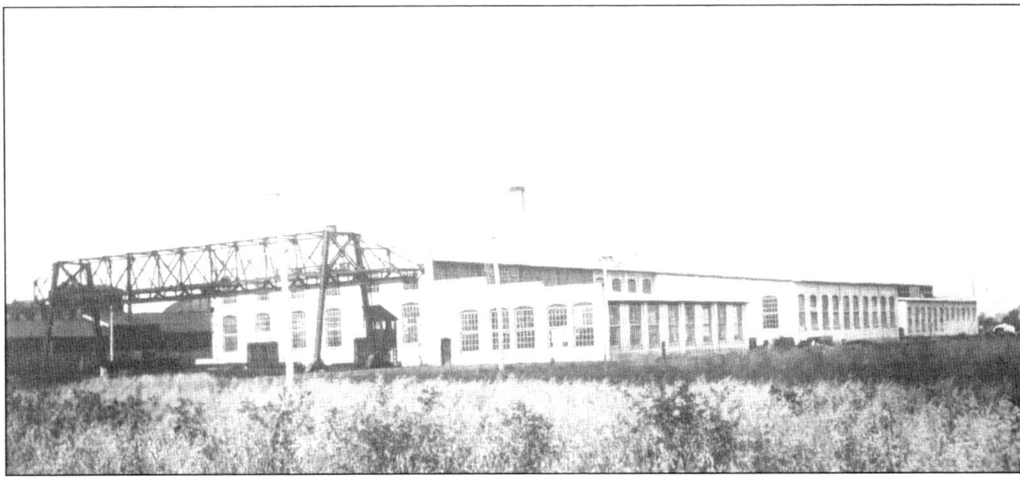

INDIANA BRIDGE CO. The oldest manufacturing firm in the city of Muncie is the Indiana Bridge Company. It was founded on May 17, 1886, to manufacture metal for the construction of bridges. In 1887, Charles M. Kimbrough became general manager of the plant. Emily, another member of the Muncie Kimbrough family, gained fame as an author. (Unidentified printer and publisher.)

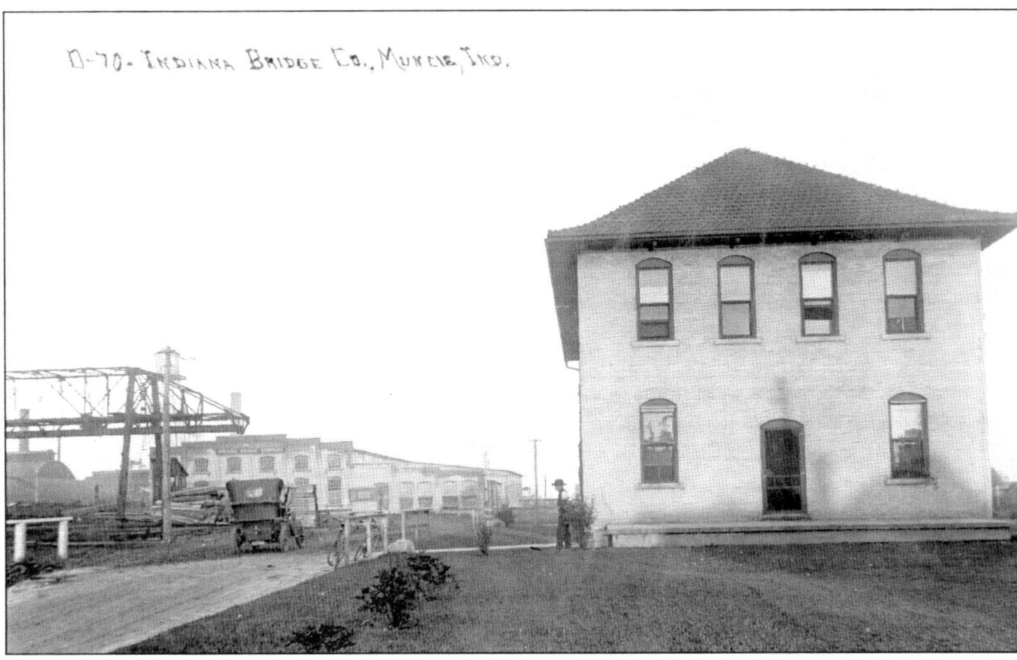

INDIANA BRIDGE CO. In the later years of the factory, production was expanded to include the design, manufacture, and construction of steel work for powerhouses along with steam and electric railway bridges. (Real photo, published by Galion View Co.)

Seven

Commercial Buildings and Businesses

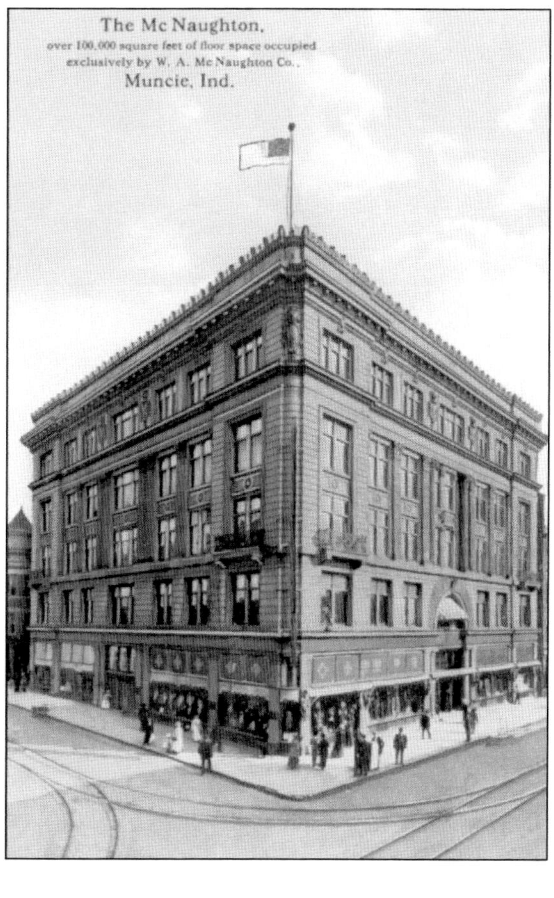

THE MCNAUGHTON. The McNaughton block at 400 South Walnut Street was designed by the Cincinnati architectural firm of Crapsey & Lamm and constructed from 1901 through 1903. Later, the Beaux Arts-style building was used as Ball Stores department store. In 1989, after the City of Muncie did not purchase the building for a "steal," it was unfortunately demolished to make room for empty space. (Curt Teich & Co.)

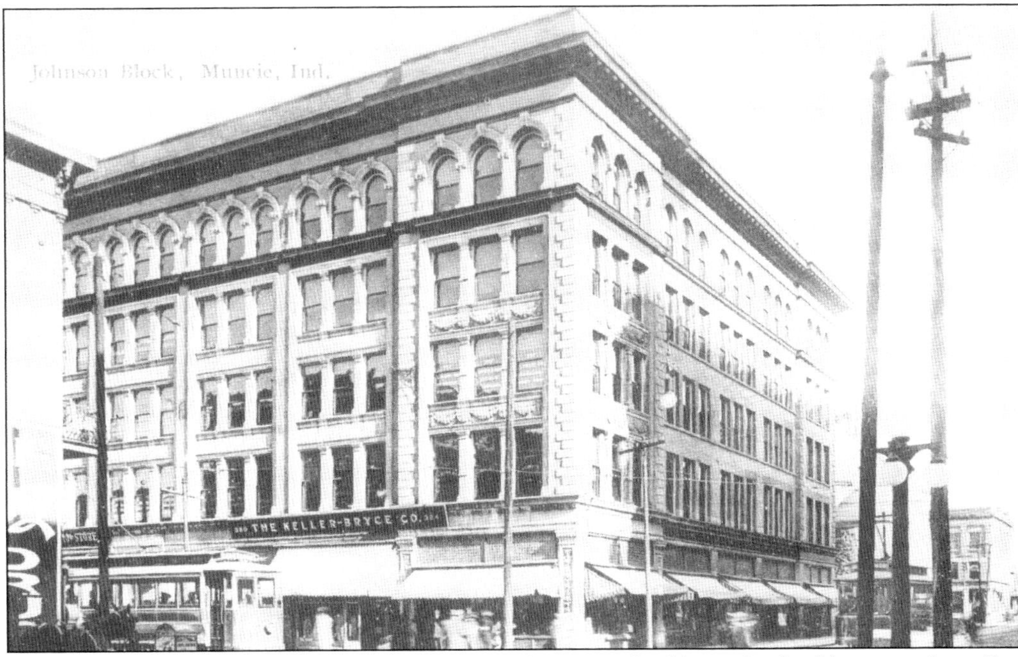

JOHNSON BLOCK. Also known as the Johnson and Morgan building, this building was the tallest in the city when constructed from 1895 until 1896. It was located at 320 South Walnut Street, on the northeast corner with Charles Street. Williams & Andrews of Dayton, Ohio, were the architects. It was razed in 1977. (Kraemer Art Co.)

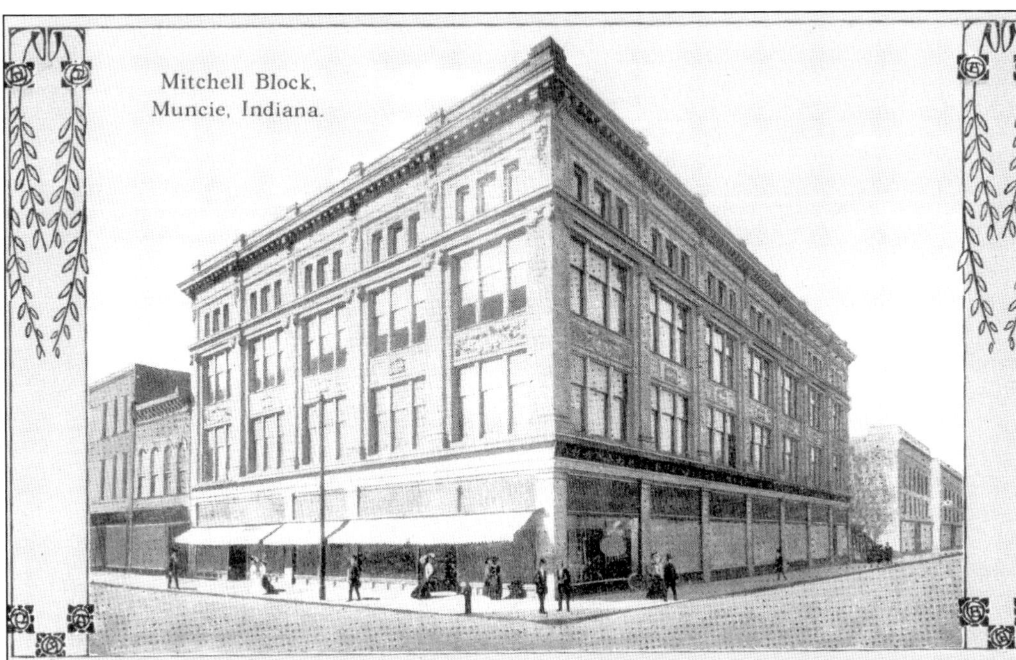

MITCHELL BLOCK. This Beaux Arts building at 301 South Walnut Street was completed in 1908 from plans drawn by Cuno Kibele of Muncie. It is currently used as a luxury apartment building. (S.H. Knox & Co.)

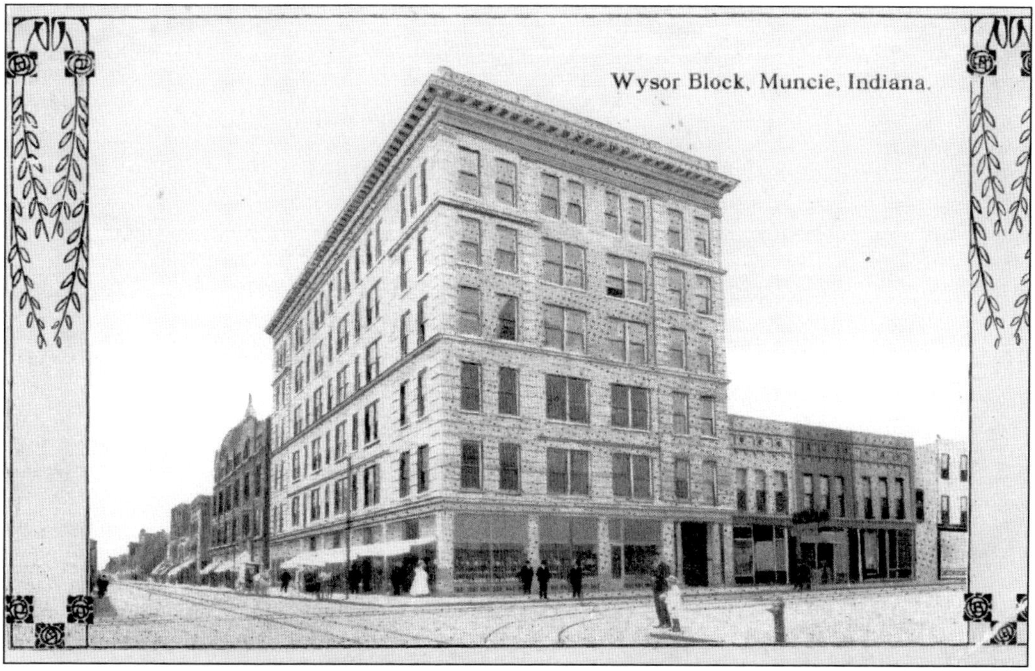

WYSOR BLOCK. Just after the turn of the century, Jacob H. Wysor hired Cuno Kibele to design a three-story addition to a three-story building that he owned on the southwest corner of Walnut and Main Streets. The addition was completed in 1906. In 1978, a major fire seriously damaged the abandoned building. Nine years later, it was razed and replaced by a small park. (S.H. Knox & Co.)

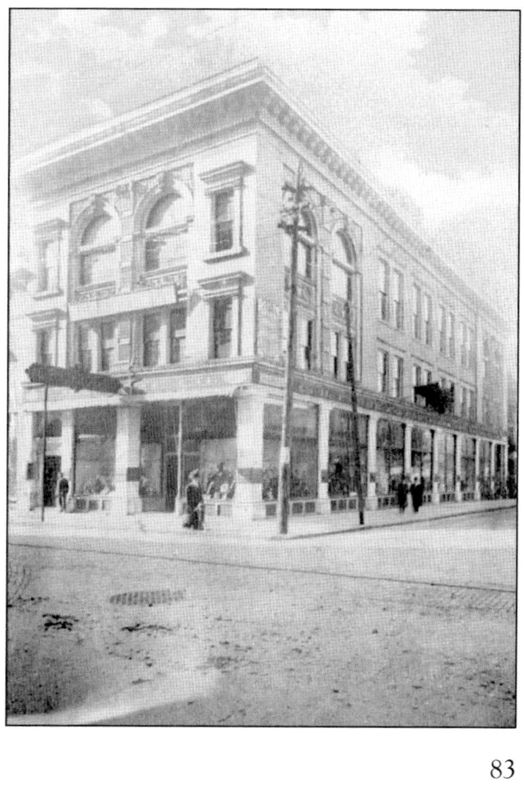

FUDGE'S CORNER, CHARLES AND WALNUT STREETS. Also known as the Jones or Freund building, this Classical Revival structure was completed for Mrs. C.C. Jones in 1906. Designed by Grindle & Cramer, it cost $25,000. The building was home to the Indiana Business College for several decades. In the 1924 city directory, the Indiana Business College was headed by Charles C. Cring, president; Fred W. Case, vice-president; Roy H. Puterbaugh, secretary; Ora E. Butz, treasurer and general manager; and John C. Pickerill, resident manager. The Fudge building is located on the southwest corner of Charles and Walnut Streets. (Union News Co.)

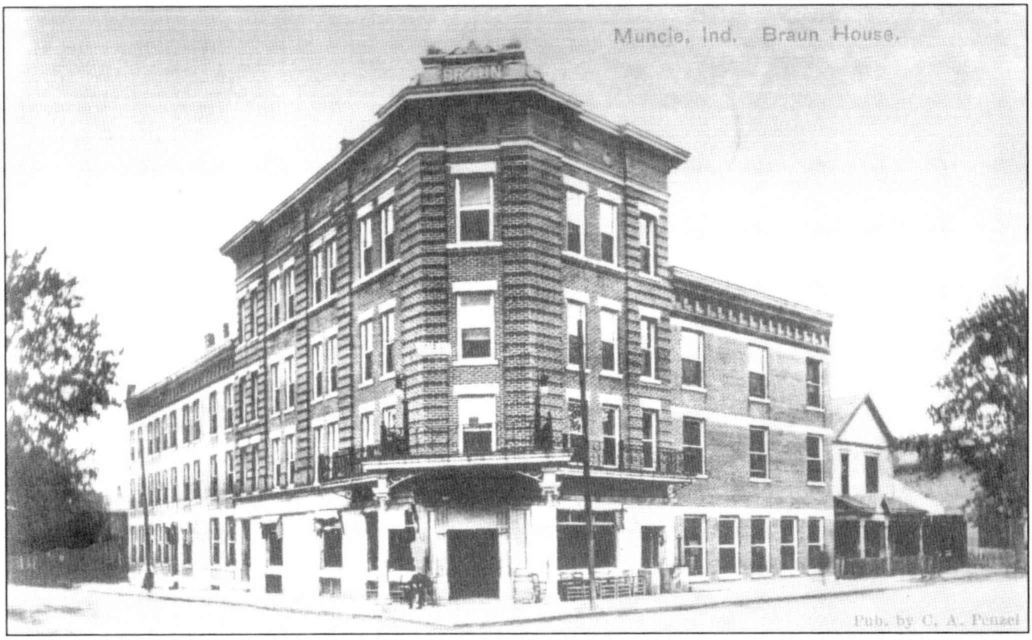

Braun House. August Braun was the proprietor of this hotel at 200 West Washington Street. Morrow and Morrow and Lane and Pyke of Lafayette, Indiana, contracted the construction of the original building [front of picture] for around $18,000. (The Metropolitan News & Publishing Co.)

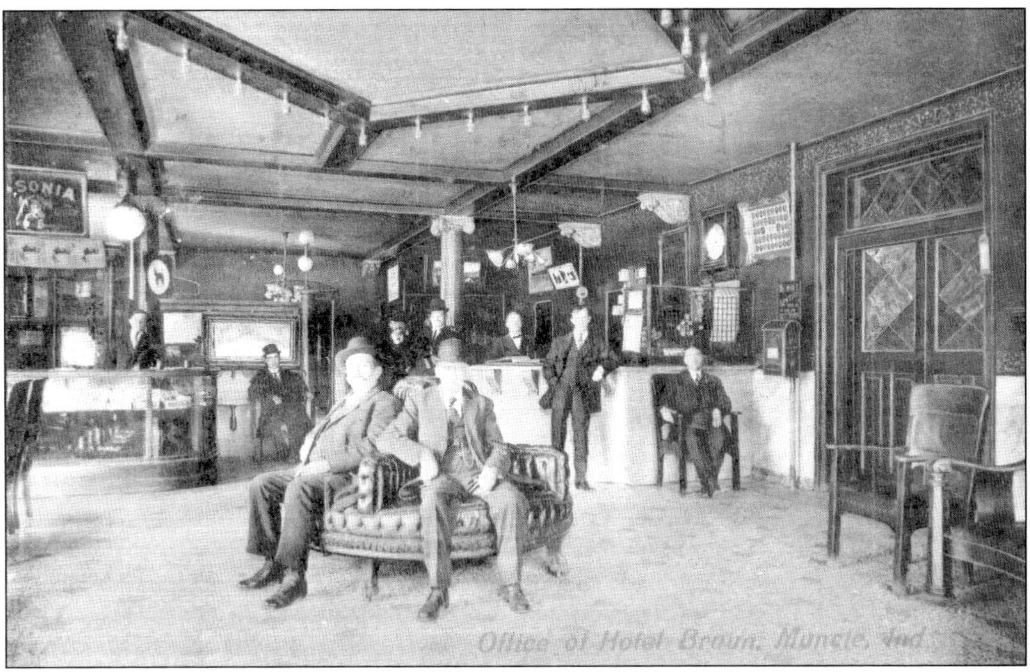

Office of the Hotel Braun. Demolition of the Braun Hotel, completed by the Rogers Wrecking Company of New Castle, Indiana, occurred in 1951. (Kraemer Art Co.)

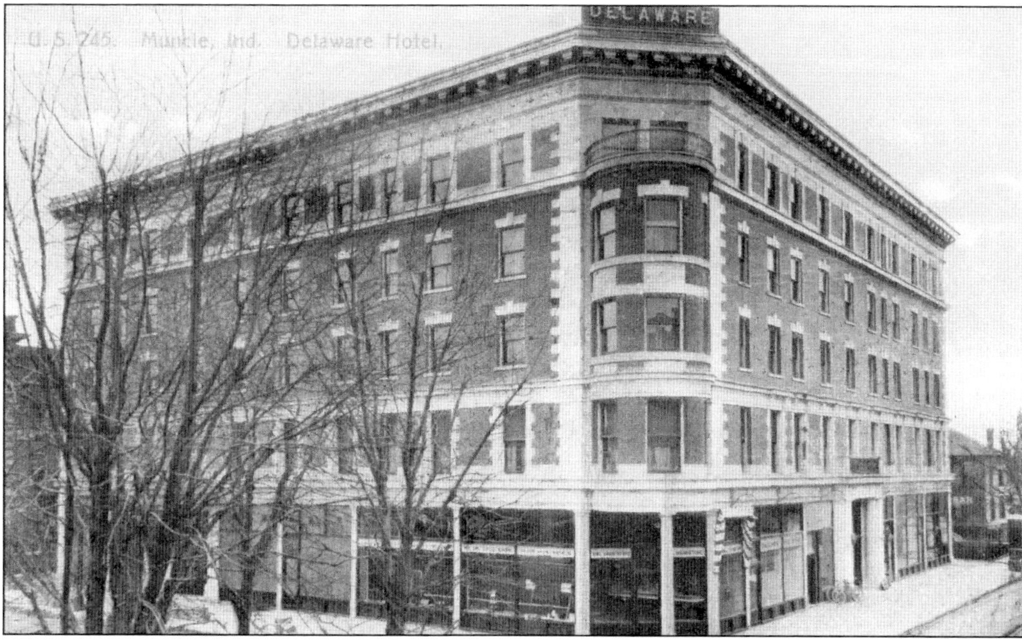

DELAWARE HOTEL. Built in 1905 by Theodore Rose for an estimated $200,000, the Delaware served as Muncie's largest hotel for two decades. It was located at 206 South Mulberry Street, at the southeast corner with Adams. (F. Von Bardelben.)

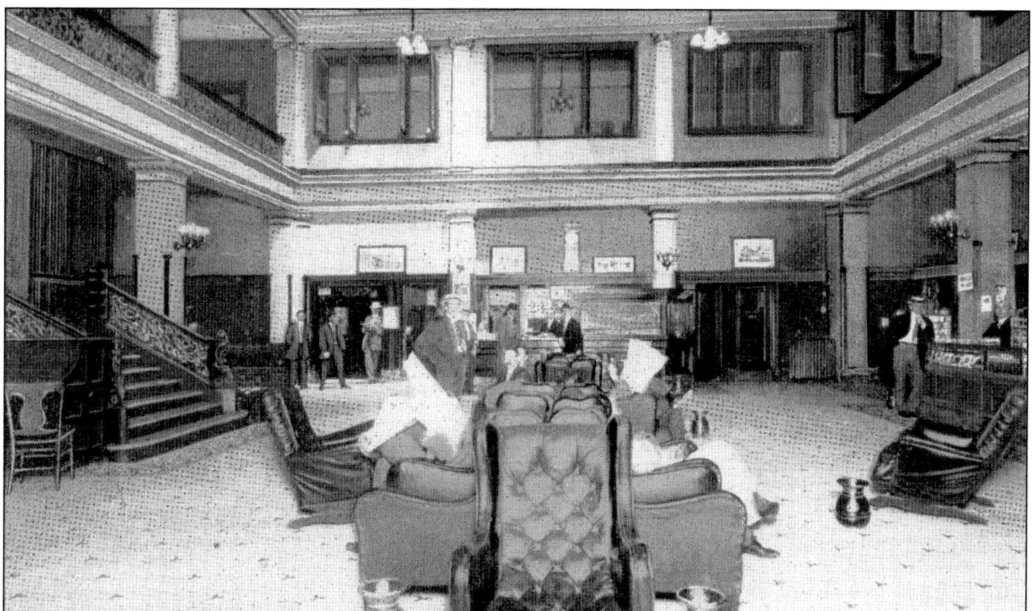

DELAWARE HOTEL LOBBY. The lobby of the Delaware was a large room with a high ceiling that was a precursor to many designs of hotel lobbies today. The building was torn down in the fall of 1970. (Curt Teich & Co.)

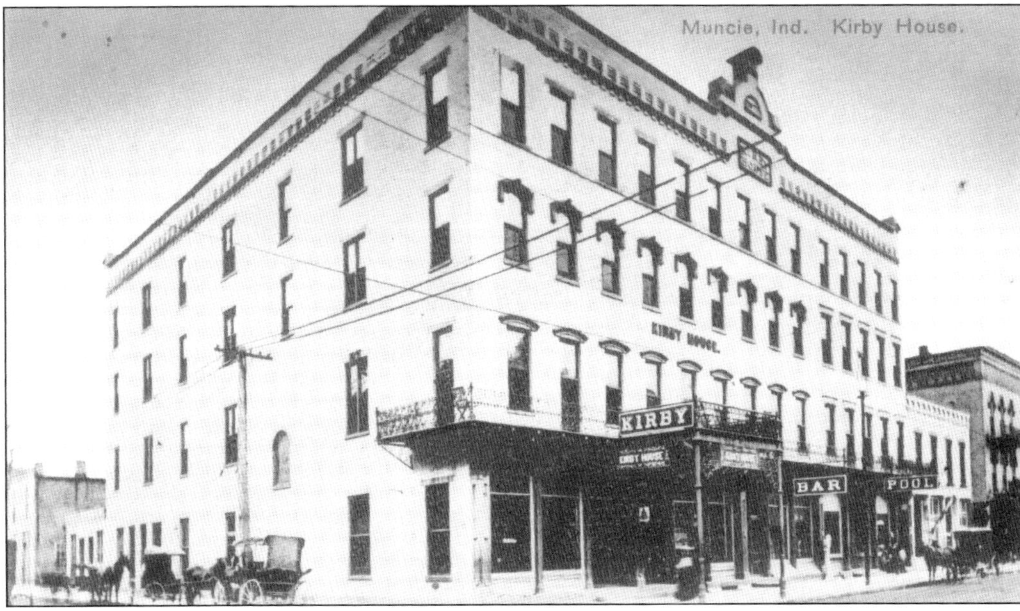

KIRBY HOUSE. Constructed 1870–72, the Kirby House, when dedicated in January of 1872, was a large three-story building with a mansard roof. It was located on the southwest corner of Main and Jefferson Streets. Sometime near 1880, the building was remodeled to remove the mansard roof and add a fourth floor. The building was torn down in 1962. (The Metropolitan News & Publishing Co., for C.A. Penzel.)

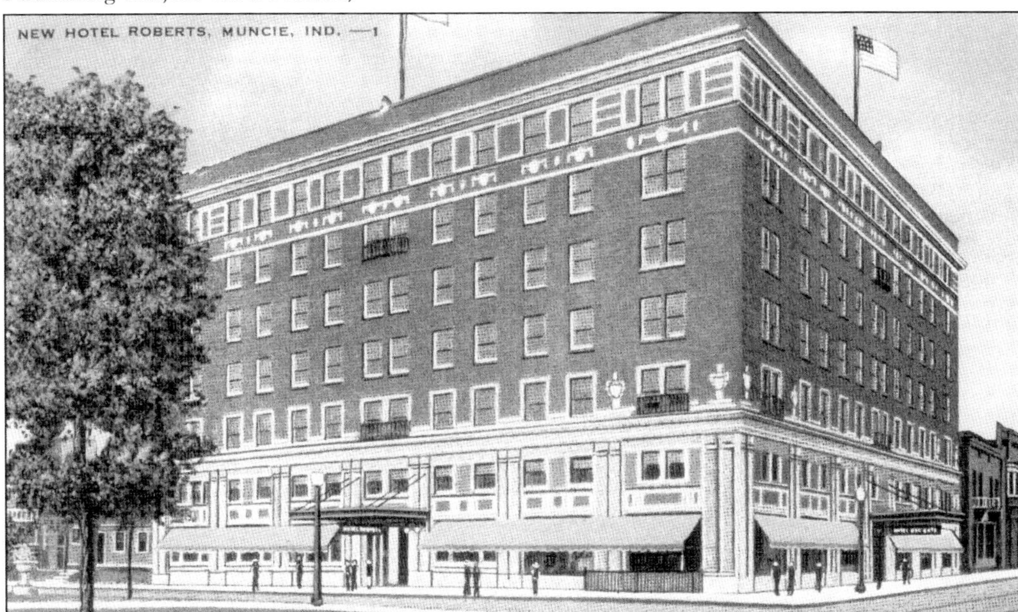

THE NEW HOTEL ROBERTS. In 1921, George C. Roberts built this hotel according to plans by architect Charles W. Nichol of Lafayette, Indiana. From 1986 through 1987, the building was enlarged at a cost of nearly $10 million and renamed the Radisson Hotel. Sebree, Craig, & McKnight of Indianapolis drew the plans for the addition, which was contracted to Oberle & Associates. (E.C. Kropp Co.)

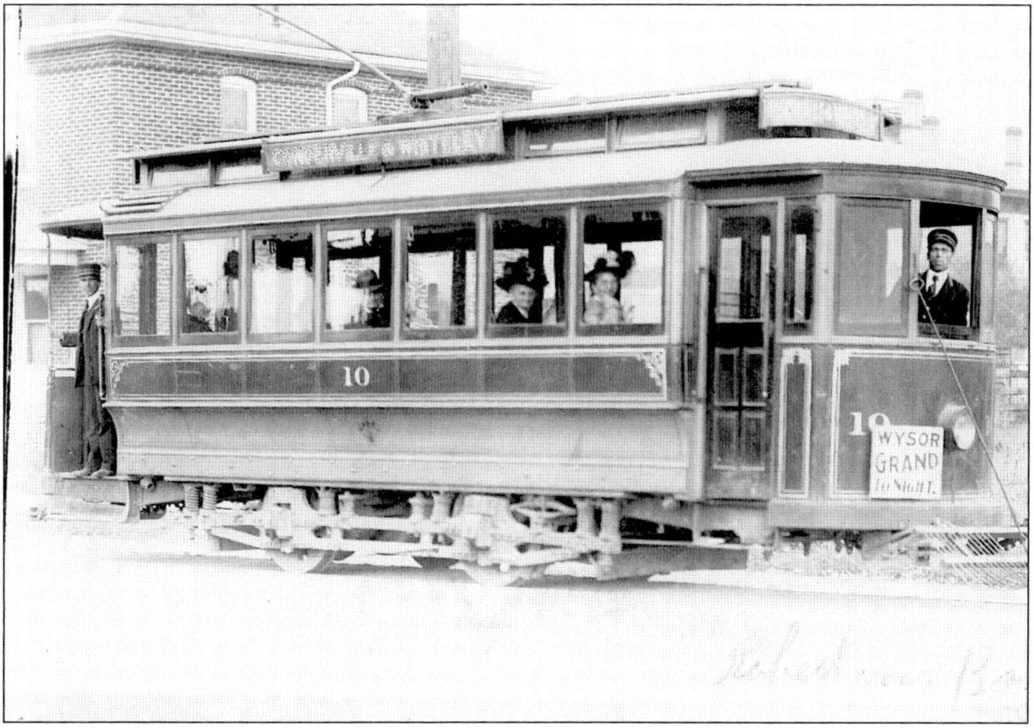

INTER-URBAN CAR. At the time of this photo in 1908, this particular car was being used to service the suburbs of Congerville and Whiteley. Both suburbs are now a part of the city of Muncie. (Real photo, unidentified photographer.)

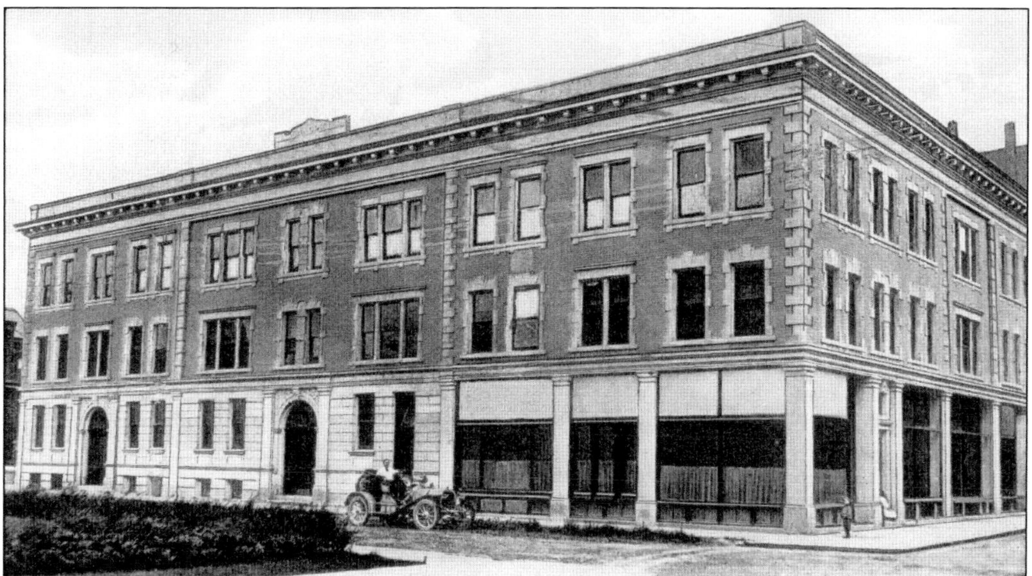

NEW SHIRK BLOCK. (INDIANA NEWS CO./UNION NEWS CO.) Built by W.W. Shirk, this building was later known as the Canopic Apartments. It is located at 217-225 East Jackson Street. A 1906 addition designed by Cuno Kibele more than doubled the size of this building, originally constructed in 1896.

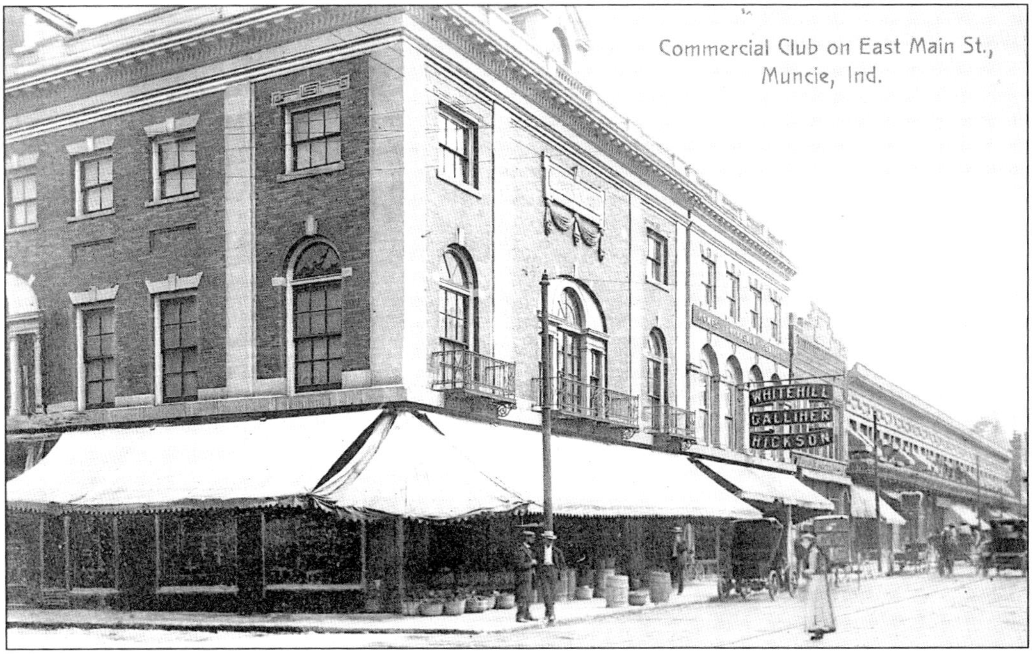

COMMERCIAL CLUB ON EAST MAIN STREET. Little substantial data could be found regarding this building. One source says that Charles Russey was contracted for the construction of this building and completed the work in 1901. The Delaware County Interim Report of 1985 estimates the building to have been constructed around 1920 in the Renaissance Revival style of architecture. (Kraemer Art Co., for C.A. Penzel.)

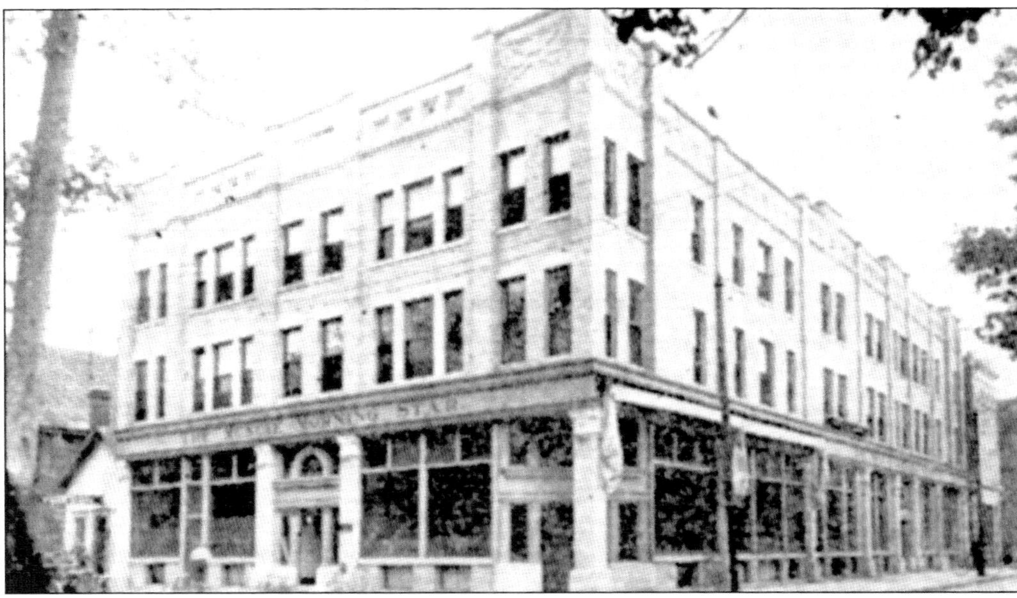

THE MUNCIE MORNING STAR BUILDING. This building, completed in 1905 at 308 South Mulberry Street, housed the city's largest newspaper. John C. Shaffer was the owner of the paper at the time the building was constructed. When the newspapers of Muncie consolidated in 1947, this building was abandoned as a newspaper office. In 1978, it was razed. (Unidentified printer, unidentified publisher.)

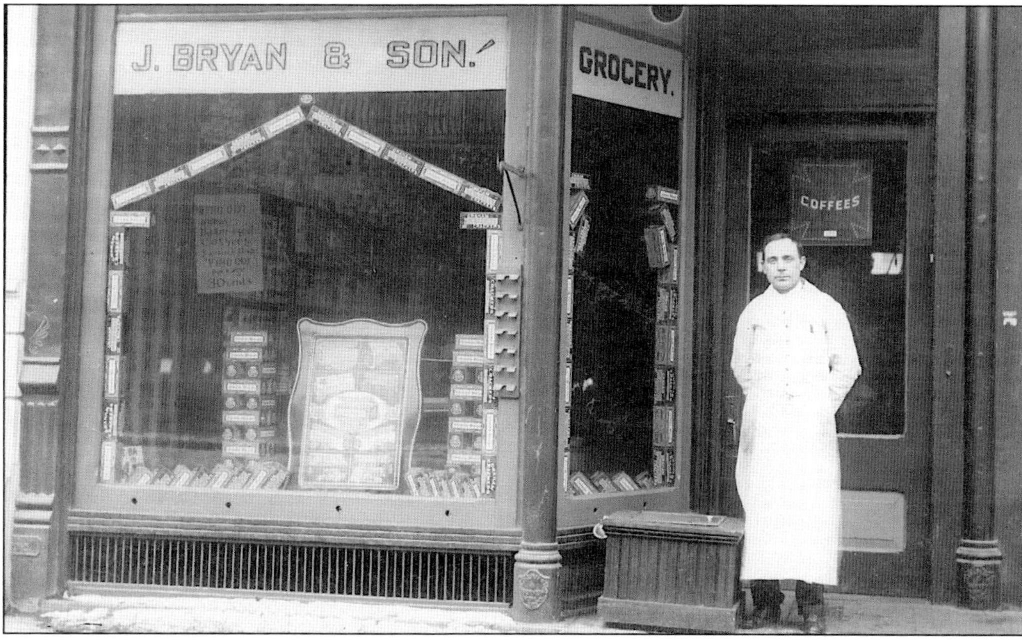

J. Bryan & Son Grocery. This photo postcard was mailed in Muncie in 1909. The 1909–10 Muncie City Directory shows the store to be operated by John and Charles C. Bryan at 325 East Main Street. The directory states that they were "dealers in staple and fancy groceries, country produce, etc." (Real photo, unidentified photographer.)

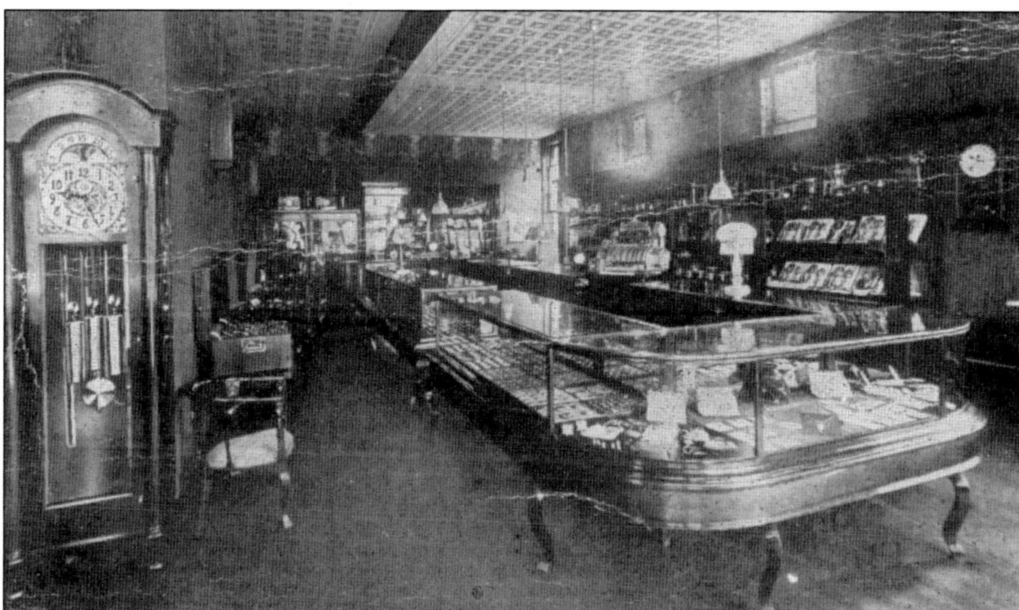

Muncie Jewelry and Plating Works and the J.F. Kisor Store. The J.F. Kisor Co. and the Muncie Jewelry & Plating Works were both operated from 401 West Howard Street when this postcard was mailed in 1910. In 1914 and 1919, when the companies were incorporated, J. F. Kiser was the president, A. Kiser was vice-president, and Frank Kiser served as both secretary and treasurer. (Real photo, unidentified photographer.)

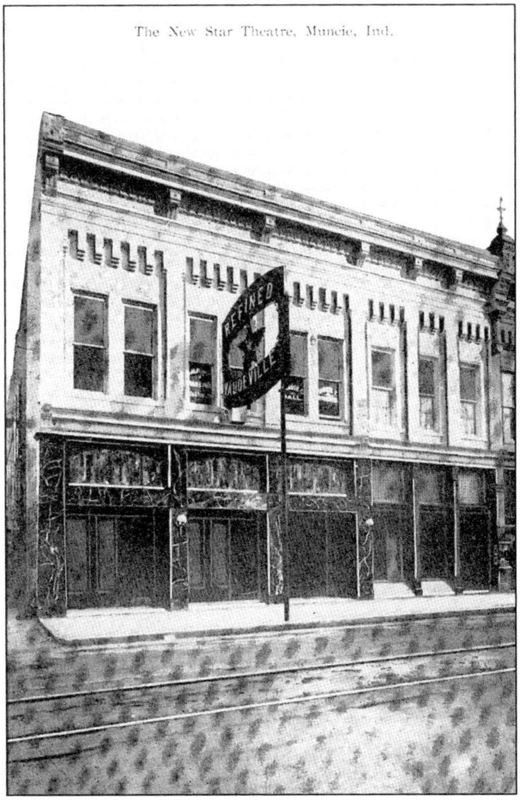

THE NEW STAR THEATRE. The Star Theatre was located at 214-216 East Main Street in the Boyce block, which was constructed in 1880. In 1909, the theater advertised to have "High-Class Vaudeville."

Matinees were held daily at 3 p.m., 10¢ to all. Evening entertainment occurred at 7:45 and 9 p.m. and cost between 10¢ and 20¢. It was "Some Place To Go." Throughout the early lifetime of this Masing author, the theater was known as the Hoosier Theater. In 1955, the Hoosier went out of business, and the building sat vacant for eight years. In 1963, it was purchased for use as the Muncie Civic Theatre. It has continued in that capacity ever since. (Watson, Stationer.)

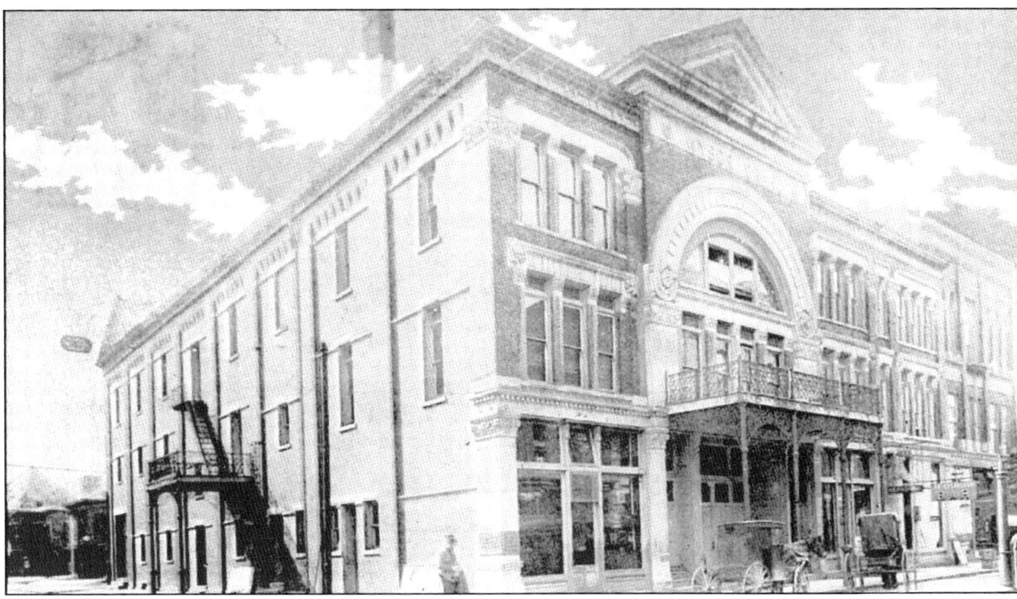

THE WYSOR GRAND OPERA HOUSE, AT THE CORNER OF JACKSON AND MULBERRY STREETS. The Wysor Grand Opera House (later a motion picture theater) was built by Jacob H. Wysor and completed in 1892. It was located at 123 East Jackson Street. In 1963, the building was torn down. (Union News Co.)

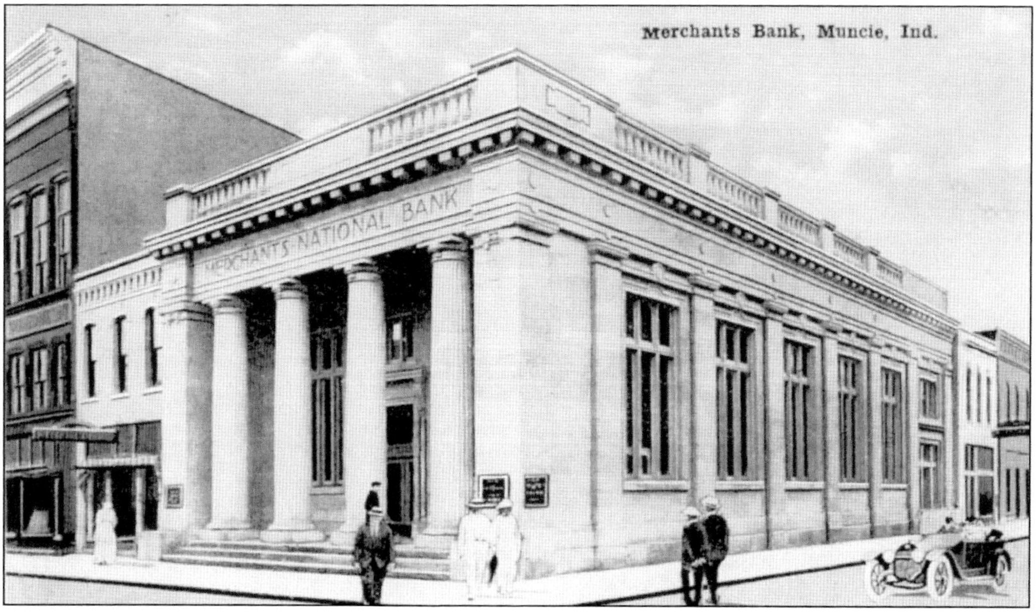

MERCHANTS NATIONAL BANK. This Merchants National Bank building, located at 122 South Mulberry Street, was built in 1913 and 1914 at a cost of $45,000. It was designed by Muncie architect Cuno Kibele. On July 6, 1914, the bank held an open house in its Classic Revival-style edifice. In 1972, another building, modern in style, was completed from plans by Bank Builders Corporation. This led to a 1977 razing of the old building. (E.C. Kropp Co.)

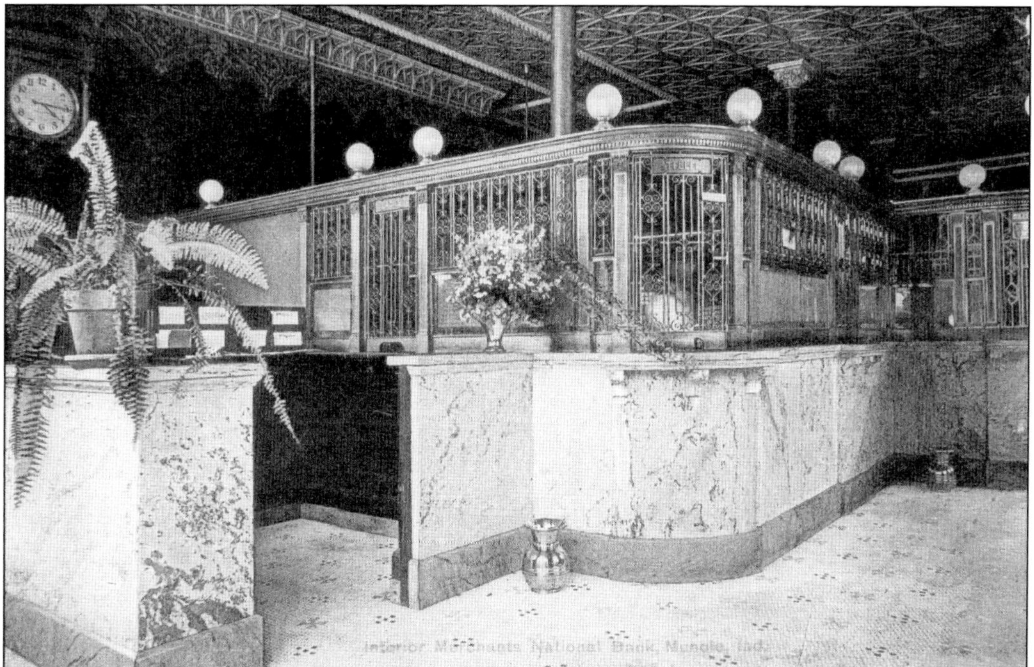

INTERIOR, MERCHANTS NATIONAL BANK. This is an interior view of the bank shown above. (A.N.C., New York, for Watson, Bookseller and Stationer.)

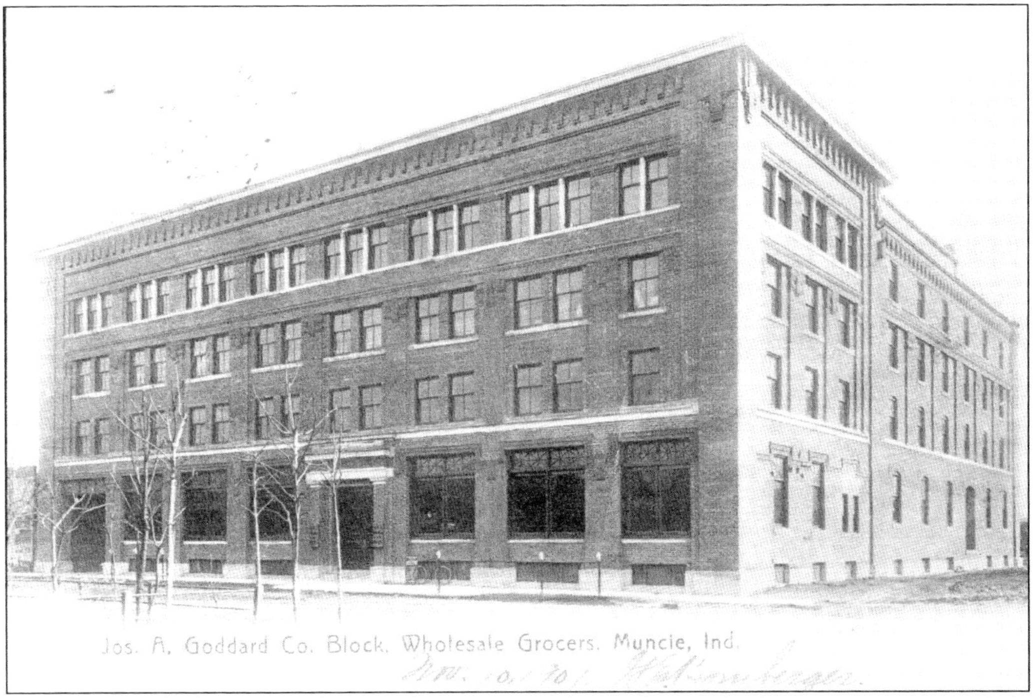

JOS. A. GODDARD CO. BLOCK, WHOLESALE GROCERIES. Wing & Mahurin of Fort Wayne drew the plans for this 1905 building at 215 West Seymour Street. During the winter of 1989, a major fire gutted the interior of the empty structure, causing the building to be torn down in 1991. (Marion Stewart.)

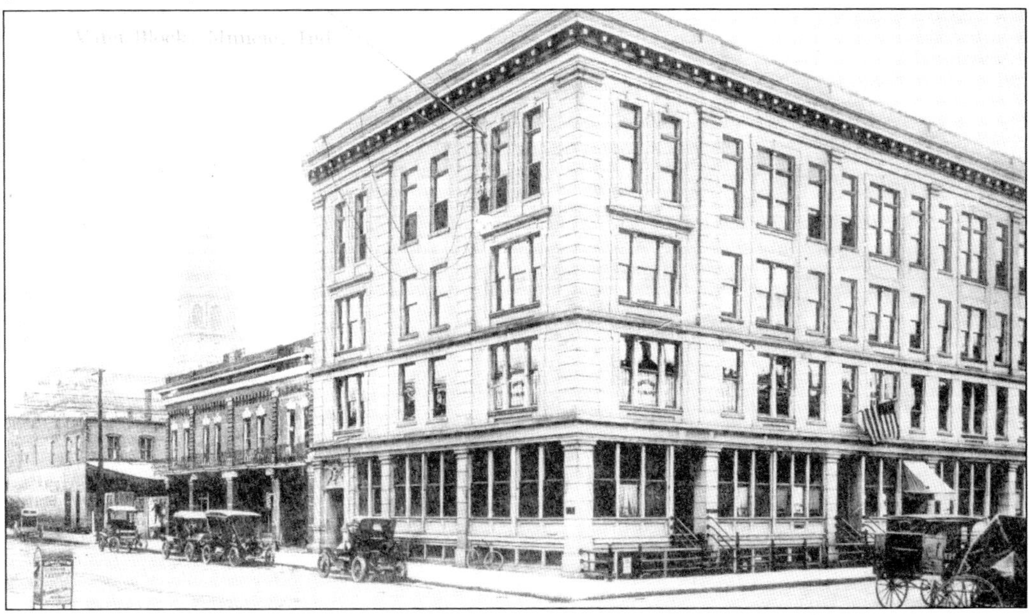

VATET BLOCK. Built by Eugene Vatet, this building was also referred to as the Western Reserve Building. It was constructed from 1904 though 1906 at a cost of approximately $45,000 from plans drawn by Cuno Kibele of Muncie. In 1965 and 1966, it suffered from a Muncie illness called "wreck it." It was located at 124 West Jackson Street. (Kraemer Art Co.)

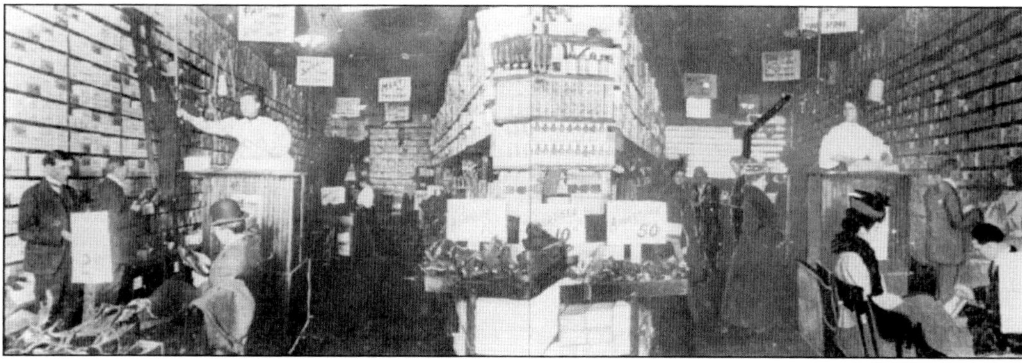

Interior View of Frank V. Sowar's Shoe Store, 221-23 Walnut Street. Sowar's Shoe Store was located on the west side of Walnut Street in a building that was replaced in 1930 by a J.C. Penney department store. (Tom Jones Pub. Co.)

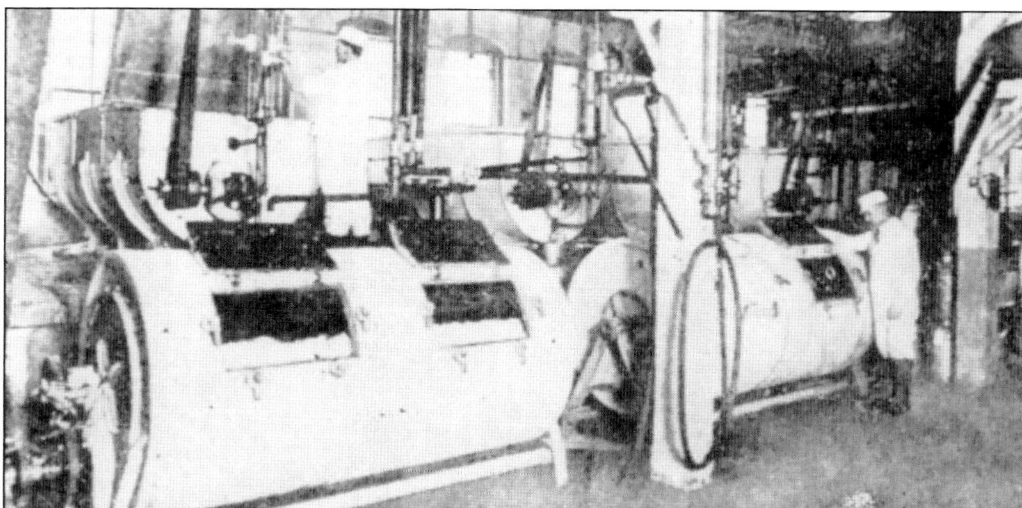

Churn Room of the White River Creamery, Where a Million Pounds of Butter a Year are Manufactured. The 1909–10 Muncie Directory states, "The White River Creamery Co., Muncie, Ind., is completing a large, modern, pure Pasteurized Cream Butter Manufacturing Plant at about even date with the issuance of this directory." (Unidentified printer and publisher.)

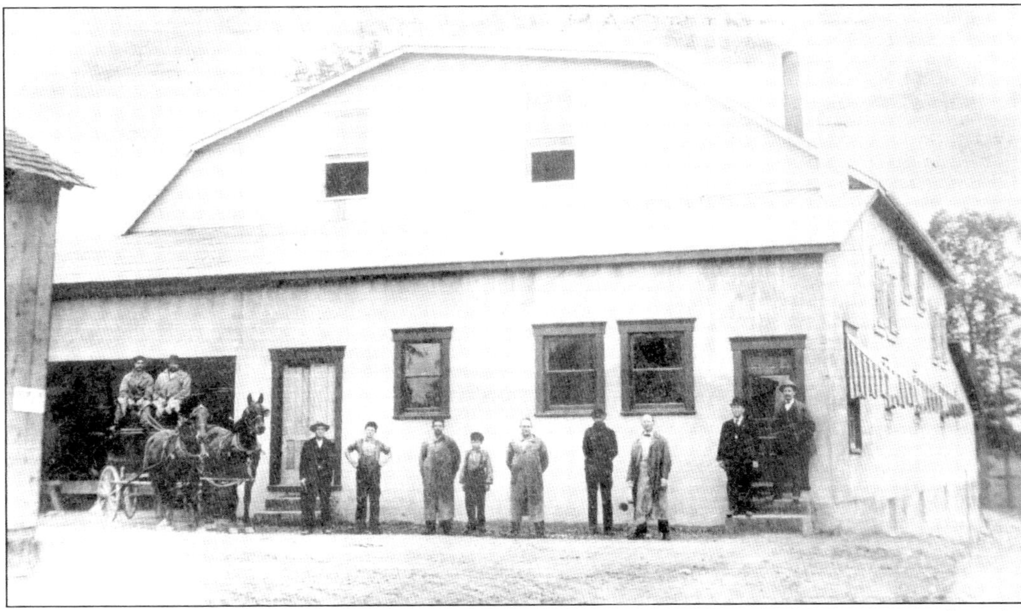

Cavanaugh Meat Packing Co. On the back of this card, someone has written that the opening of this company was October 15, 1908. In the 1909–10 Muncie City Directory, the address for the company was not given. Jacob D. Cavanaugh, J.A. Guthrie, Orrin S. Lenon, Fred O. Jackson, and Frank Kennedy were listed as officers at the time. (Real photo, unidentified photographer.)

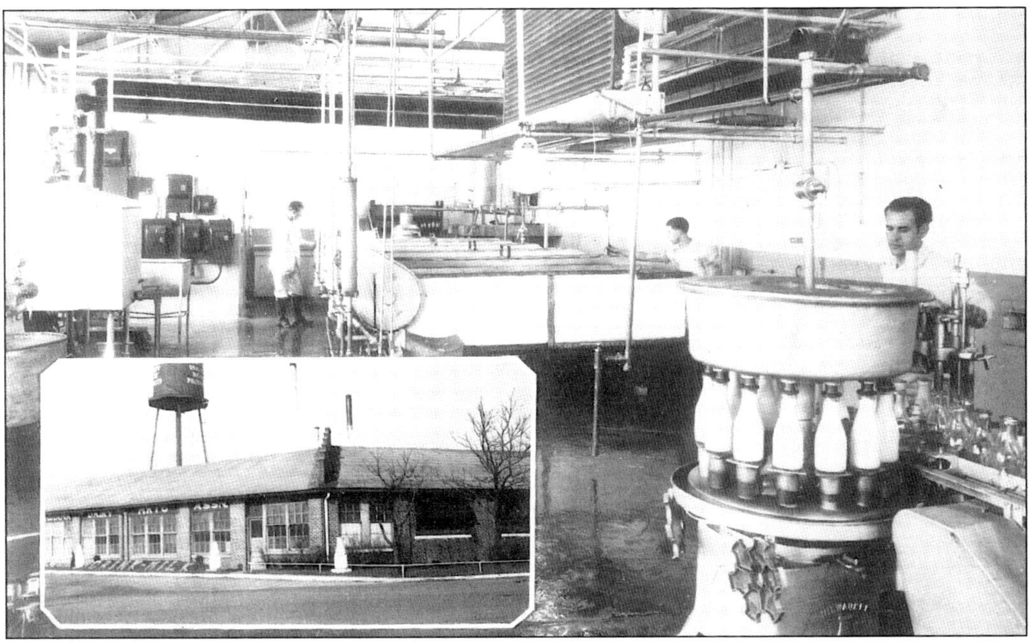

Producer's Quality Dairy Products, Always Uniform, Always Safe, Call 484 for Prompt and Courteous Service—Indiana Dairy Marketing Association. (Real photos, unidentified photographer.)

Eight

RESIDENCES

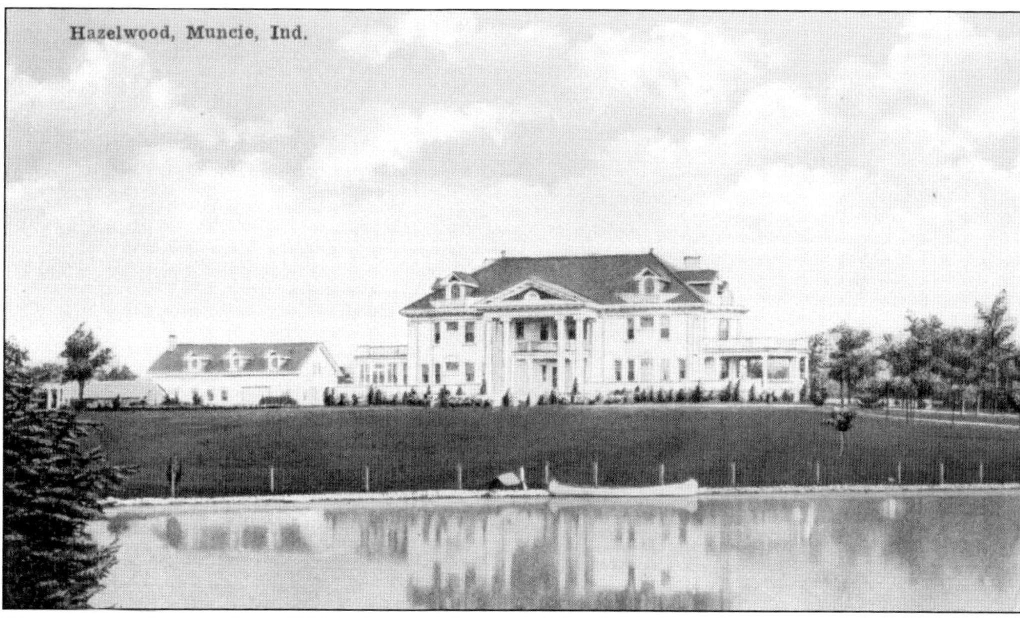

HAZELWOOD. Located at 1400 University Avenue, Hazelwood was designed by Muncie architect Cuno Kibele for local industrialist Alvah LaSalle Kitselman. The house was completed in 1920. The Classic style, the grandiose size, and the extensive grounds surrounding the house all combine to make this one of the city's most impressive houses. The house is now part of the Hazelwood Christian Church complex, and even though it is no longer used as a residence, the house is well maintained by the church in a historically accurate manner. (E.C. Kropp Co.)

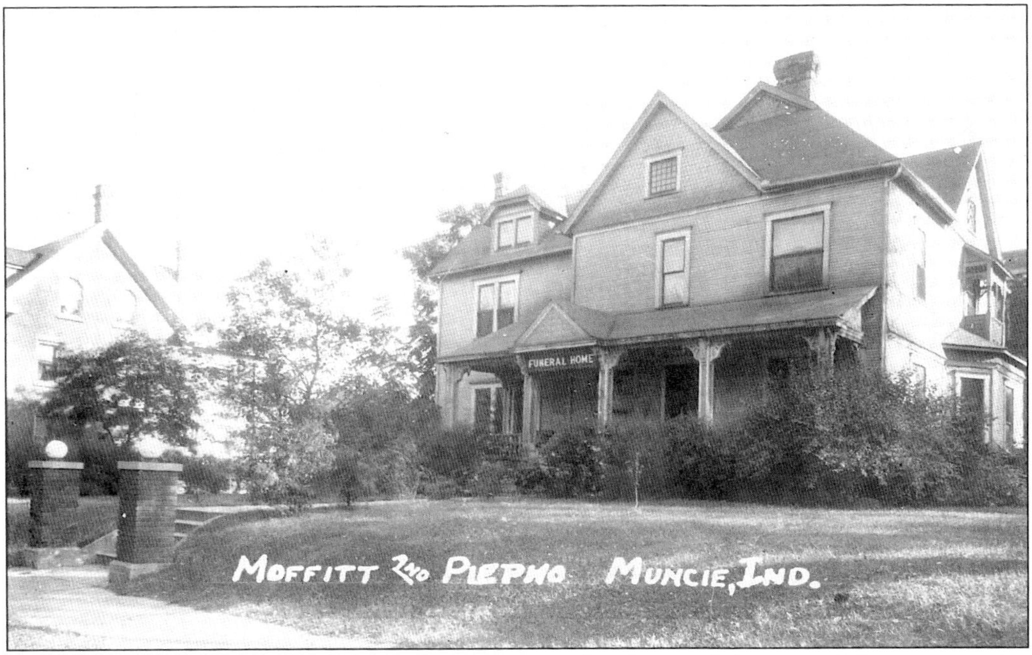

MOFFITT AND PIEPHO (FUNERAL HOME). When completed around the turn of the century, this home was used as a regular residence. Since 1920, it has been used as a funeral home with variations to the name of the business. Located at 307 East Charles Street, it is still used as a funeral home today. (Real photo, unidentified photographer.)

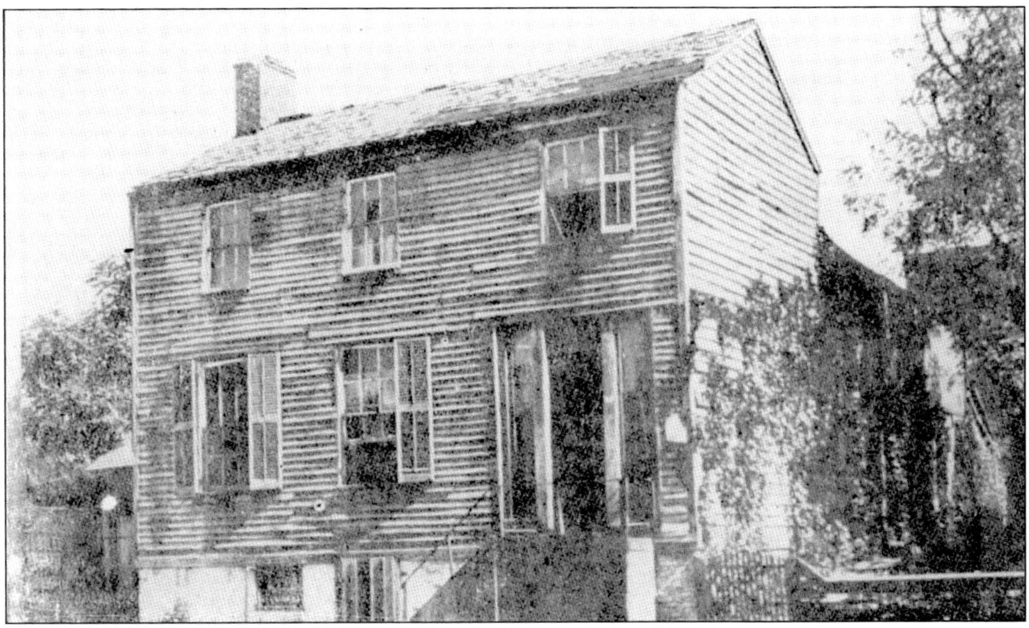

OLD HOME OF DR. SAMUEL P. ANTHONY, PRIOR TO 1843. Dr. Samuel P. Anthony was born in Virginia, studied medicine in Cincinnati, and first arrived in Muncie in 1831. While in Muncie, Dr. Anthony not only practiced medicine, but he also played a very active role in the business life of the city. (Unknown printer, for the Delaware County Centennial, September 27, 28, and 29, Muncie, Indiana.)

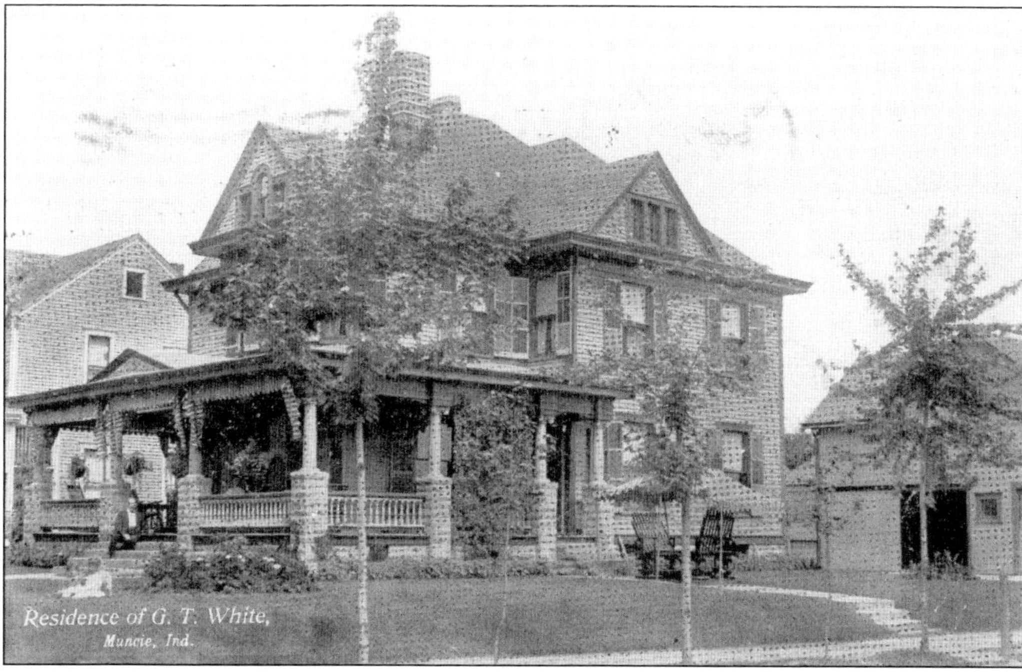

RESIDENCE OF G.T. WHITE. This house, previously known as the W.A. McNaughton residence, was located on East Adams Street at the corner of Elm Street. Mr. McNaughton was the owner of the W.A. McNaughton Company, the predecessor to Ball Stores. (Unidentified printer and publisher.)

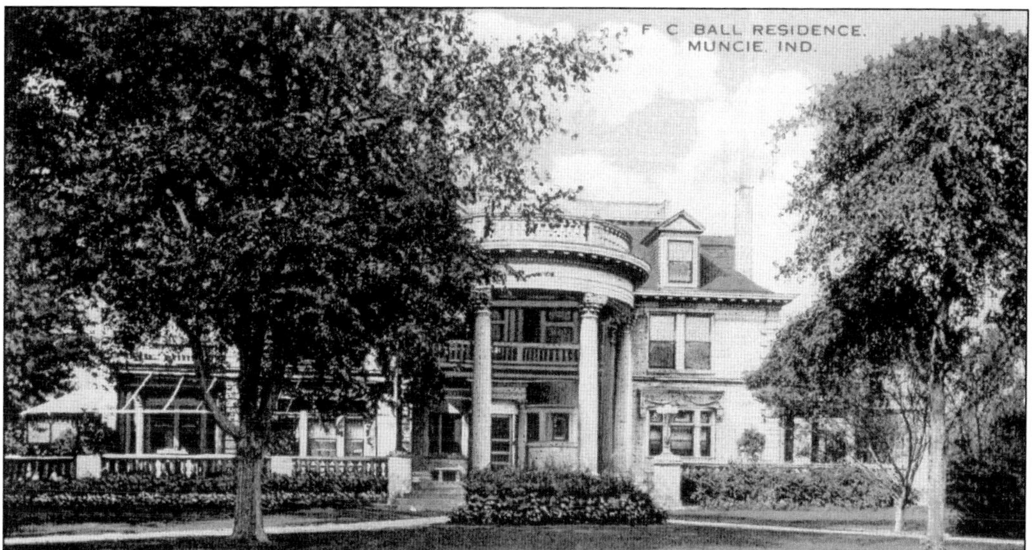

F.C. BALL RESIDENCE (IDENTIFIED ONLY WITH THE SLOGAN: COMMERCIAL-CHROME). The Frank C. Ball residence was located at 220 Minnetrista Boulevard on the horseshoe bend of the White River. The house was constructed between 1894 and 1896 from plans drawn by Indianapolis architect Louis H. Gibson. On February 28, 1967, the house was destroyed by fire. The columns remain as a gateway to Minnetrista Cultural Center. (Unidentified printer and publisher.)

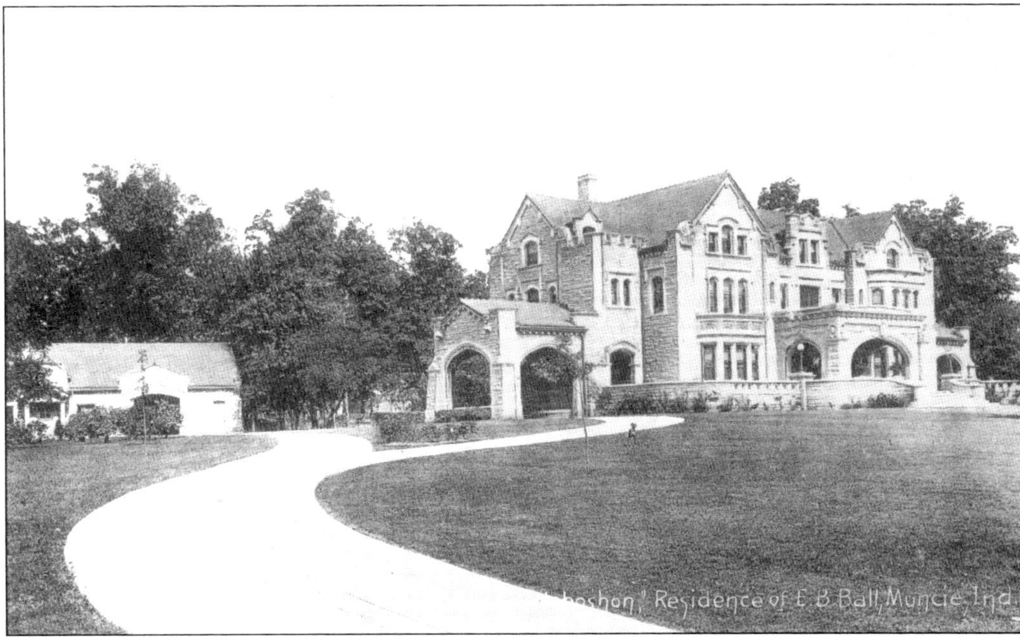

"NEBASHON," RESIDENCE OF E.B. BALL. Wing and Mahurin of Fort Wayne, Indiana, drew the plans for this 1907 residence for Edmund Burke Ball. It is located at 400 Minnetrista Boulevard, adjacent to the homes of the four other Ball brothers that settled in Muncie. In 1963, the home was given to Ball State, and in 1977, extensive restoration work was completed to revive the English Tudor style of the home. (Kraemer Art Co., for C.A. Penzel.)

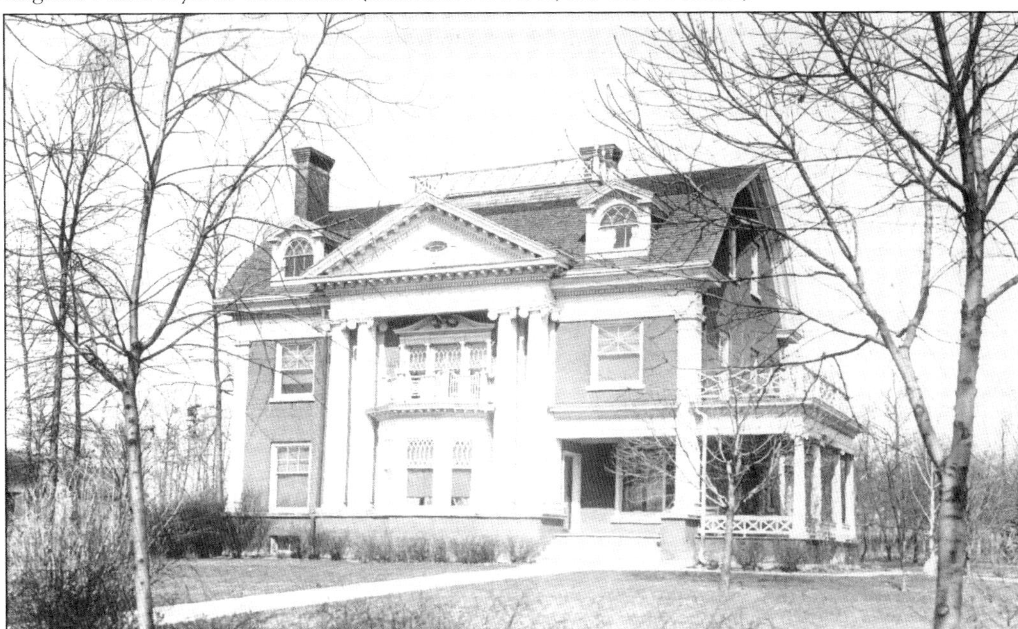

RESIDENCE OF WILLIAM C. BALL. This photo shows the home with a rather different appearance than it now has. Changes made to the house include an enlarged front porch, a second-floor addition on top of the right wing, and another wing on the left side of the house. The house was first built in 1898. (Kraemer Art Co., for C.A. Penzel.)

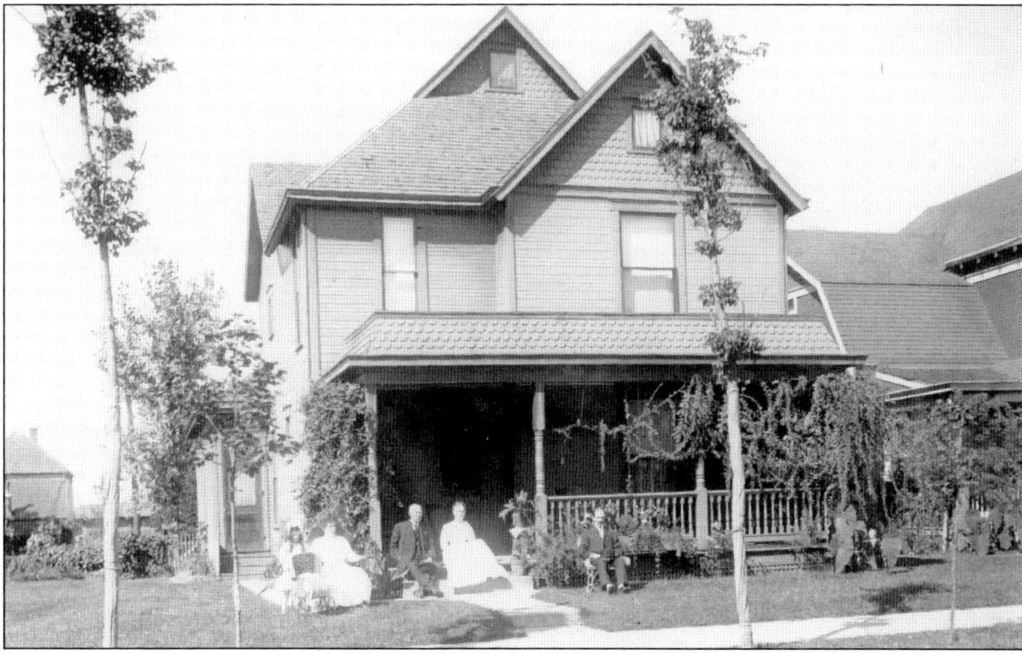

RESIDENCE OF JOSEPH A. AND AMANDA M. LEONARD. The location of this house was, and still is, 1320 East Main Street. The Leonard family occupied the house during the "golden age" of postcards. (Real photo, unidentified photographer.)

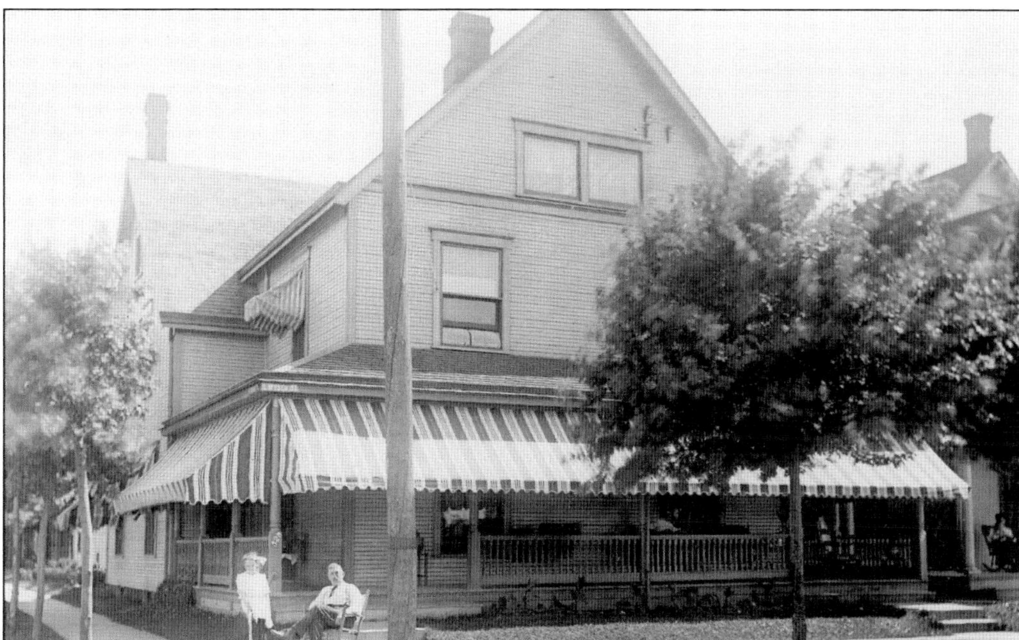

S.R. GIBSON RESIDENCE. This house is still standing today—although somewhat altered. It is located on the southwest corner of Wysor and Monroe Streets at 525 West Wysor Street. (Real photo, unidentified photographer.)

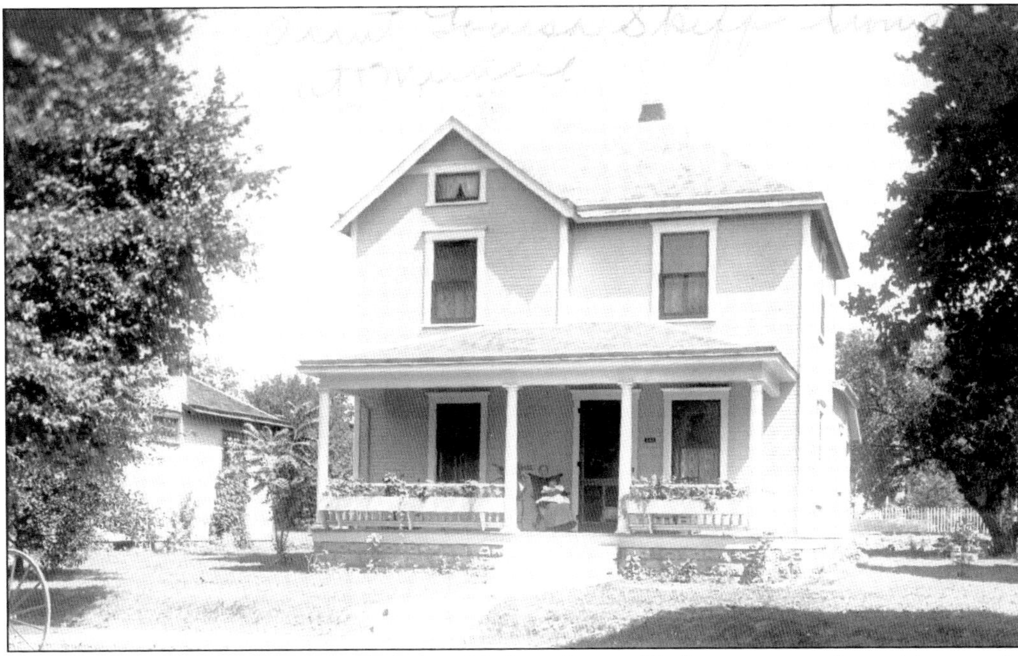

Residence of Louisa Skiff. Mailed in 1908 from Louisa Skiff to a niece, the writing on the correspondence side of this card declares this place to be "my new home." According to the early city directories, the house was located at 616 Sutton in Riverside addition. Louisa Skiff was the widow of Dr. Clark Skiff. (Real photo, unidentified photographer.)

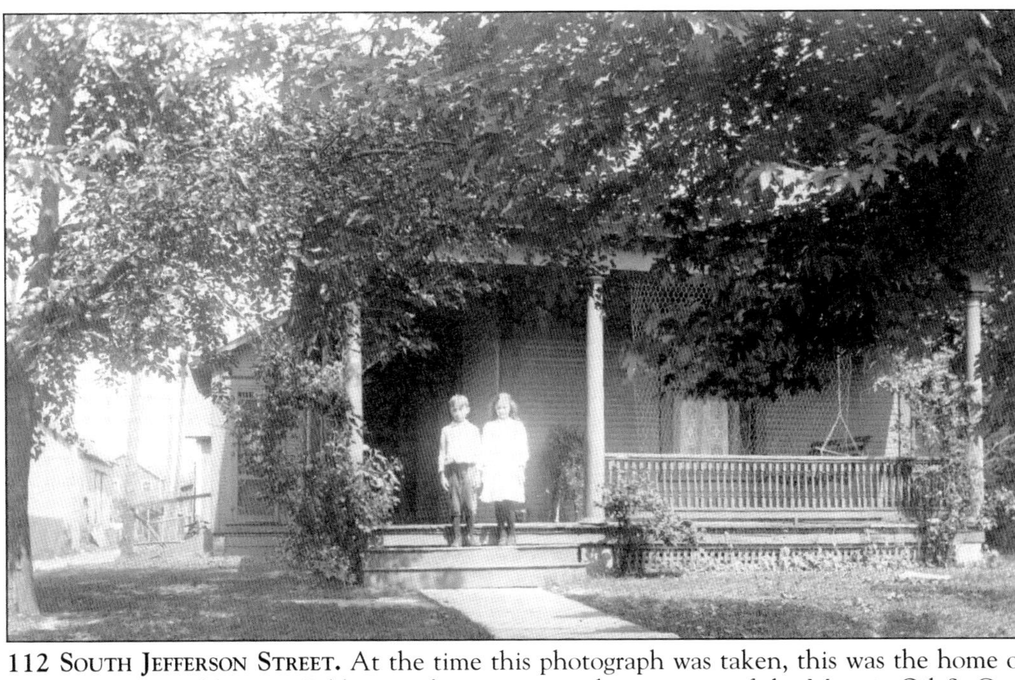

112 South Jefferson Street. At the time this photograph was taken, this was the home of A.A. and Rosa Bibler. Mr. Bibler was for some time the manager of the Muncie Oil & Coal Company on South Liberty Street. (Real photo, unidentified photographer.)

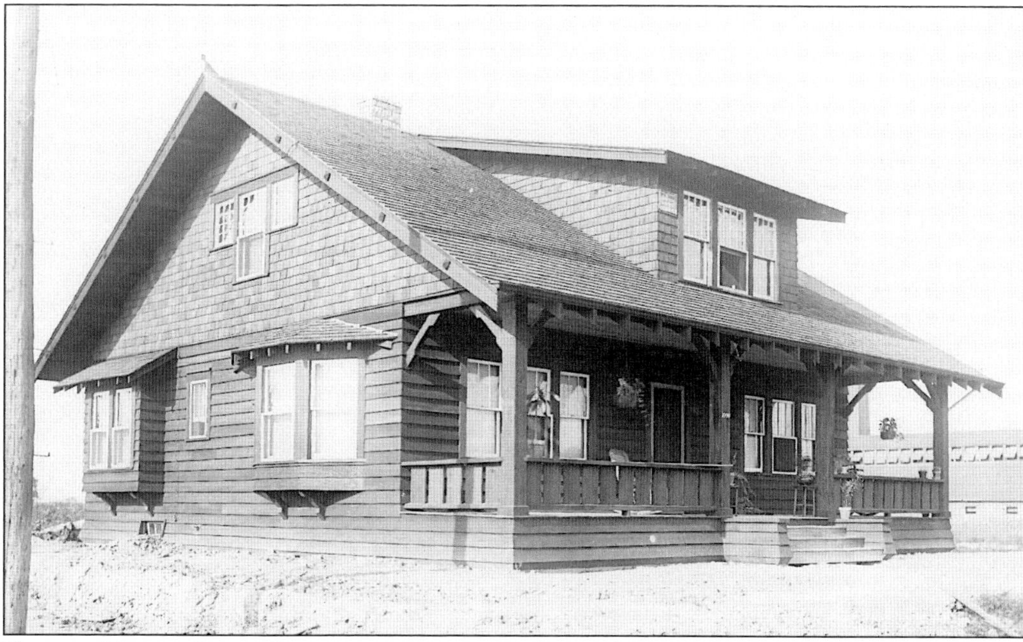

Horace M. and Irene Caldwell Residence. This card, identified in pencil on the back, was never mailed. City directories for the time period indicate that Horace M. Caldwell lived at several addresses, but the number "1000" on the front of this house probably refers to 1000 North Elm Street. (Real photo, unidentified photographer.)

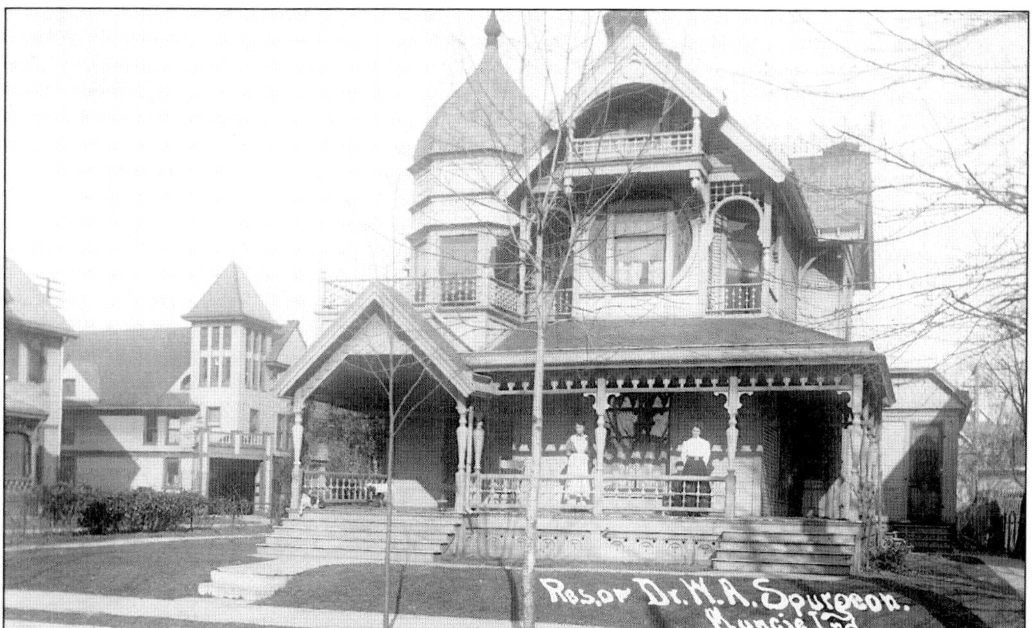

Residence of Dr. W.A. Spurgeon. Ornate porches and extensive decorative detail dominated this 1890s home at 322 East Charles Street. Unfortunately, the home was razed in the 1960s. (Real photo, unidentified photographer.)

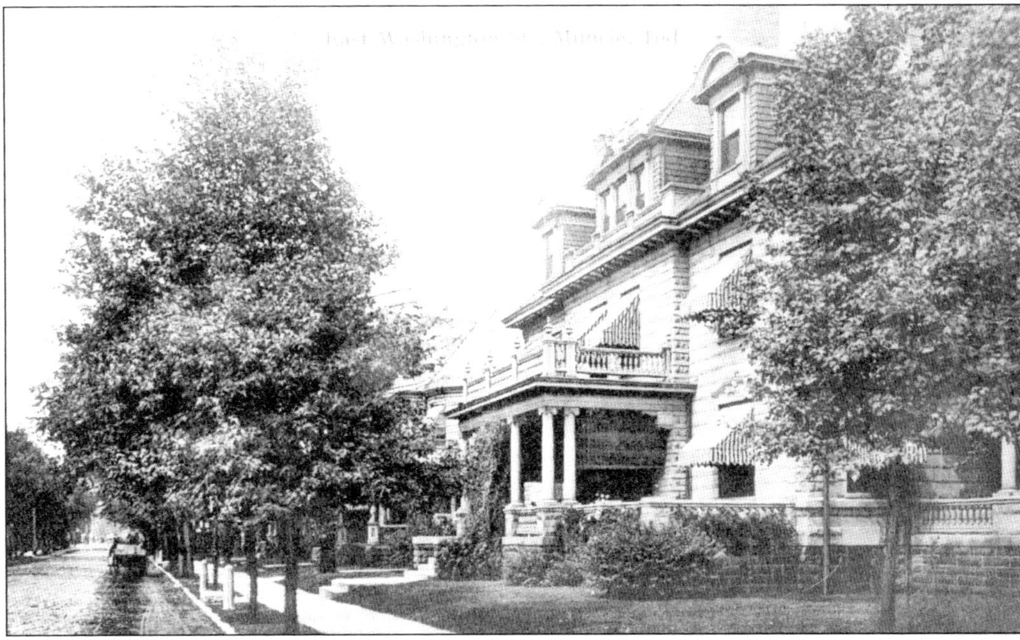

East Washington Street. The focus in this picture is the 1901 house at 330 East Washington Street, which was originally built for A.L. Johnson. The Delaware County Interim Report of 1985 identified this house to be "Chateau-esque" style. The house was used as administrative offices for the Muncie City Schools for several years. Later, these offices were moved to the former Anthony Elementary School. (Kraemer Art Co.)

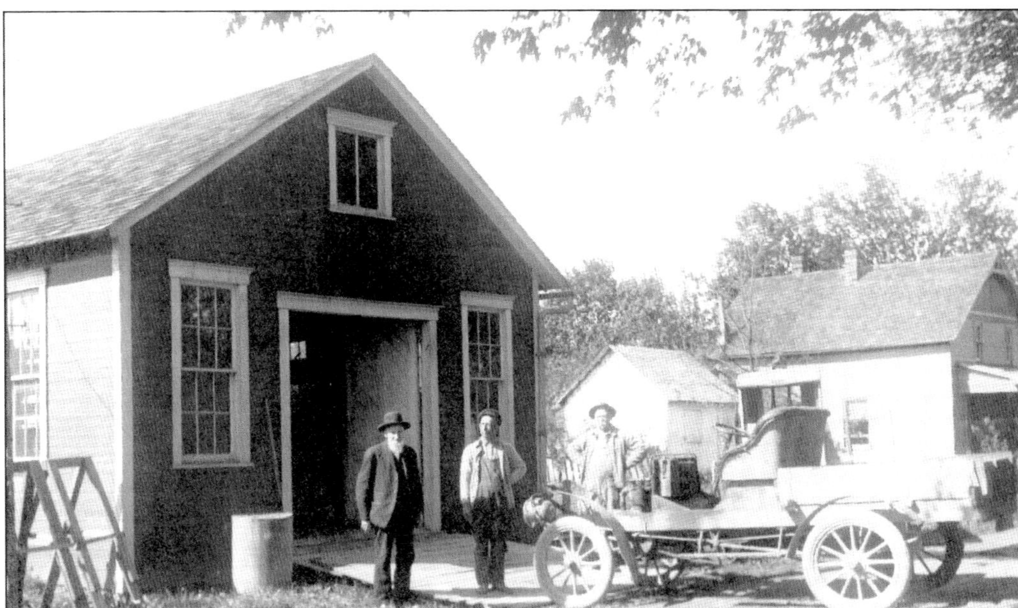

Unknown Location, Probably in Muncie. Although it has not been possible to determine the location of this scene, the interesting subject matter of the picture warranted inclusion in this volume. (Real Photo, published by Burkey Bro's Studio.)

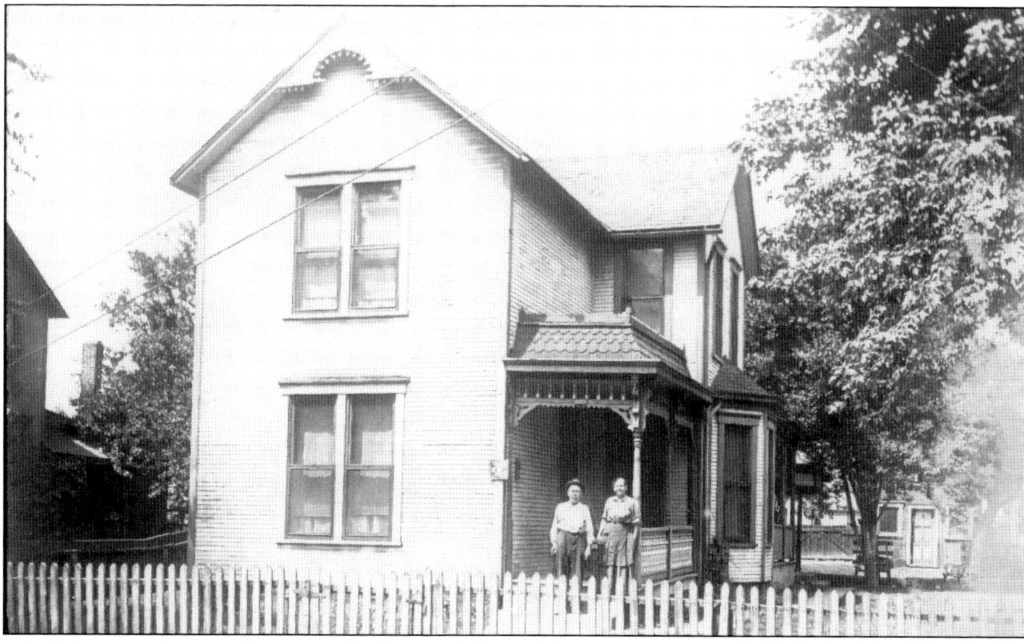

1607 SOUTH BLAINE STREET. The back of this card indicates the address of this house and also that it was purchased in 1919, but it does not identify the owner or writer of the data. The city directories indicate the occupants to be John and Anna M. Karlin. John's occupation is listed as a machinist, and Anna's as a laborer. (Real photo, unidentified photographer.)

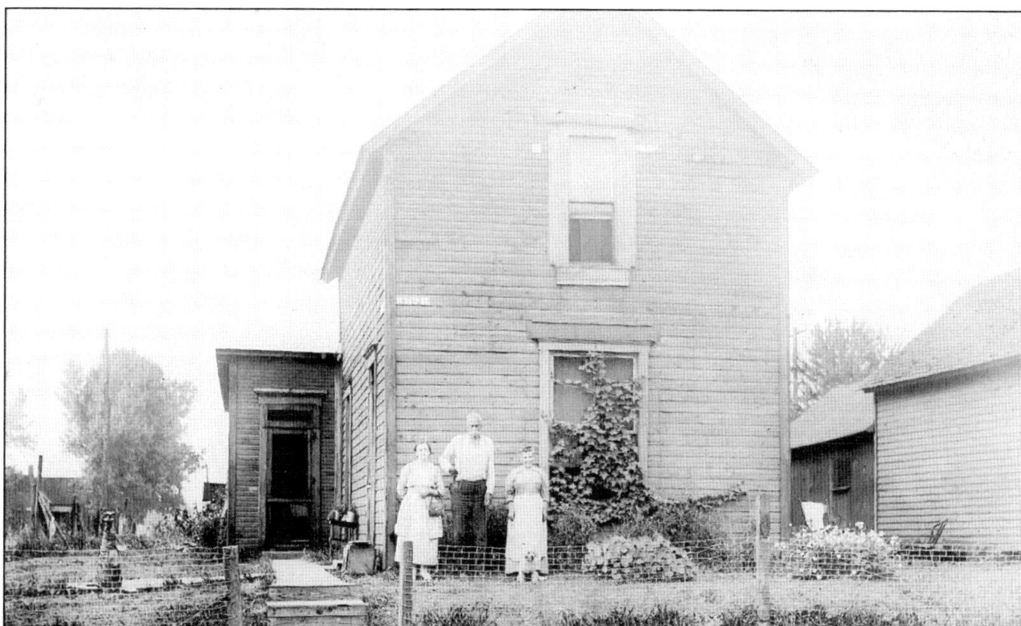

1340 WEST FOURTEENTH STREET. City directories for the first two decades of the century indicate the residents of the house pictured here to be John D. and Jeanetta McCoy. (Real photo, unidentified photographer.)

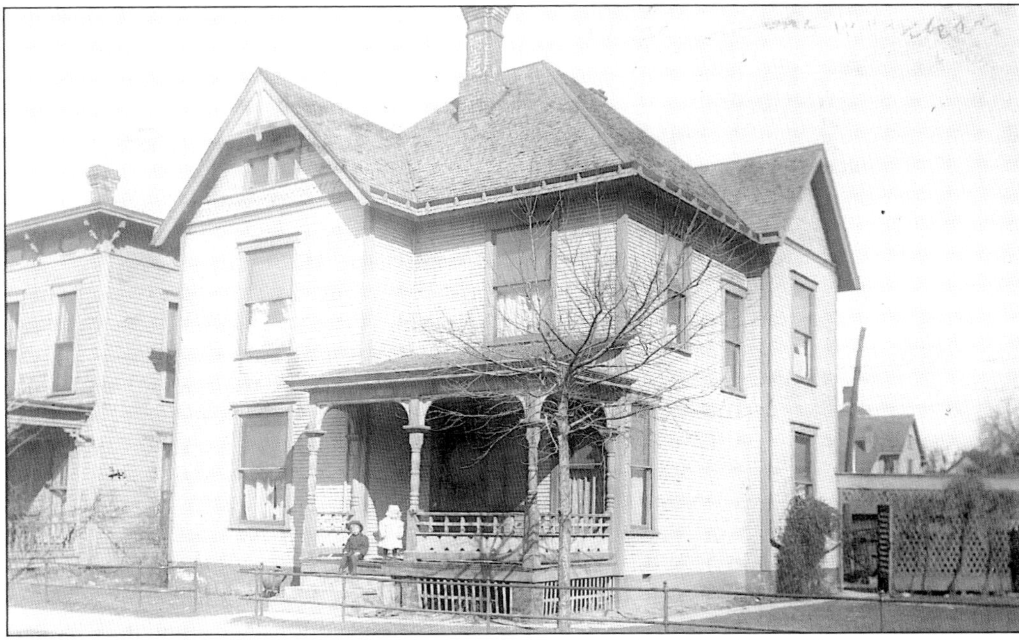

306 WEST JACKSON STREET. This card was postmarked 1910. The address was identified in pencil on the back, and the card was sent by a Fred H. The space formerly occupied by this house now contains one of Muncie's many parking lots. (Real photo, unidentified photographer.)

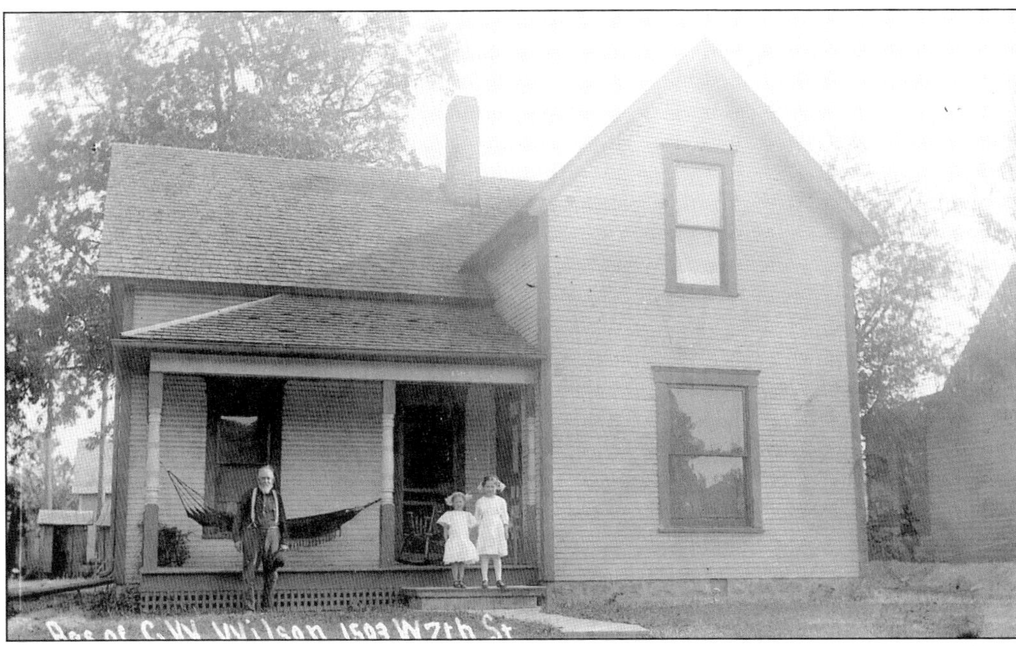

RESIDENCE OF C.W. WILSON, 1503 W. SEVENTH STREET. Corey W. and Julia Wilson lived in this house when this picture was taken, but they apparently sold the house. The 1907–08 Muncie directory indicates that they lived here, but subsequent directories do not. (Real photo, unidentified photographer.)

Nine

Parks, Rivers, Cemeteries, and Monuments

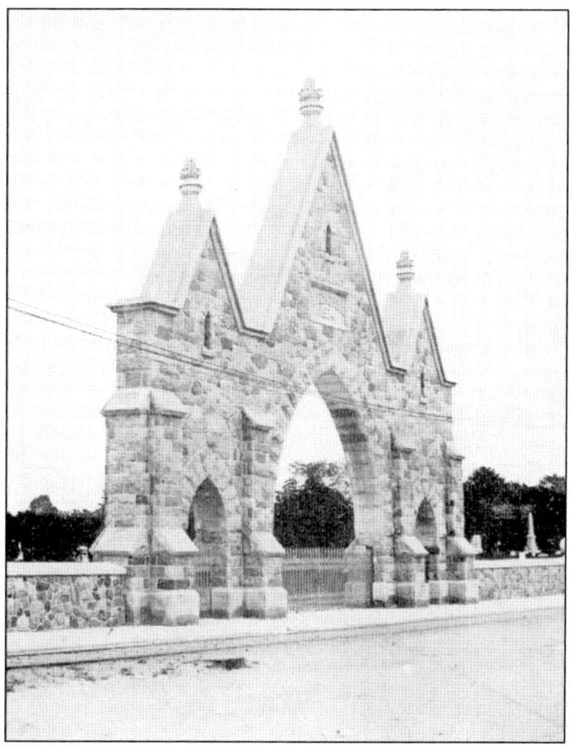

Entrance to Beech Grove Cemetery. The municipally owned Beech Grove Cemetery dates back to the early 1840s when the city was officially named "Munceytown." Since that time, the cemetery space has been expanded several times. The stone archway shown above is the main entrance to the cemetery. It was completed in 1904 from plans drawn by Muncie architect Cuno Kibele. At the time of the construction of the gate, the superintendent of the cemetery, which was located on Kilgore Avenue, was O.W. Crabbs. (Unidentified printer and publisher.)

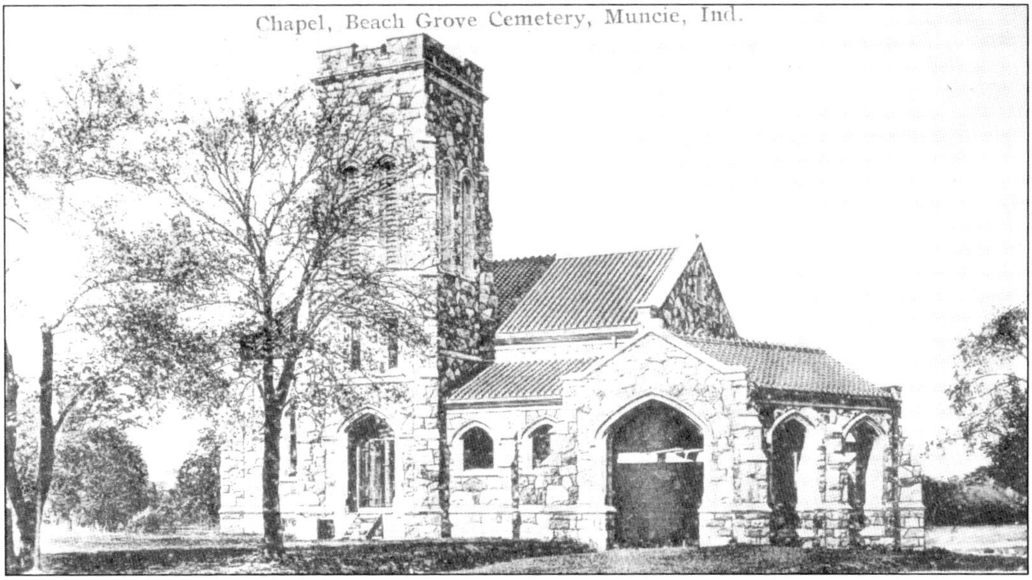

CHAPEL, BEECH GROVE CEMETERY. The chapel to Beech Grove Cemetery was dedicated on Memorial Day in 1912. Like the entrance gate, the chapel was designed by Cuno Kibele. The chapel was used for only a few short years before it became obsolete due to the increasing number of spaces provided by private funeral directors. In 1955, it was demolished. (Dexter-Fawley Co.)

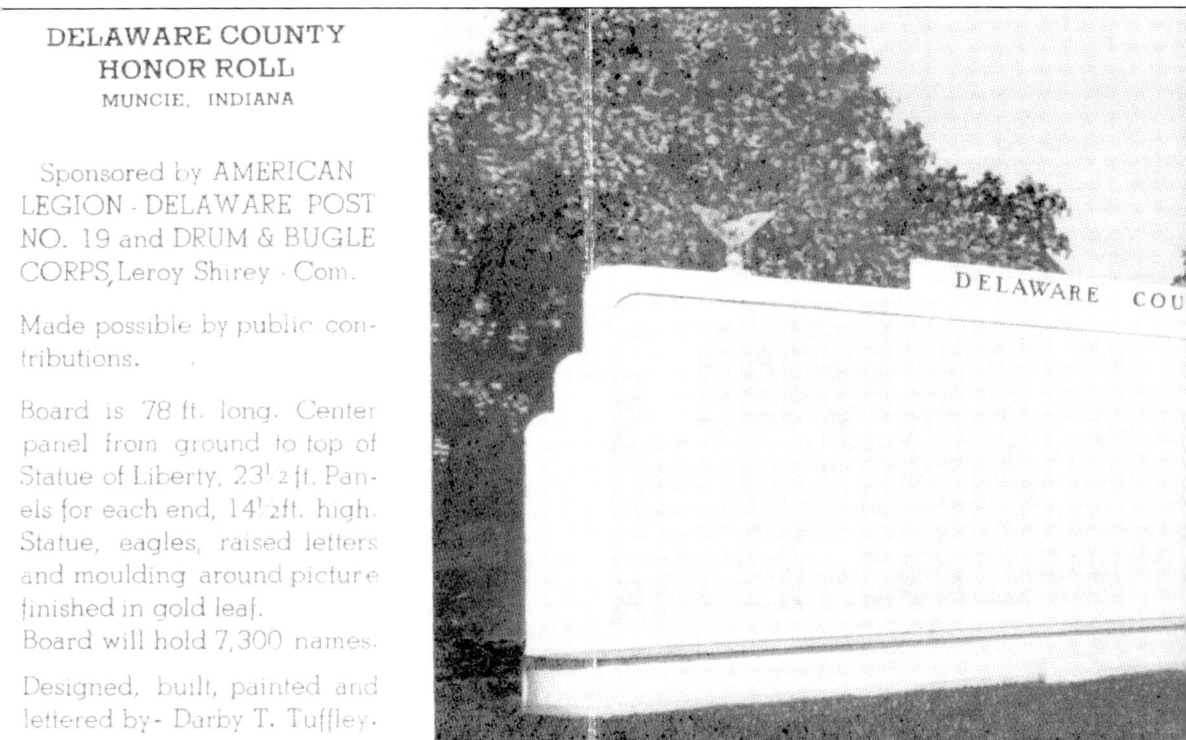

DELAWARE COUNTY HONOR ROLL. The Delaware County Honor Roll was sponsored by the American Legion, Delaware Post No. 19, from public contributions. The board is 78 feet long

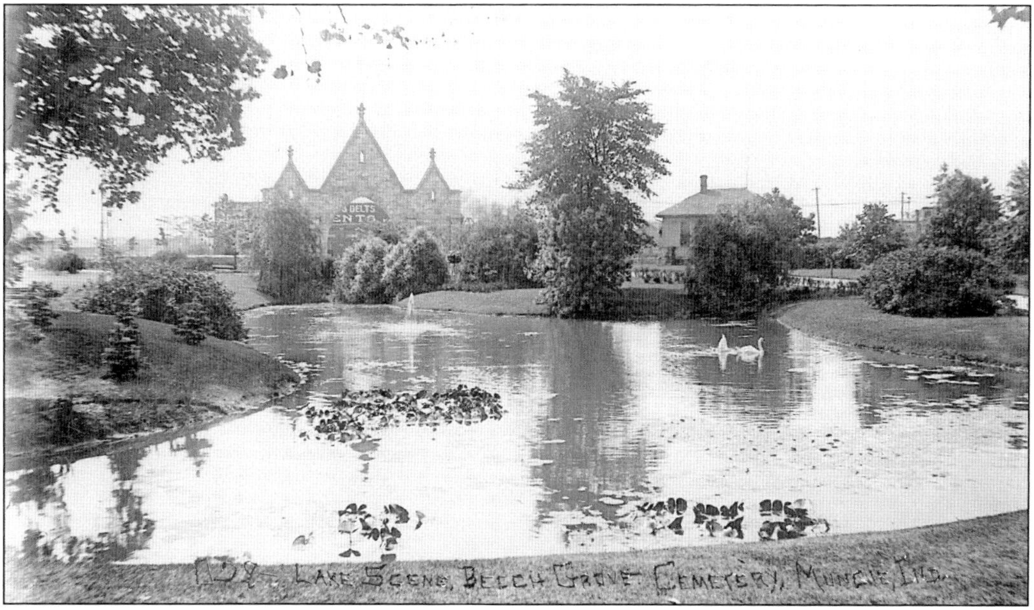

Beech Grove Cemetery Lagoon. Seen here is one of two lagoons built in the cemetery. The lagoons were fed by fountains of fresh water piped in from city water lines. As can be seen here, they were abundant with plant and bird life. The lagoons were later filled. (Real Photo, produced by Galion View Co.)

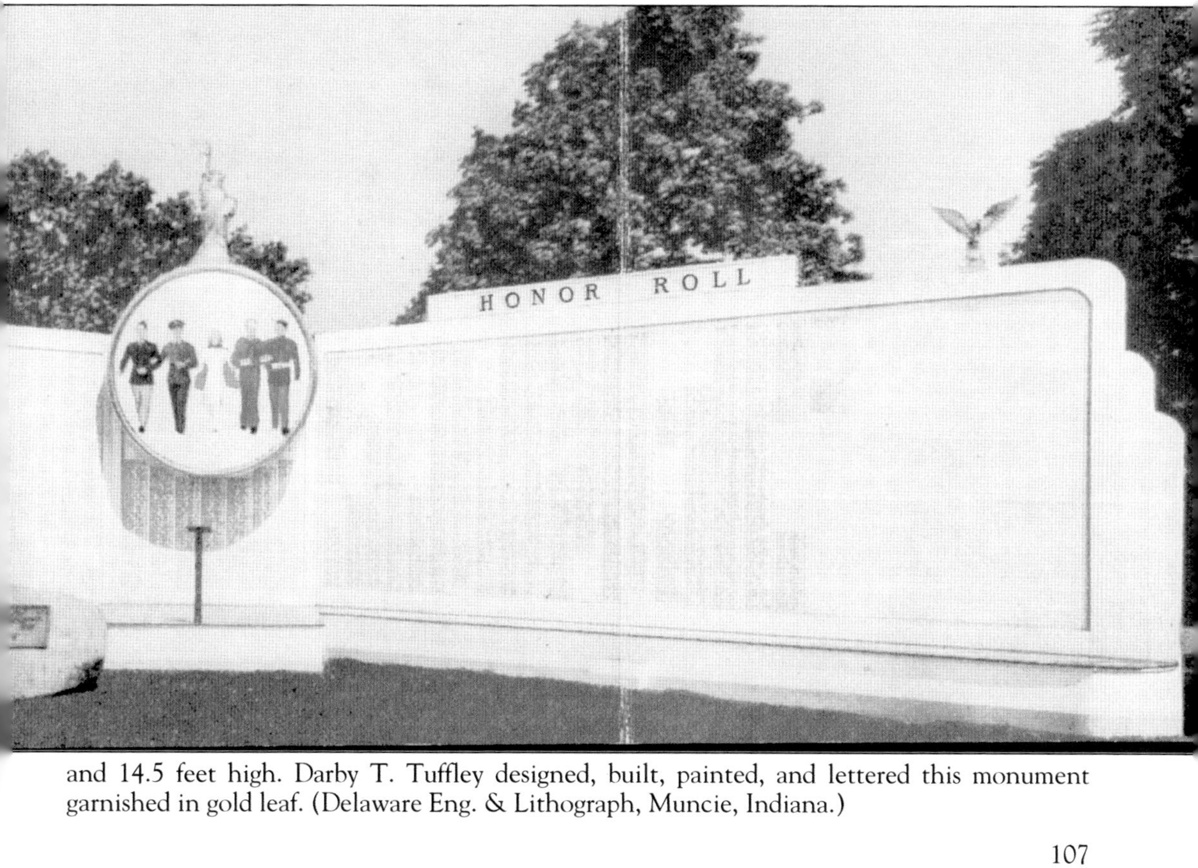

and 14.5 feet high. Darby T. Tuffley designed, built, painted, and lettered this monument garnished in gold leaf. (Delaware Eng. & Lithograph, Muncie, Indiana.)

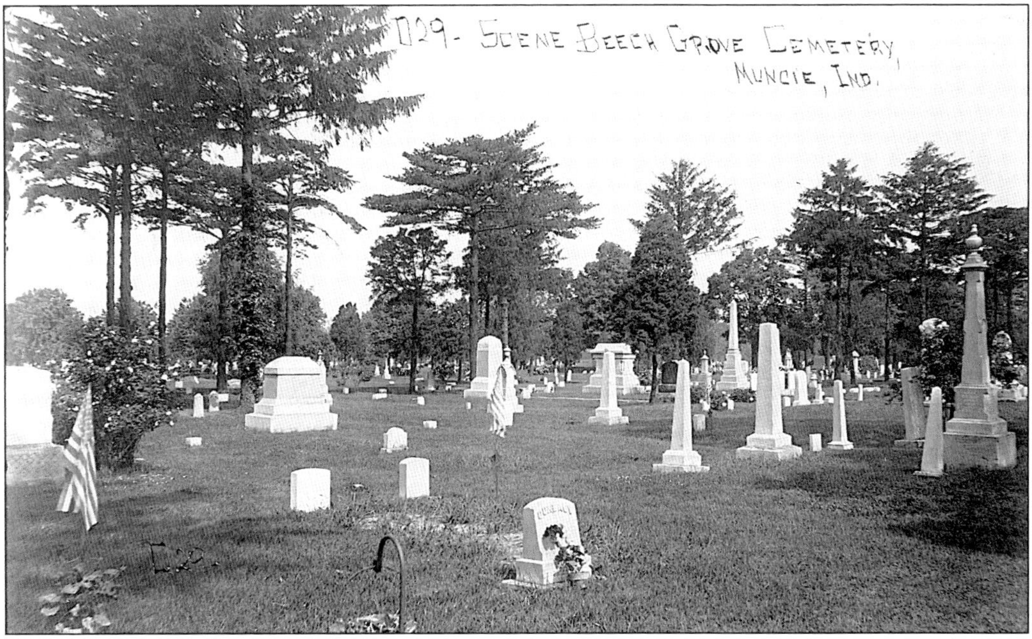

SCENE FROM BEECH GROVE CEMETERY. In the early part of this century, Beech Grove Cemetery was one of the most beautiful cemeteries in Indiana. The grounds were extensively landscaped and were immaculately maintained under the direction of Superintendent Crabbs. (Real Photo, produced by Galion View Co.)

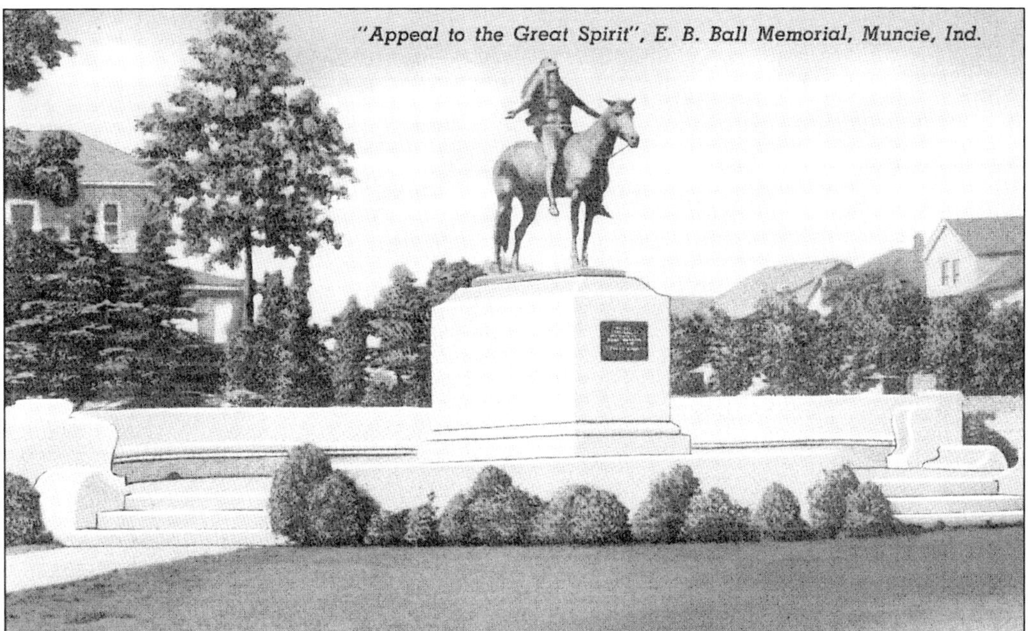

"APPEAL TO THE GREAT SPIRIT," E.B. BALL MEMORIAL. This memorial to Edmund Burke Ball was erected in Muncie in 1929. The statue itself, however, is a 1908 product of sculptor Cyrus E. Dallin. It is located just north of White River, near the residences of the five Ball brothers. (Curt Teich Co., for Muncie News Co.)

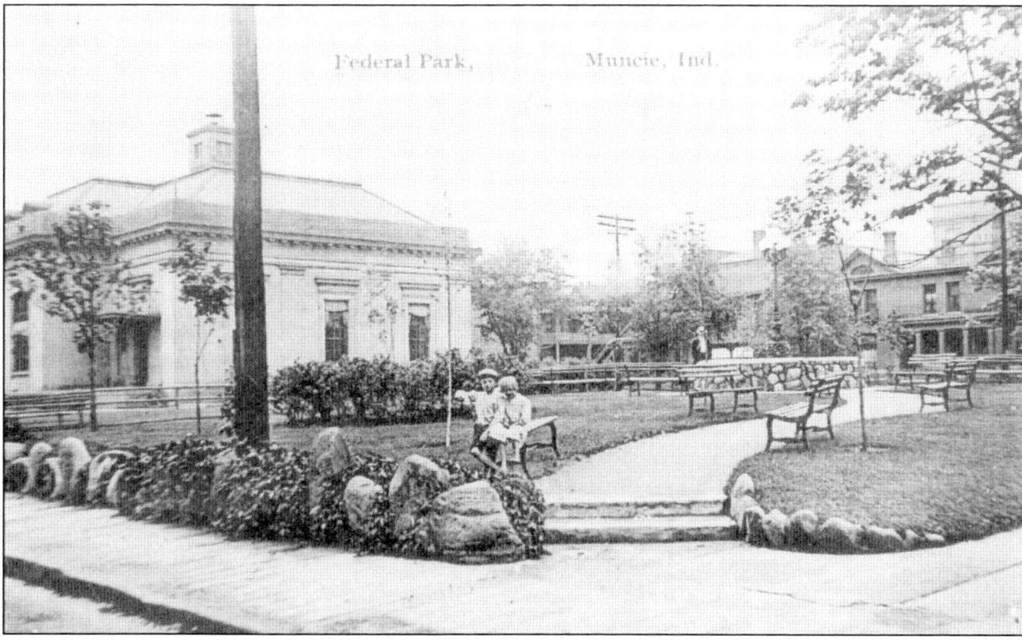

FEDERAL PARK. This small park, built in 1908, was located at the south end of the post office, also called the federal building; hence, it was named Federal Park. When the post office was sold to the City and made into the Horizon Convention Center, this park was used for the construction of an expansion to the building. (Kraemer Art Co.)

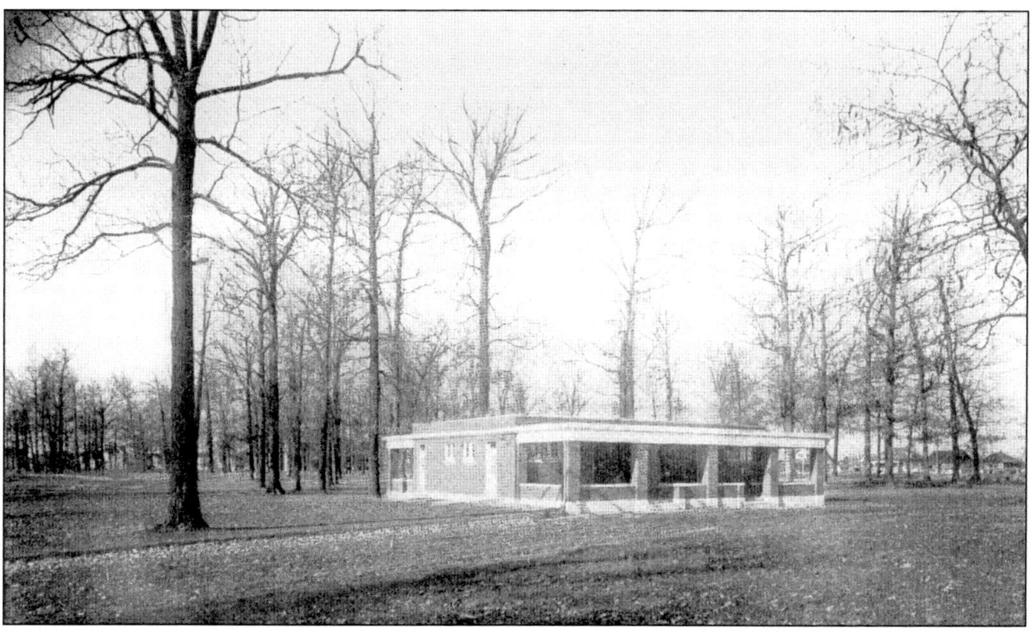

SHELTER HOUSE, HEEKIN PARK. Heekin Park is Muncie's second largest park. It contains some 83 acres of land on the south side of the city. In addition to the shelter house shown here, the park was also built to contain playground equipment, a picnic area, and ball fields. (Unidentified printer and publisher.)

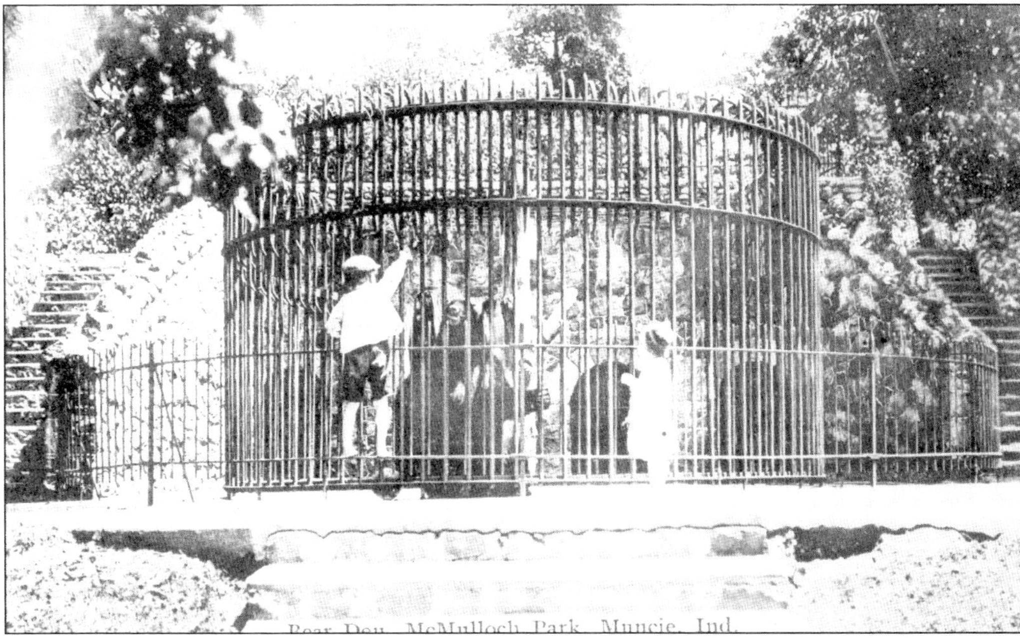

BEAR DEN, MCCULLOCH PARK. The oldest and largest park in Muncie is McCulloch (the name is incorrectly spelled on the front of the card) Park. It was opened in 1903 on land given to the city by industrialist George Foulke McCulloch. McCulloch owned a large portion of the traction railway and felt that the park would help promote that business. Both authors recall thinking as a youngster that the Bear Den shown here always had a very unpleasant odor. (Dexter-Fawley Co., Muncie, Indiana.)

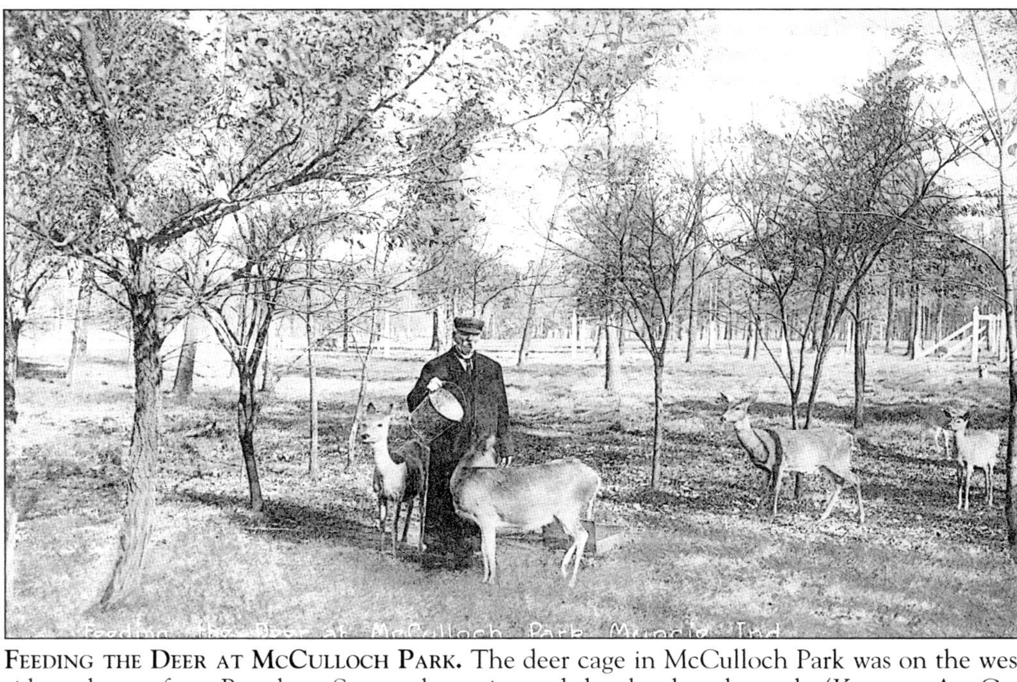

FEEDING THE DEER AT MCCULLOCH PARK. The deer cage in McCulloch Park was on the west side and away from Broadway Street, the main road that borders the park. (Kraemer Art Co., for C.A. Penzel.)

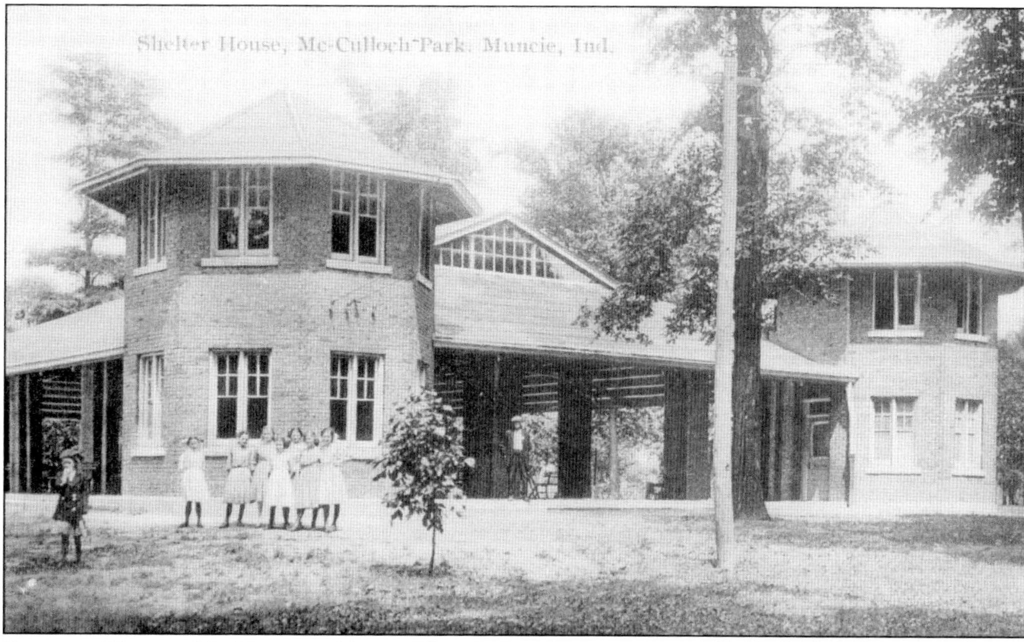

SHELTER HOUSE, McCULLOCH PARK. The shelter house at McCulloch Park was a very popular place to have family reunions, a pastime that is unfortunately losing popularity. During the shelter house's later years of existence, it was a popular meeting place for the participants in Muncie's famous Soap Box Derby. (Kraemer Art Co.)

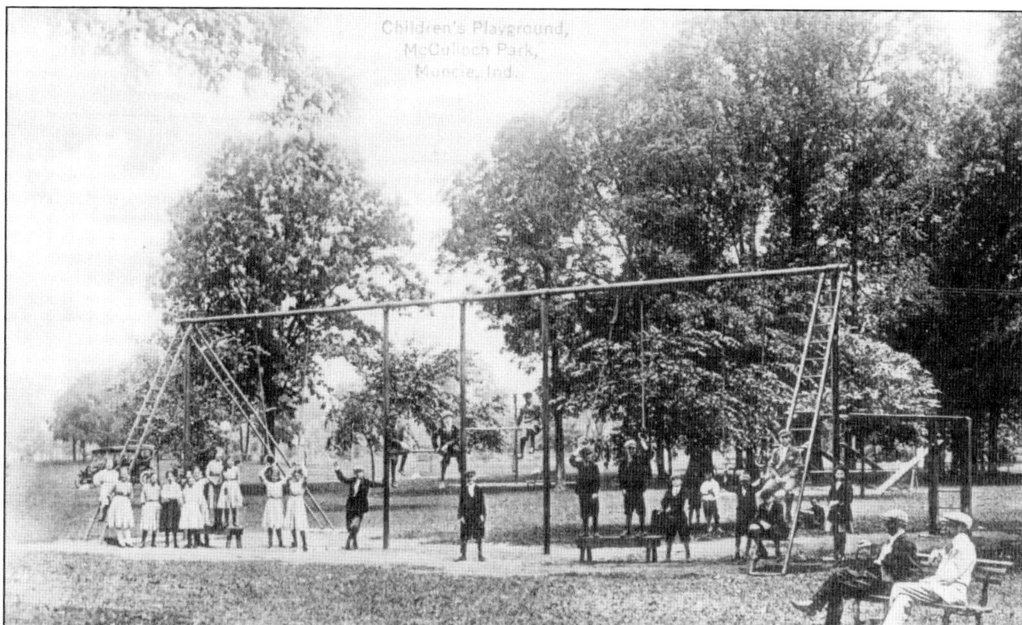

CHILDREN'S PLAYGROUND, McCULLOCH PARK. McCulloch Park has always had a very extensive play area for children. It has also been the site of many firework displays, a grand stand for the minor league Muncie Reds, as well as being the site of extensive displays of peonies, snack bars, and a large monkey pen that entertained and amused this author on several different occasions. (Kraemer Art Co.)

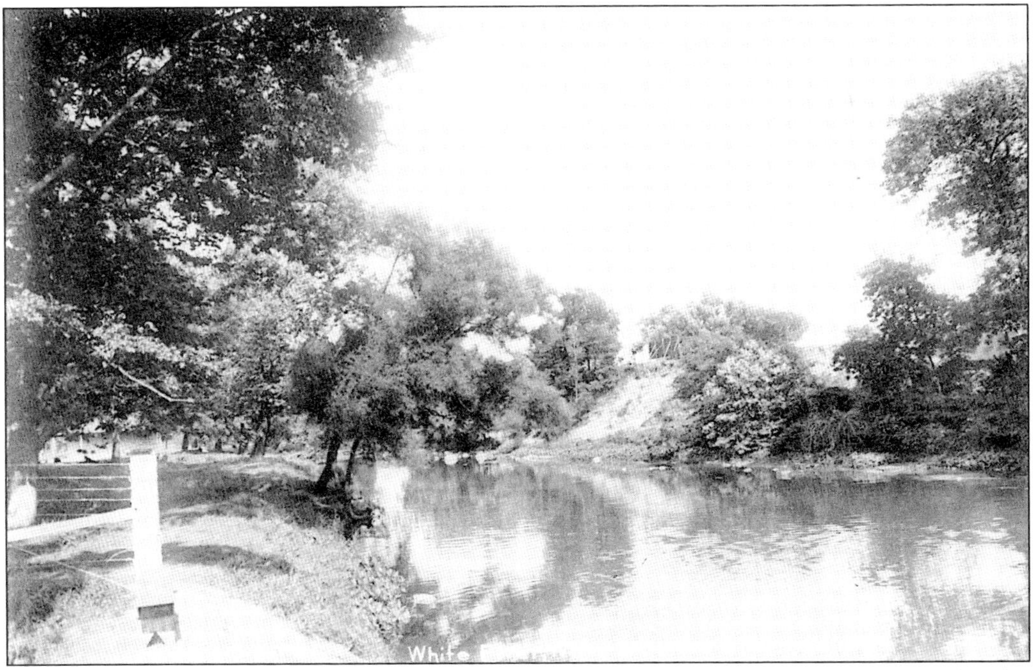

WHITE RIVER, WEST SIDE PARK. The West Side Park was one of Muncie's most colorful parks. Unfortunately, its tendency to flood greatly limited later use of this park. From this picture, it can clearly be seen that the park was located on the "low" bank of the White River. (The Rotograph Co.)

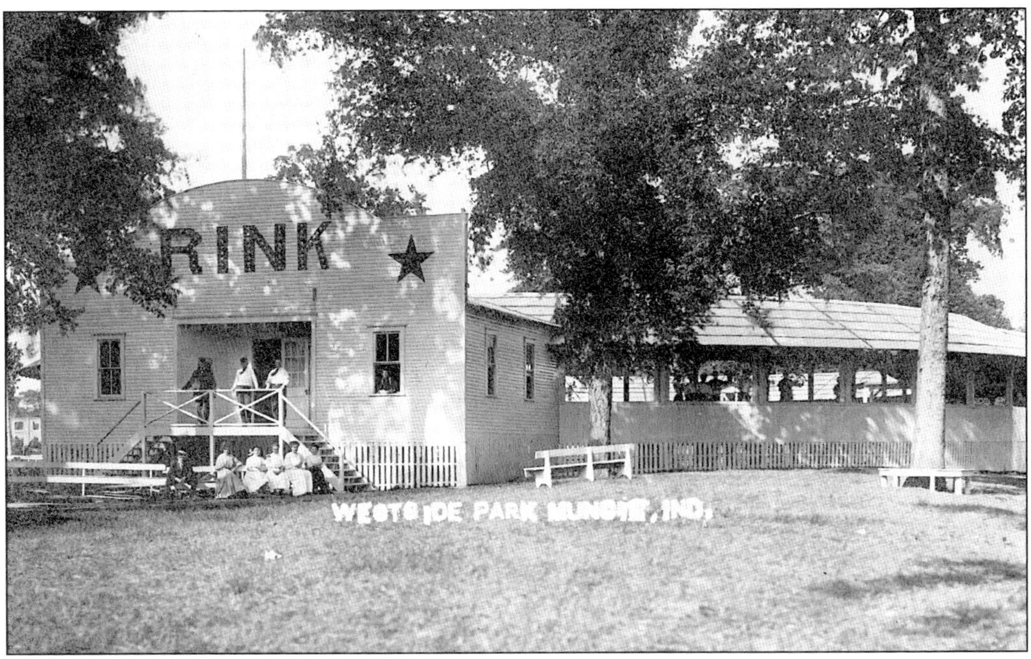

WEST SIDE PARK. One of the several attractions at this park was the roller rink shown in this picture. When this card was mailed in 1908, the rink was described on the back of the card as "brand-new." (Real photo, unidentified photographer.)

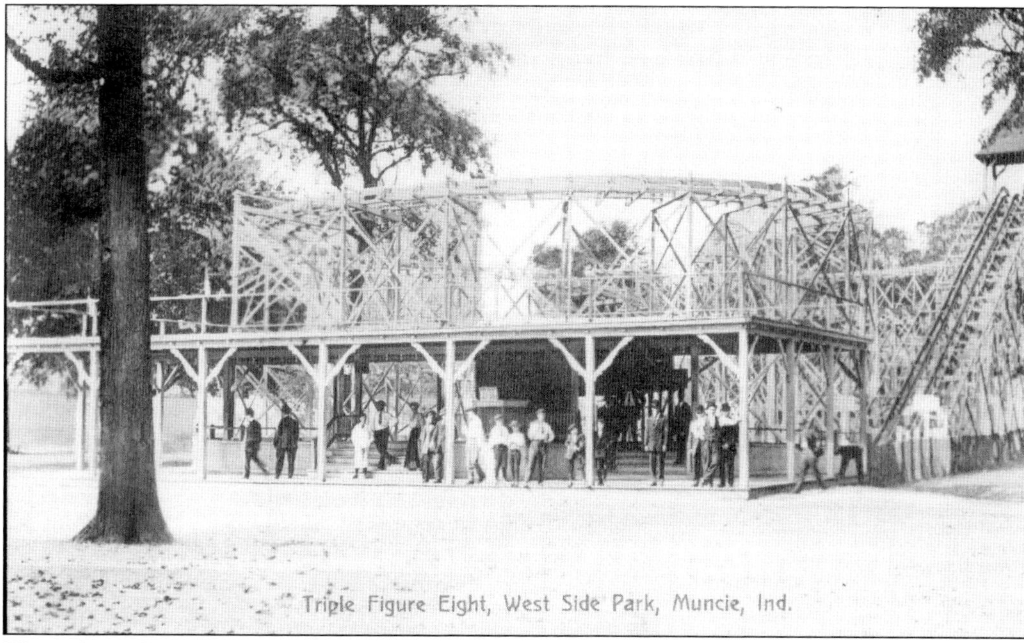

WEST SIDE PARK TRIPLE FIGURE EIGHT. This was probably the only roller coaster built for Muncie. By the roller coaster standards of today, the Triple Figure Eight would be considered very small. But, when this card was mailed in 1910, it must have been quite impressive. (Kraemer Art Co., for C.A. Penzel.)

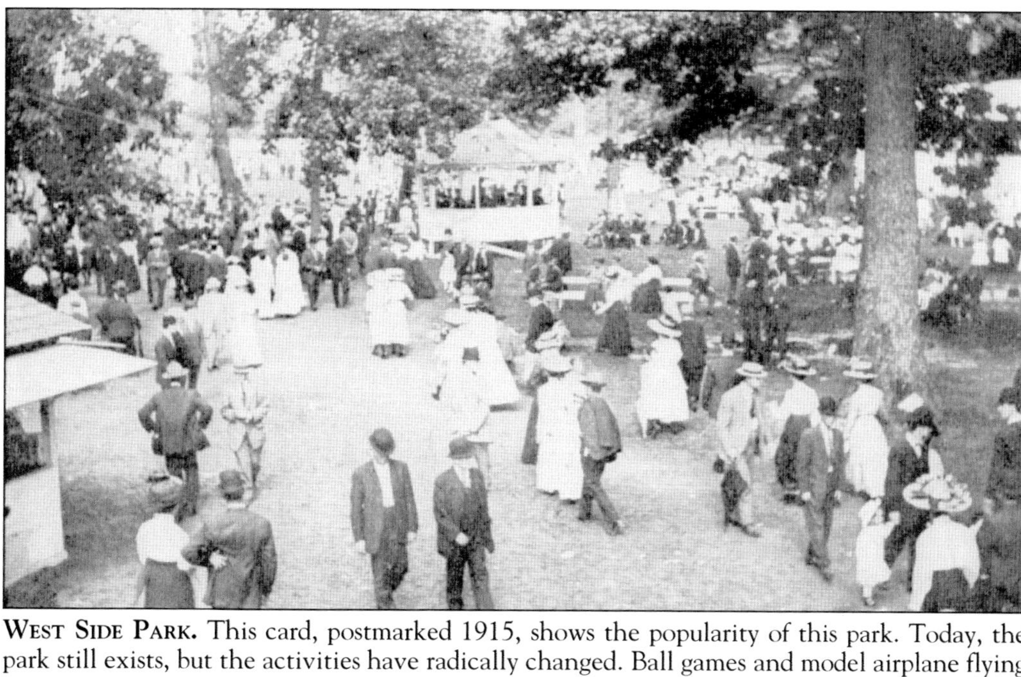

WEST SIDE PARK. This card, postmarked 1915, shows the popularity of this park. Today, the park still exists, but the activities have radically changed. Ball games and model airplane flying are some of the more recent activities that have been enjoyed in the park. (Unidentified printer and publisher.)

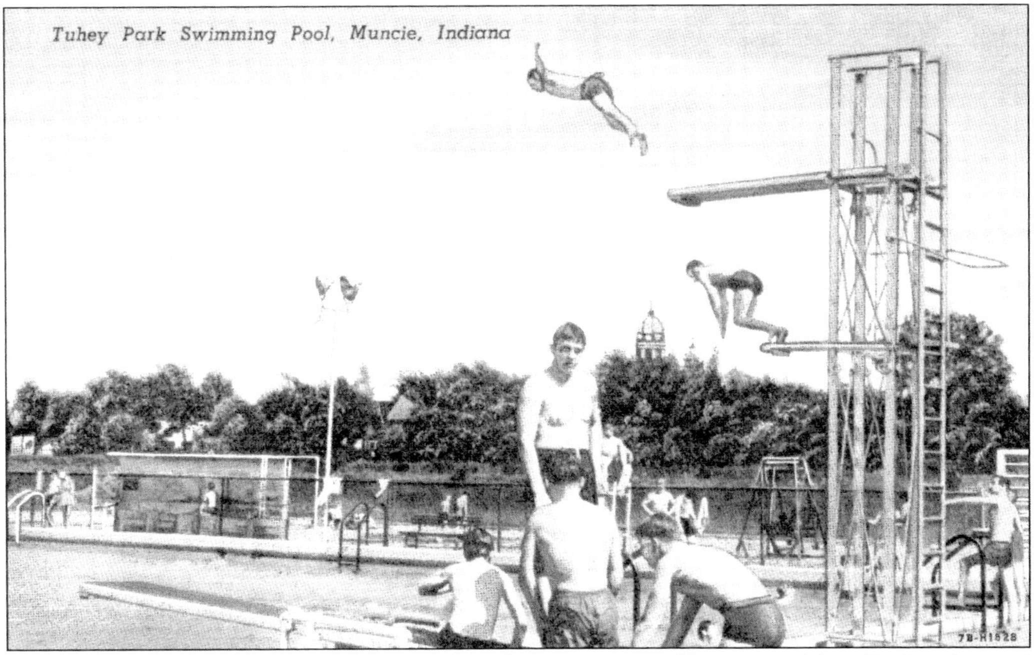

TUHEY PARK SWIMMING POOL. Named for a former mayor of Muncie, Tuhey Park is located at White River Boulevard and Wheeling Avenue. The Olympic-size swimming pool, built in 1934, is the park's main attraction. This card was published about ten years after the pool was completed. (Curt Teich Co., for Muncie News Co.)

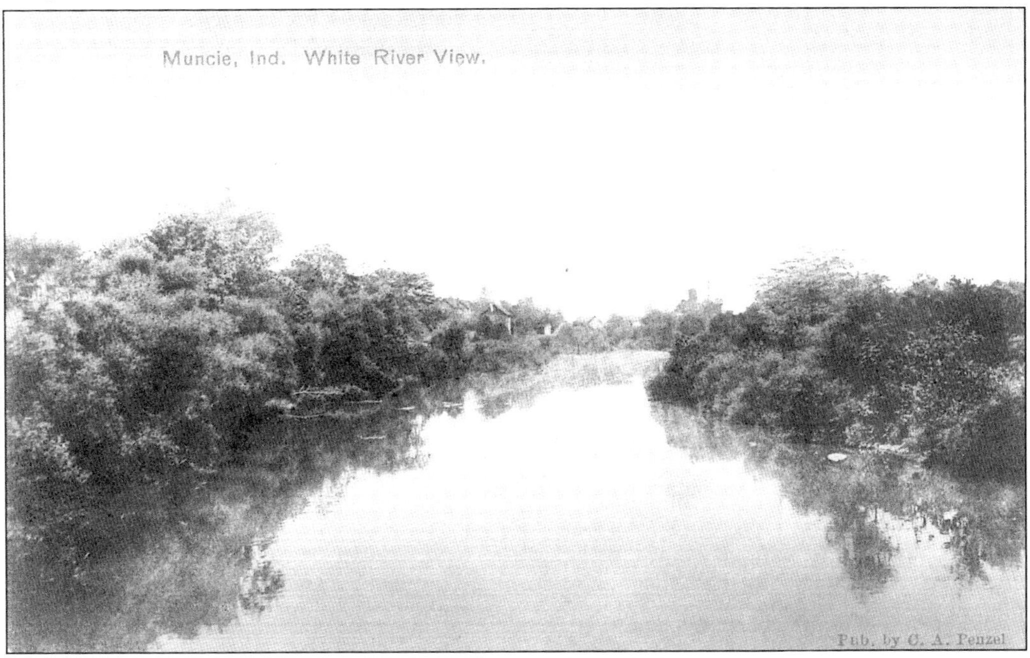

WHITE RIVER VIEW. According to American Indian legend, the unique "horseshoe" bend in the White River accounts for why the city of Muncie has never experienced a destructive tornado. The view in this picture is just after the bend, looking south toward the city center. (The Metropolitan News Co., for C.A. Penzel.)

Ten

Ball State and Before

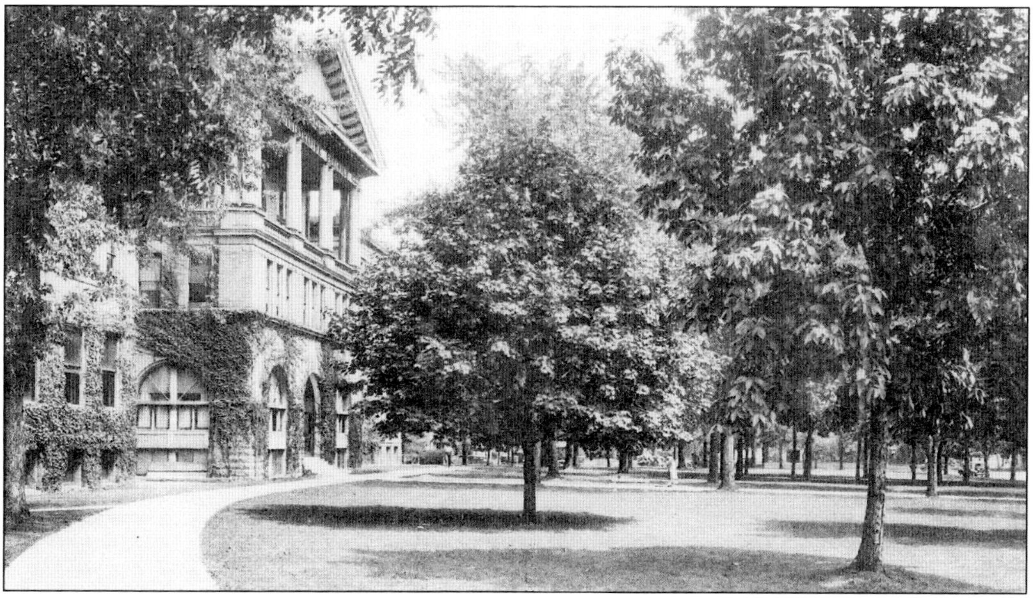

Administration Building, Ball State Teachers' College. The administration building was built in the Normal City area between 1898 and 1899. It was designed by J.F. Alexander of Lafayette, Indiana, at a cost of $32,949 to serve as the home to the Eastern Indiana Normal University. It operated under this name until 1902, when it became Palmer University. In 1904, it was closed as Palmer University and reopened a year later as Indiana Normal School and College of Applied Science. It closed again in 1907 for a period of about five years, but reopened in 1912, this time as Muncie Normal Institute. In 1922, this name was changed to Muncie National Institute, and the school continued until 1917. From 1918 until 1922, the school operated under the name Eastern Division Indiana State Normal School. When Frank C. Ball and his brothers contributed a quarter of a million dollars for the construction of a new science hall, the school was renamed Ball Teachers' College and later Ball State Teachers' College. In 1965, the school gained university status and became known as Ball State University. The view shown here is from the southwest. (The Albertype Co.)

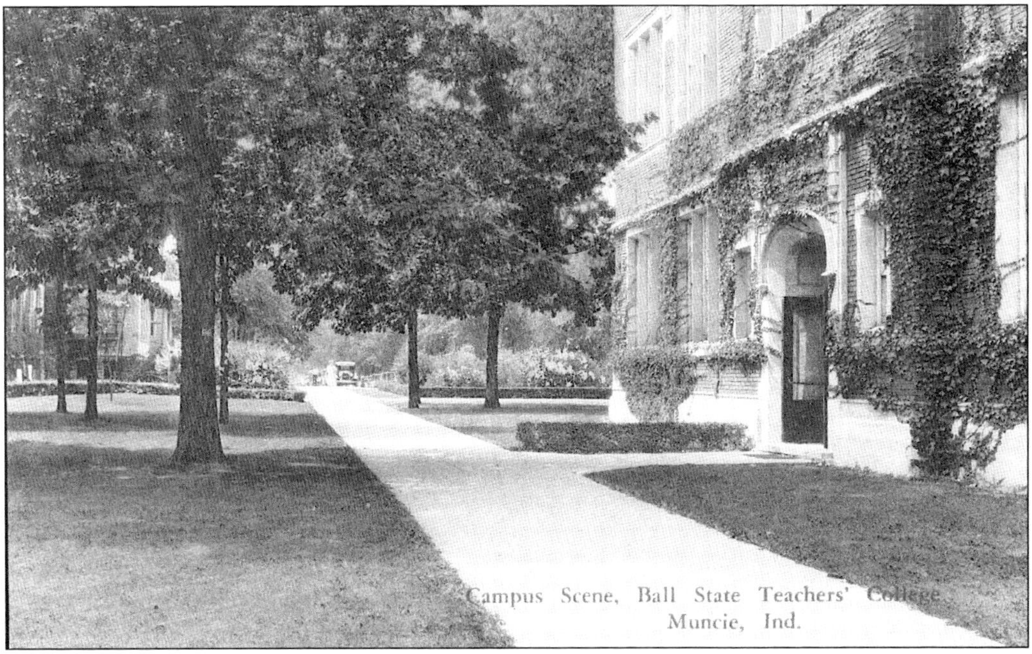

CAMPUS SCENE, BALL STATE TEACHERS' COLLEGE. This view looks to the west and is past the science building. The science building was constructed in 1922–24 in a style that might be termed "Collegiate Gothic." It was designed by Muncie architect Cuno Kibele. (The Albertype Co.)

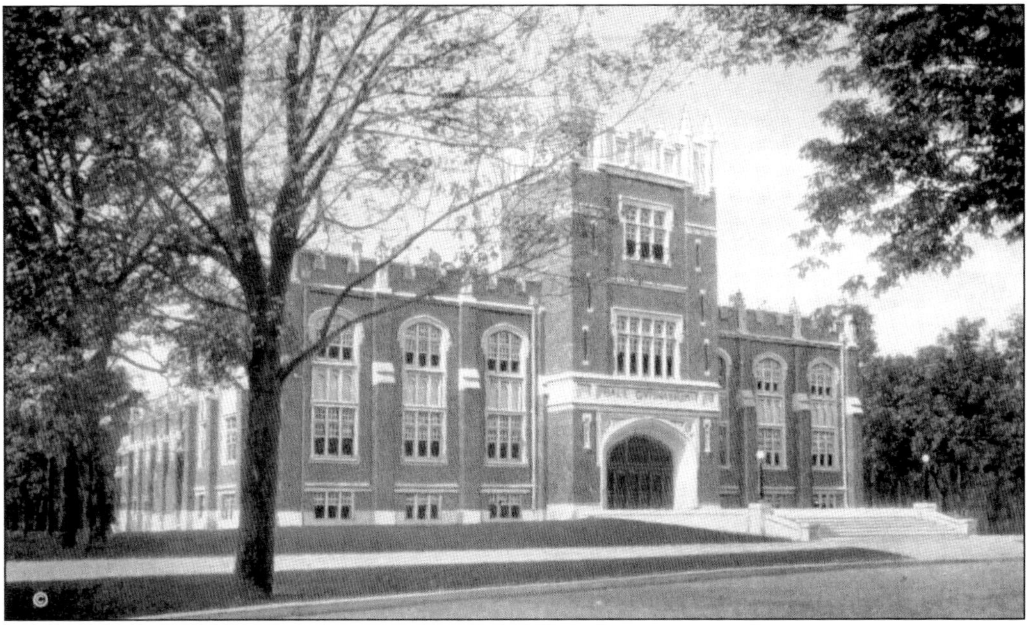

BALL GYMNASIUM, INDIANA STATE NORMAL SCHOOL, EASTERN DIVISION. Opened in 1925—and dedicated on January 9 of that year—the Ball Gymnasium was designed by Kibele & Garrard of Muncie in a Tudor Gothic style. Besides a gymnasium, the building was also planned to include a swimming pool, bowling alleys, and several other rooms for physical education. (Hermann Post Card Co.)

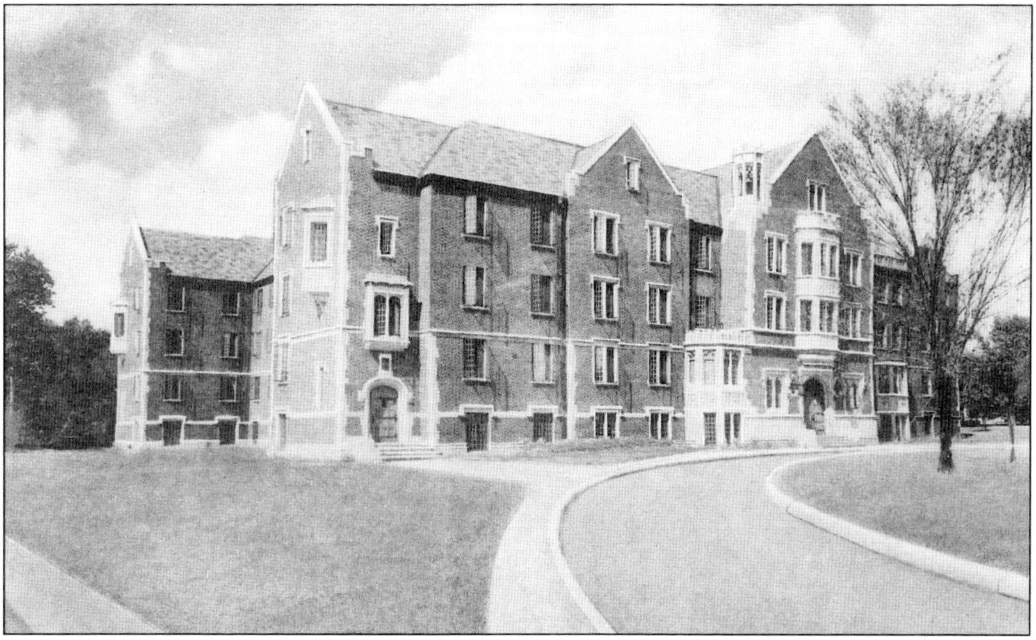

LUCINA HALL, BALL STATE TEACHERS' COLLEGE. Looking from University Avenue, this view shows Lucina Hall, a building planned as a girls' dormitory. Snyder and Babbitt of Columbus, Ohio, designed the building in the English Tudor style of architecture. It was completed in 1927 by the A.J. Glaser Construction Company of Muncie and dedicated on February 2, 1928. (The Albertype Co.)

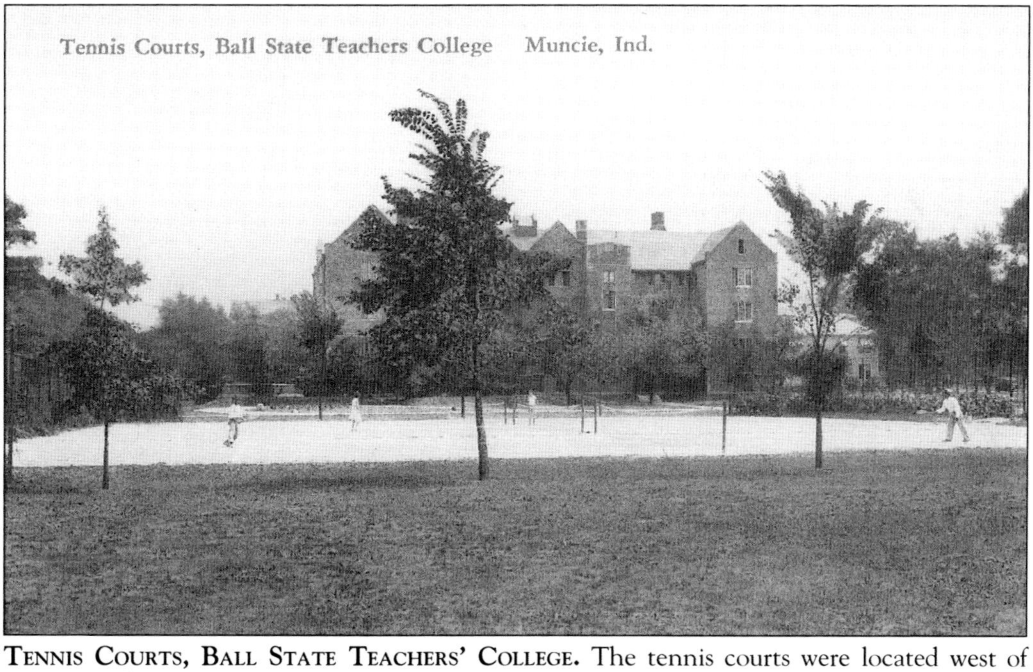

TENNIS COURTS, BALL STATE TEACHERS' COLLEGE. The tennis courts were located west of Lucina Hall, across University Avenue, and to the north of Burris School. Although still in use today, they have a much different appearance than when this picture was taken. (The Albertype Co.)

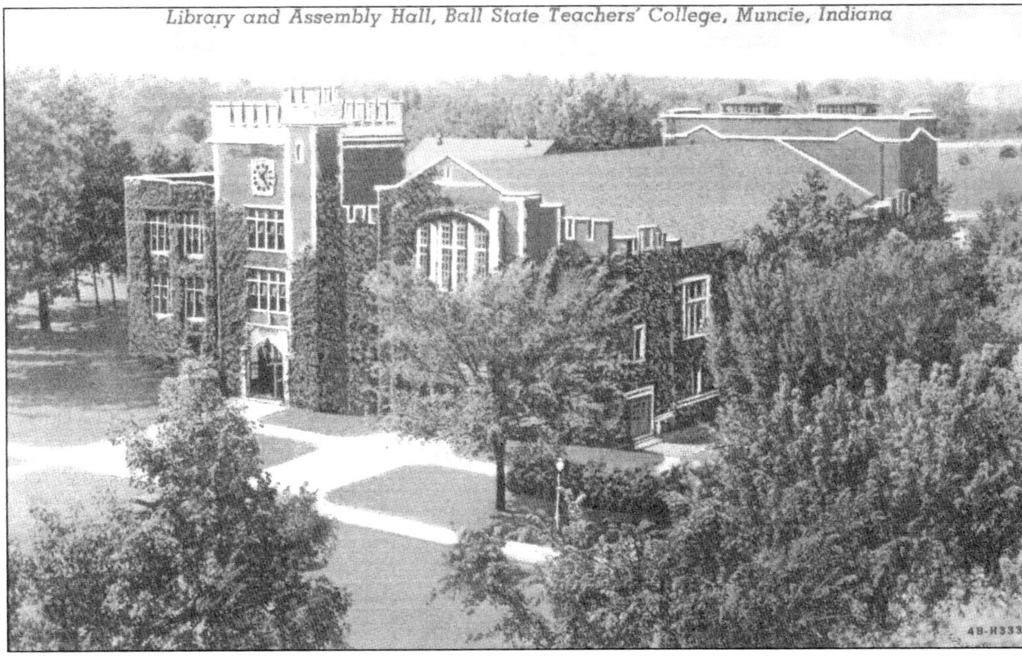

LIBRARY AND ASSEMBLY HALL, BALL STATE TEACHERS' COLLEGE. The library and assembly hall on the north side of the "old quad" lies between Riverside Avenue and Campus Drive. It was constructed from 1926 until 1927 according to the drawings by Snyder and Babbitt of Columbus, Ohio. (Curt Teich Co., for Muncie News Co.)

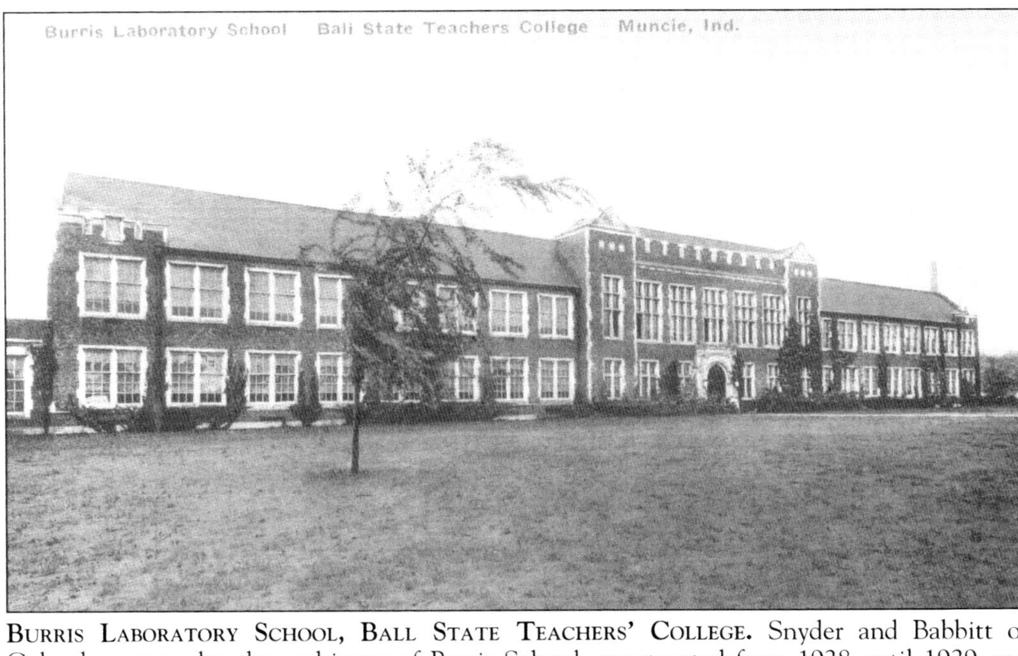

BURRIS LABORATORY SCHOOL, BALL STATE TEACHERS' COLLEGE. Snyder and Babbitt of Columbus were also the architects of Burris School, constructed from 1928 until 1929 and enlarged a decade later. This school served as a training school for education students at Ball State. Both authors of this book graduated from Burris. (The Albertype Co.)

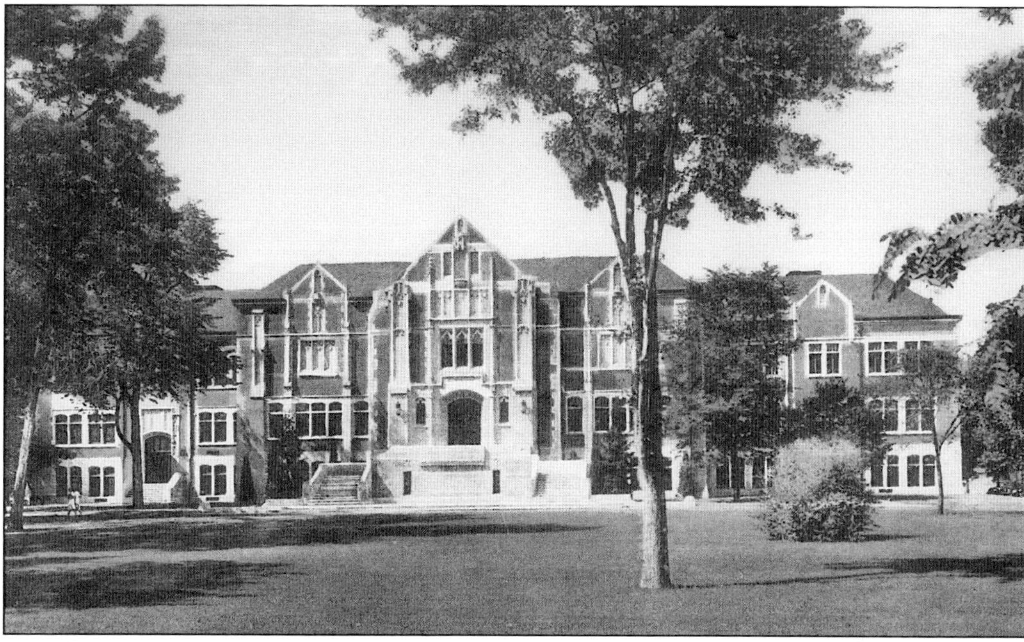

ARTS BUILDING, BALL STATE TEACHERS' COLLEGE. The Gothic Revival-style arts building at Ball State was built from 1933 through 1935 by James I. Barnes & Co. of Logansport, Indiana. The plans were drawn by George Schriebner, an Indianapolis architect. The cost of the building was nearly a half million dollars. (The Albertype Co.)

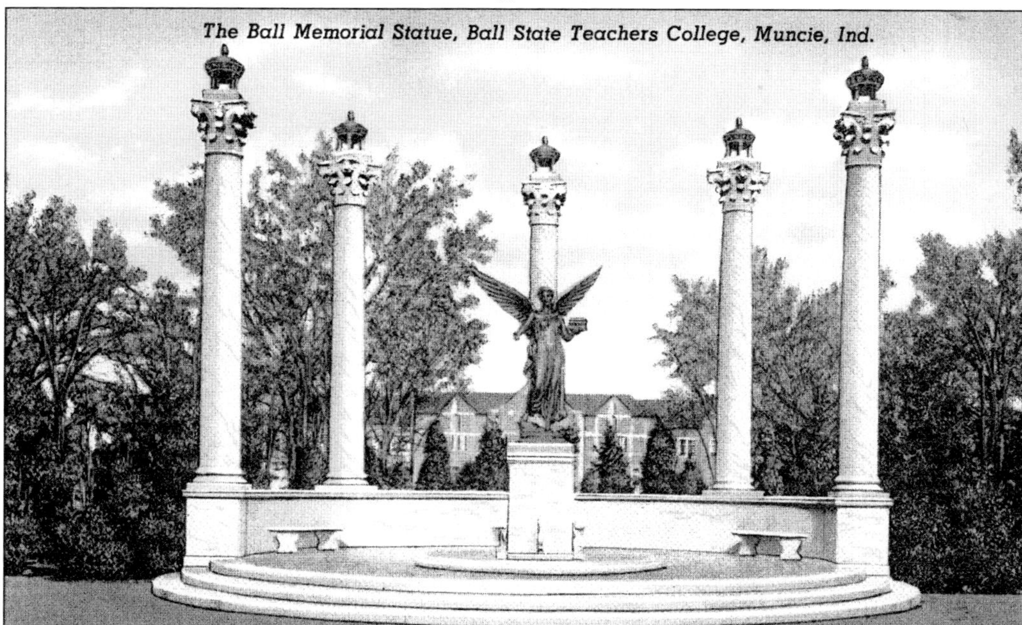

THE BALL STATE MEMORIAL STATUE, BALL STATE TEACHERS' COLLEGE. Daniel Chester French was the sculptor for this monument that is often referred to as the Beneficence. The Corinthian columns and Neo-Classical styling was designed by Richard Henry Dana of New York. Construction of the monument began in 1930 and ended seven years later. (Curt Teich Co., for Muncie News Co.)

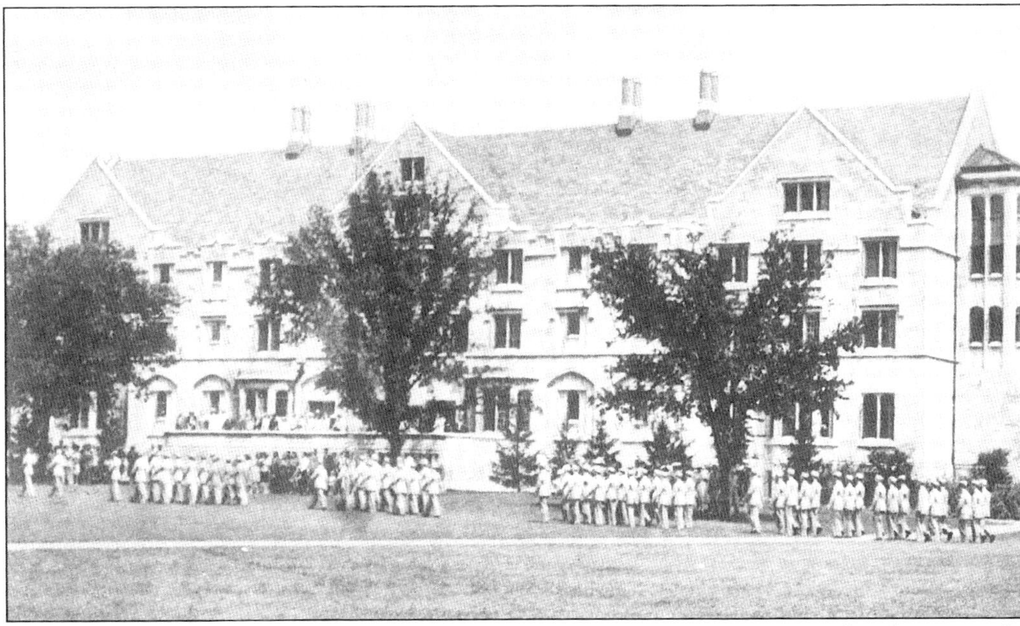

Frank Elliott Ball Residence Hall, Ball State Teachers' College. This dormitory for men was opened in 1939 after two years of construction. George F. Schrieber made the plans. This is one of the few buildings on campus that is not predominantly red brick. The view here shows the west facade of the building as a backdrop for students in military training. (The Albertype Co.)

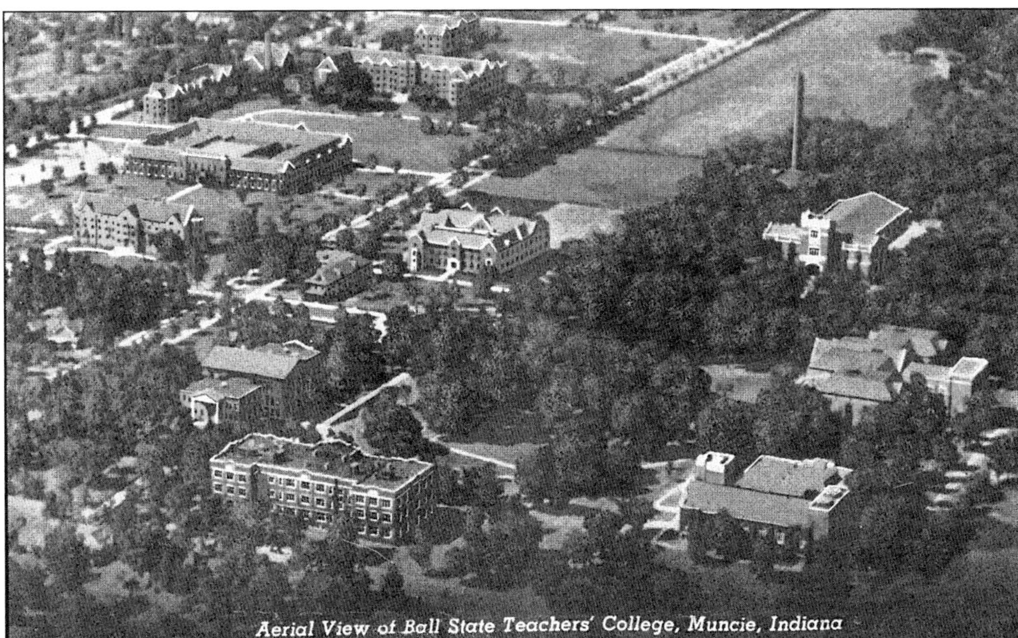

Aerial View of Ball State Teachers' College. This view shows the campus as it appeared before Forest Hall was torn down in 1941. It is unclear if Elliott Hall (1939) was under construction or just recently finished. (Curt Teich Co., for Muncie News Co.)

Eleven

Floods and Events

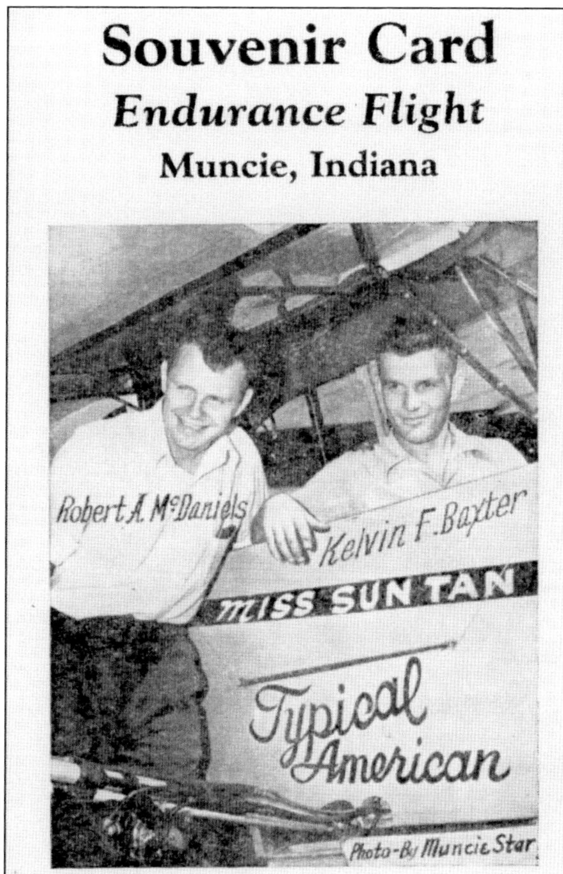

Souvenir Card, Endurance Flight. On October 1, 1939, a second endurance flight was started at 10:55 a.m. The *Muncie Star* photo shown here identifies Robert A. McDaniels and Kelvin F. Baxter sitting in the plane *Miss Suntan*. The words "Typical American" probably refer to Lynds's 1930s book, in which Muncie is declared the typical American city. (Unidentified printer and publisher.)

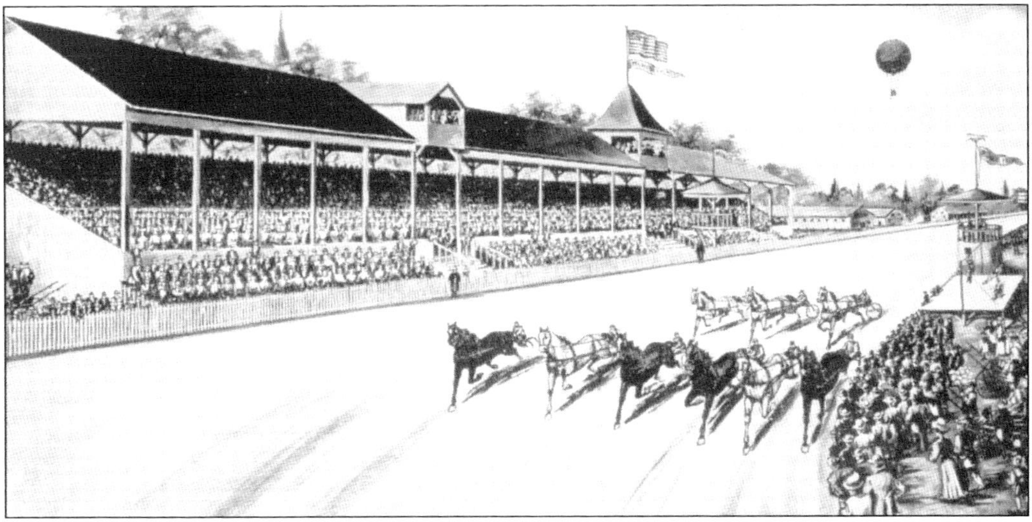

A View of the Muncie Fair. The back of this card includes a "speed program" for the Muncie Fair held August 16–19, 1910. The program lists starting times, type of race, and the purse for each race. C.H. Anthony is listed as the president, and F.A. Swain as the secretary. (Unidentified Printer and Publisher.)

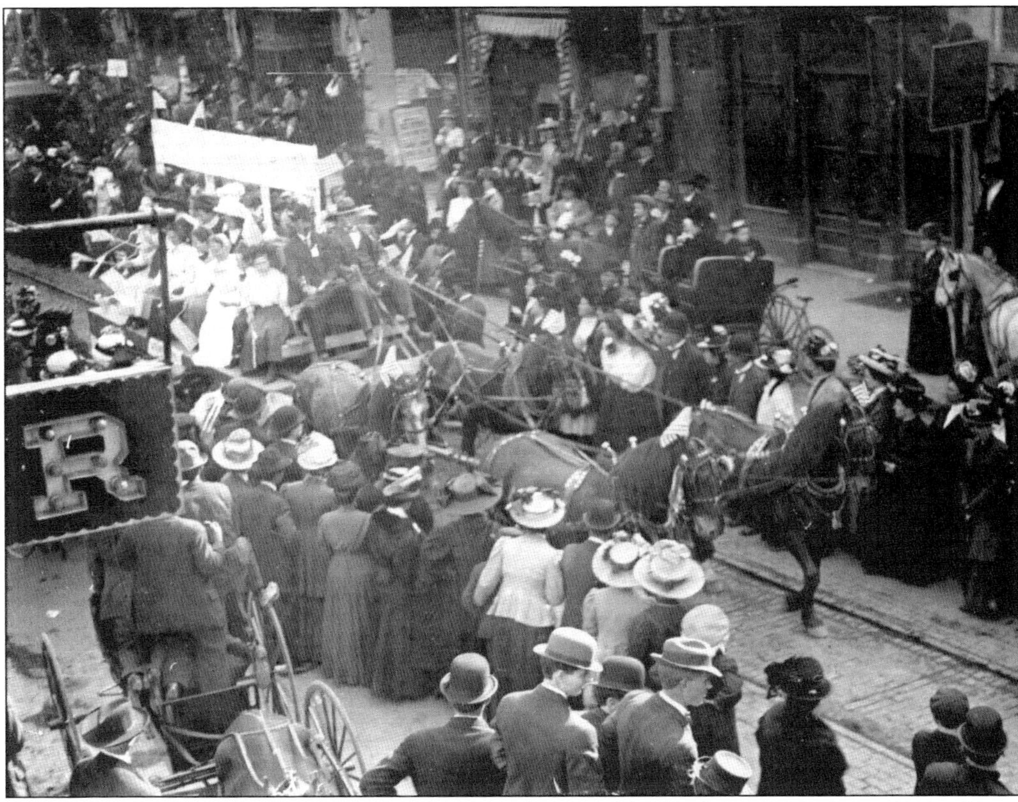

Crowd of People. This crowd is gathered in the 200 block of South Walnut Street for an option-election parade. The view is looking toward the west side of the street. The card was mailed in May of 1909. (Real Photo, unidentified photographer.)

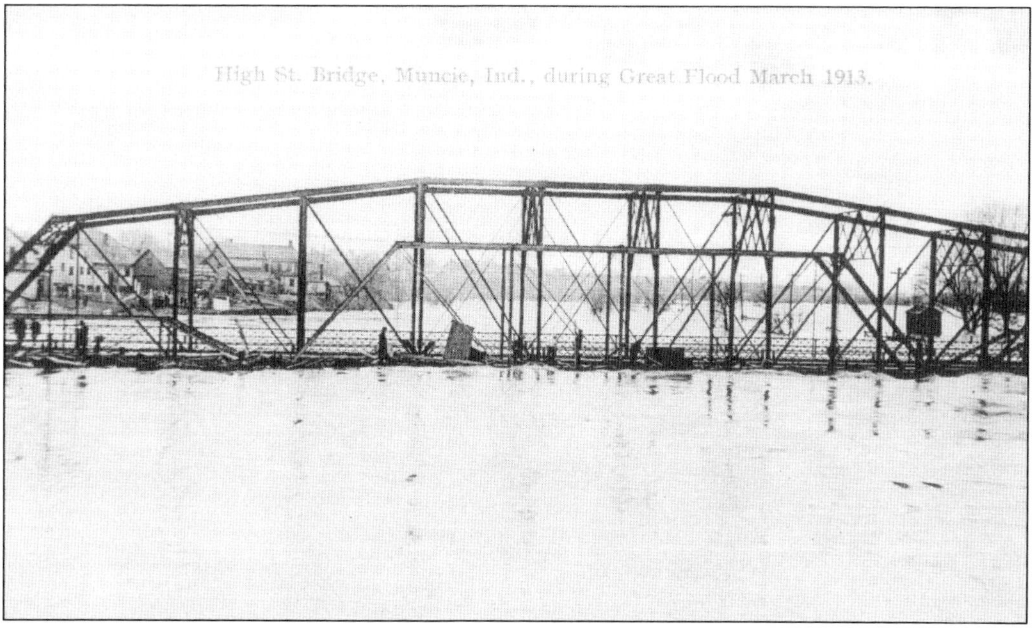

HIGH STREET BRIDGE DURING THE GREAT FLOOD, MARCH 1913. Severe flooding occurred in the Riverside area just to the north of downtown. The High Street Bridge connected Riverside and downtown. It is also sometimes referred to as the Wheeling Avenue Bridge. (Kraemer Art Co.)

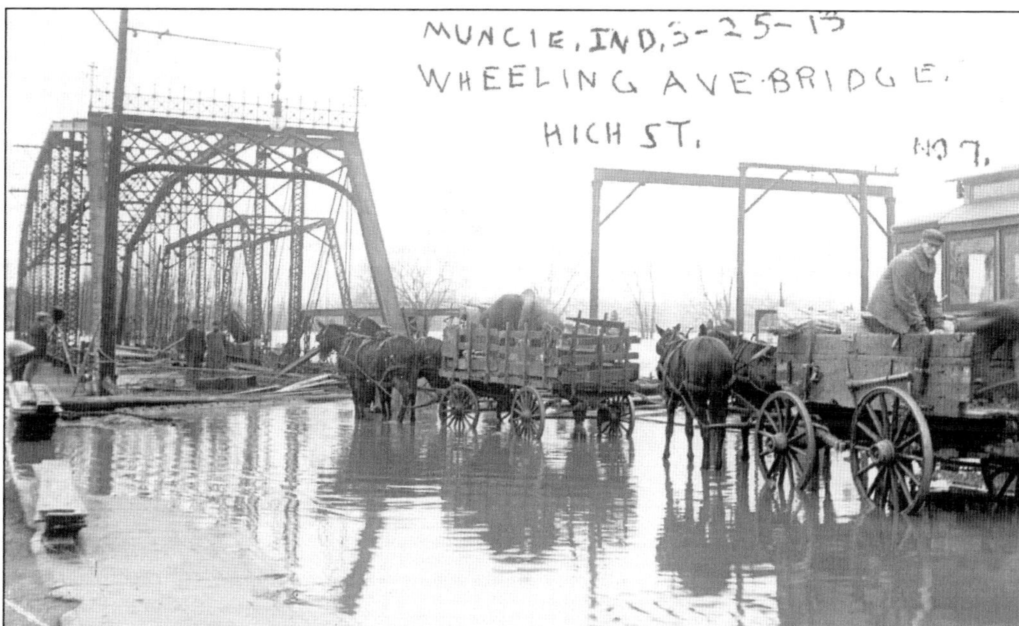

MARCH 25, 1913: WHEELING AVENUE BRIDGE AT HIGH STREET. This view shows the same bridge as the picture above. This view, however, is taken from the southern approach to the bridge. (Real Photo, unidentified photographer.)

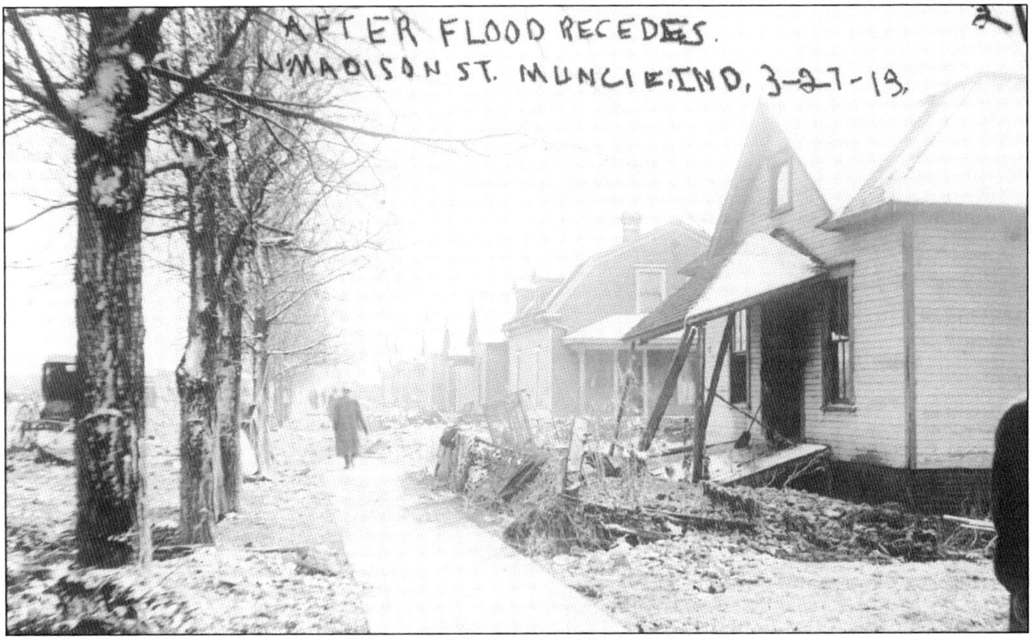

MARCH 7, 1913: MADISON STREET AFTER FLOOD RECEDES. Debris covers most of the front yards of these homes fronting North Madison Street in March of 1913. Hundreds of homes suffered severe damage from the flooding during the week of March 24–30. (Real Photo, unidentified photographer.)

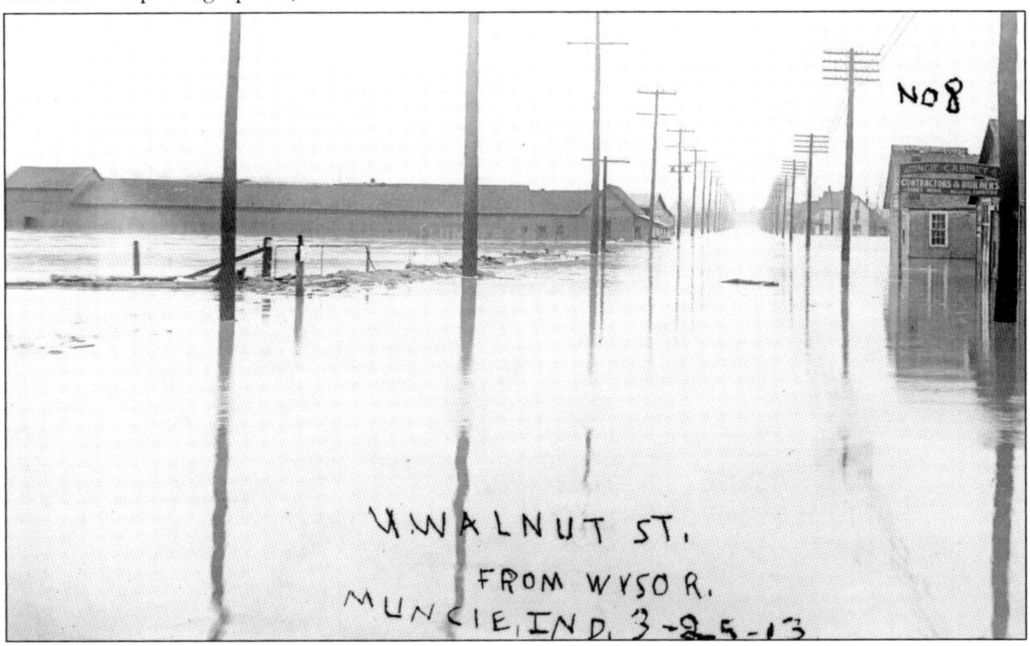

MARCH 25, 1913: NORTH WALNUT STREET FROM WYSOR. Taken before either the Muncie Fieldhouse or McKinley Junior High School was constructed, this view shows the west side of North Walnut Street during the flood of 1913. The visible buildings on the west side of Walnut Street in this photo include the Grouleff & Mauck Lumber Company. (Real Photo, unidentified photographer.)

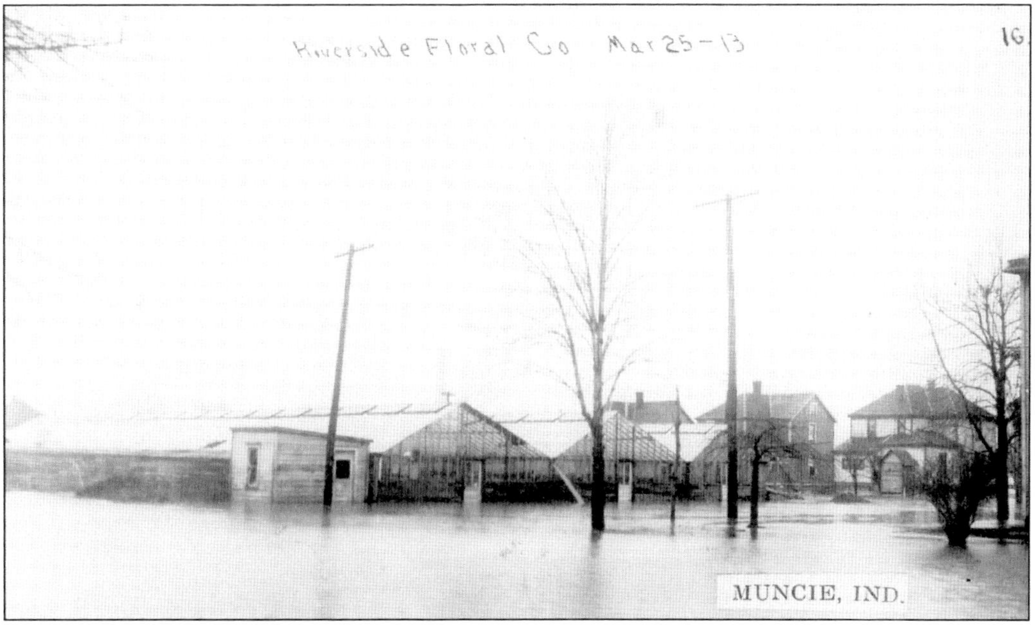

MARCH 25, 1913: RIVERSIDE FLORAL COMPANY. When the flood of 1913 hit Muncie in March, it was the worst flood ever recorded in the Midwest. The Riverside Floral Company, pictured here, was located on the corner of Beechwood Avenue and Reserve Street. (Real Photo, unidentified photographer.)

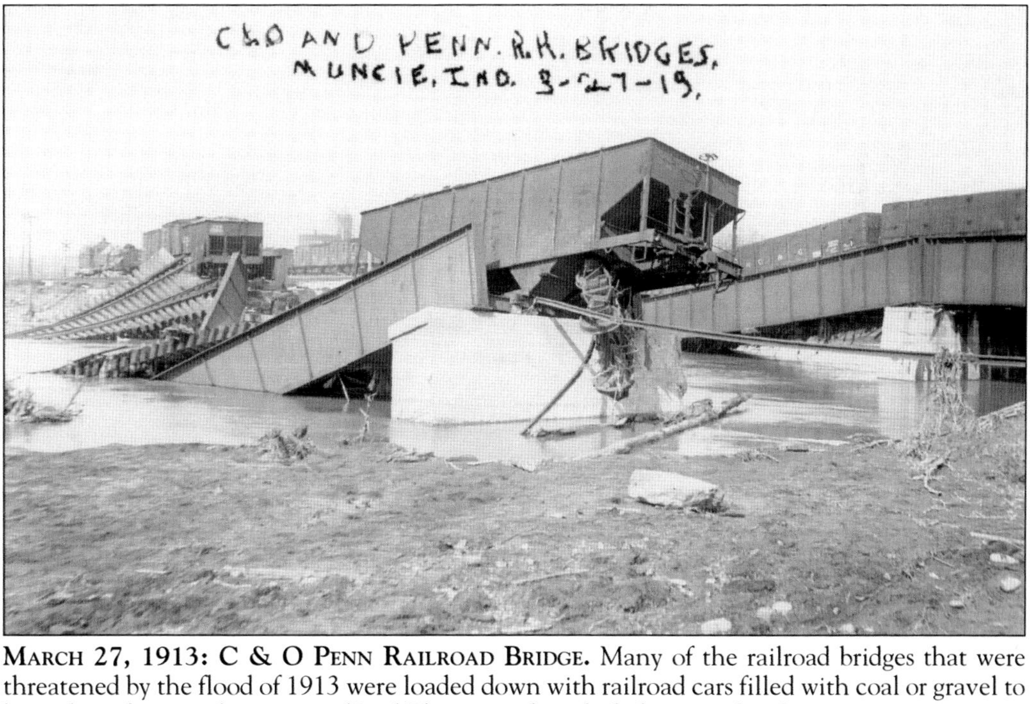

MARCH 27, 1913: C & O PENN RAILROAD BRIDGE. Many of the railroad bridges that were threatened by the flood of 1913 were loaded down with railroad cars filled with coal or gravel to keep them from washing away. (Real Photo, unidentified photographer.)

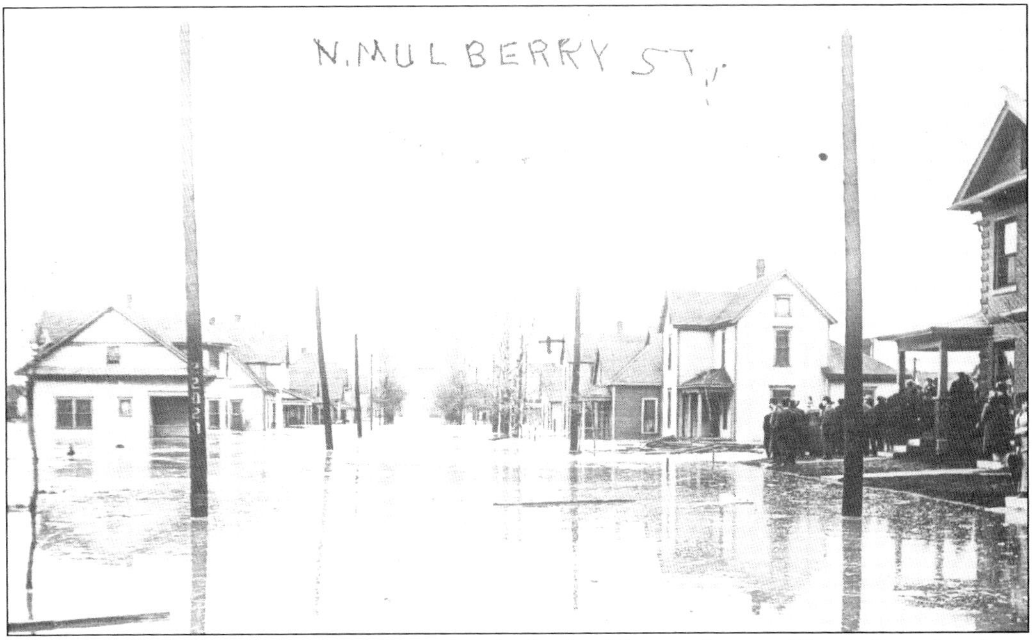

NORTH MULBERRY STREET. The message on the back of this card states: "Frank Deterling lives in the cottage where the + is. About 3 ft. of water is in his house." This is one of the few cards of this type that does not specifically identify the location of the scene as Muncie. Verification can be made from city directories. (Real Photo, unidentified photographer.)

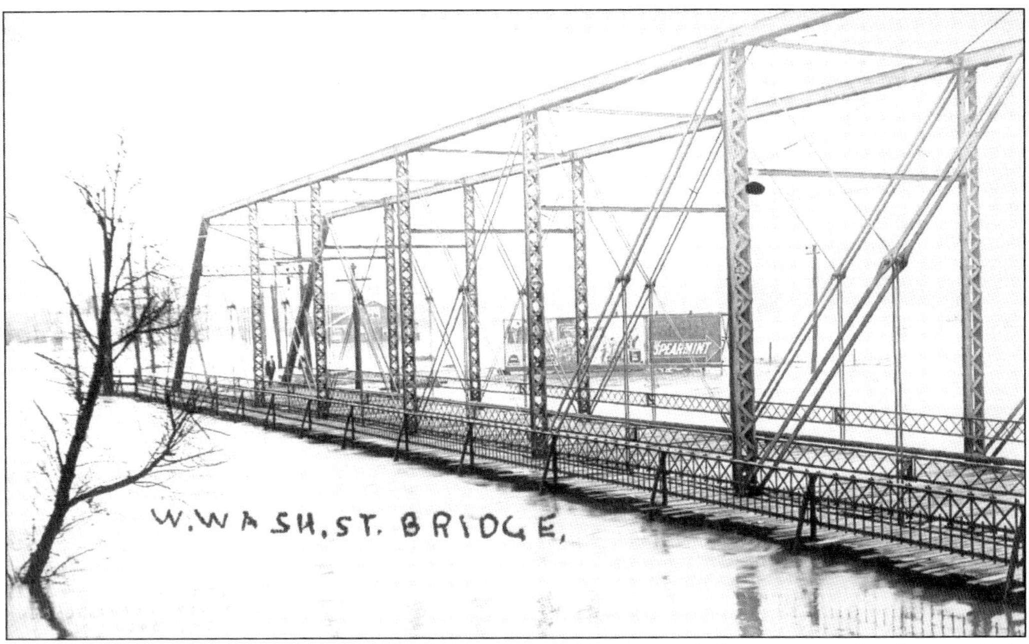

WEST WASHINGTON STREET BRIDGE. This is one of the rare real photo views that bear a C.A. Penzel hand-embossed mark. Like the card at the top of the page, this view does not identify Muncie as the location. (Real Photo, published by C.A. Penzel.)

Printers and Publishers of Muncie Postcards from Muncie

Ball State Bookstore, Administration Building, Ball State Teachers' College, Muncie, Indiana. The store published several collotype pictures printed by the Albertype Company, some black-and-white, and some handcolored. Most of the views were of campus scenes or public buildings nearby. The quality of these cards is very high.

Burkey Brothers Studio. This studio produced many real photo scenes of Muncie and the city's people with their families and/or homes in view.

Dexter-Fawley, Muncie, Indiana. Most of these cards do not identify any publisher or printer by name. A few contain the name, but all contain the double eagle trademark on the back. The earliest postmark found on one of these cards is 1912.

Muncie News Company, Washington & Mulberry Streets, Muncie, Indiana. They published mostly views printed by Curt Teich & Company. The Muncie News Co. was the major publisher of linen-era postcards, but also produced several others.

C.A. Penzel, 211 S. Walnut Street, Muncie, Indiana. Penzel used several out-of-town printers to produce several large series of Muncie scenes. Most views sold by Penzel's store were very high in quality and thoroughly represented life in the Muncie environment.

Marion Stewart, Druggist and Bookseller, Muncie, Indiana. Stewart was one of the earliest publishers of postcards of Muncie. Many of his views had undivided backs and date before 1907.

Watson, Bookseller and Stationer, Muncie, Indiana. They are another early publisher of Muncie postcards. Some Watson cards are overprinted by C.A. Penzel, possibly indicating that he was bought out by Penzel. The four series of cards known to be published by Watson are all relatively small in number.

Printers and Publishers of Muncie Postcards from outside of Muncie

The Albertype Company, 250 Adams Street, Brooklyn, New York. They used the collotype printing process to produce cards with great detail. Many of these cards are handcolored with watercolors or some other color medium.

Curt Teich Company, Chicago, Illinois. They produced lithographic images as early as the first or second decade in the 1900s, but became a national production leader when the linen era of postcards became dominant in the 1940s. Several different trademarks were used by the company, including C.T. Co., C.T. Photochrome, C.T. Art-Colortone, and C.T. American-Art.

Galion View Company, Galion, Ohio. This company created one of the largest series of postcards of Muncie, with just under a hundred real photo views of the city. This series is numbered and handprinted on the front of the cards. All of thc views have four white margins.

The Harry Hamm Company, Toledo, Ohio, and Erie, Pennsylvania. This company produced two or more series of lithograph-printed cards of Muncie. These cards are white-border cards. Some of the cards bare the trademark C.T. American-Art and were probably printed by Curt Teich Co.

Indiana News Company, Indianapolis, Indiana. The Indiana News Company published two postcard series from Muncie. They all have a "Litho-Chrome" trademark and were printed in Germany. The cards were first sold in 1909.

Tom Jones Company, Cincinnati, Ohio. They produced Muncie cards as early as 1907. Two different series of Muncie cards are known, one with a "glace" finish and the other printed with black ink on two different-colored card stocks.

S.H. Knox and Company, Cincinnati, Ohio. This company manufactured more Muncie postcards than any other company. Some carry the trademark "C.T. Photochrome." Most of these cards are full-bleed, but they include a variety of printing styles for identification.

Kraemer Art Company, Cincinnati, Ohio. This is the producer of many of Muncie's finest postcards. They are high in print and photo quality and include many rare subjects. Most are handcolored, but others are toned with green, brown, or black ink. Most of the Muncie cards by Kraemer were produced in the 1920s or the following decade.

E.C. Kropp Company, Milwaukee, Wisconsin. They produced at least five large series of views of Muncie. One series is full-bleed and dates to about 1906 or 1907. The others are white-border cards produced starting a decade or two later. These cards are some of the most common early Muncie cards. They were likely sold by several stores.

Metropolitan News and Publishing Company, Boston, Massachusetts. These cards bear a trademark of MNCo. They were printed in Germany and first sold in Muncie in 1908.

M.L. Photo, Chicago, Illinois. They were the producers of real photo postcards across most of the Midwest. These cards often depict factories and downtown scenes. The cards that are not faded are usually of very high quality and value. They are identified and numbered on the front of the card.

National Colortype Company, Cincinnati, Ohio. As early as 1907, the National Colortype Company started producing at least two series of below-average quality Muncie postcards. They are hand-colored views numbering in the 20s.

The Rotograph, New York City, New York. The Rotograph Company printed both black-and-white and handcolored Muncie postcards starting in 1906.

Superior Post Card Company. This company produced one large series of nearly 30 Muncie full-bleed lithograph postcards, probably in 1912.

Raphael Tuck and Sons, London, England. "Art Publishers to Their Majesties the King and Queen," Tuck also produced many cards that were sold in the United States. Only one series, No. 2633, was produced for Muncie. The series contains six views. Tuck also produced at least one view of Muncie that was not a part of a series.

Union News Company. Cards printed by this company are not always easy to identify. The few that do have identifications can help identify those that do not. The dates on the cards identified as being by the Union News Company start about 1910 and run through the 1940s. The print quality of these cards is rather poor, but many of the subjects represented are rare on postcards.

F. Von Bardelben, New York City, New York, and Germany. This company manufactured blue-sky, full-bleed lithograph views of Muncie sometime around 1913. These are numbered and identified in red ink on the front of the cards.

Wayne Novelty and Publishing Company, Fort Wayne, Indiana. Actually a publisher rather than a printer, this company used Curt Teich Co. to publish several white-border series of views of Muncie.

Milton Weixelbaum, Lima, Ohio, and Germany. As early as 1906 or 1907, Milton Weixelbaum was printing Muncie postcards with undivided backs. He did at least four different series of cards, one sepia-toned, one black-and-white, one handcolored, and another that was a variety of types.